**London School of Economics
Monographs on Social Anthropology**

Managing Editor: Peter Loizos

The Monographs on Social Anthropology were established in 1940 and aim to publish results of modern anthropological research of primary interest to specialists.

The continuation of the series was made possible by a grant in aid from the Wenner–Gren Foundation for Anthropological Research, and, more recently, by a further grant from the Governors of the London School of Economics and Political Science. Income from sales is returned to a revolving fund to assist further publications.

The Monographs are under the direction of an Editorial Board associated with the Department of Anthropology of the London School of Economics and Political Science.

London School of Economics
Monographs on Social Anthropology
No 61

Christina Toren

Making Sense of Hierarchy

Cognition as Social Process in Fiji

THE ATHLONE PRESS
London & Atlantic Highlands, NJ

First published 1990 by The Athlone Press Ltd
1 Park Drive, London NW11 7SG and
171 First Avenue, Atlantic Highlands, NJ 07716

© Christina Toren 1990

British Library Cataloguing in Publication Data
Toren, Christina *1947–*
  Making sense of hierarchy: cognition as social process.—
  (London School of Economics monographs on social
  anthropology, ISSN 0077-1074; no. 61)
  1. Fiji. Social life
  I. Title II. Series
  996.11

  ISBN 0-485-19561-5

Library of Congress Cataloging-in-Publication Data
Toren, Christina, 1947–
  Making sense of hierarchy : cognition as social process in Fiji /
  Christina Toren.
      p.   cm. — (Monographs on social anthropology : no. 61)
  Includes bibliographical references and index.
  ISBN 0-485-19561-5 : $70.00
  1. Fijians—Kinship. 2. Fijians—Social conditions. 3. Spatial behavior—
  Fiji—Sawaieke. 4. Social structure—Fiji—Sawaieke. 5. Sawaieke (Fiji)—
  Social conditions. I. Title. II. Series.
  DU600.T67 1990
  306.83'089995—dc20

DU
600
T67

Typeset by J&L Composition Ltd, Filey, North Yorkshire
Printed in Great Britain by Bookcraft (Bath) Ltd, Midsomer Norton

This book is dedicated to the memory
of my mother, Mary Camden Pratt,
who once held learning dear,
and to the people of Sawaieke who
made it possible.

Contents

List of figures   viii
List of tables   ix
Preface   xi
Preliminary notes   xiii

 1   Introduction   1

 2   Kinship and hierarchy within the household   29

 3   Transforming equality into hierarchy   50

 4   Hierarchy and equality beyond the household   65

 5   Containing equality – the *yaqona* ceremony   90

 6   Hierarchy and space in the church   119

 7   Government and traditional hierarchy   138

 8   Learning about seniority and gender   167

 9   Understanding above/below   196

10   Cognition as a microhistorical process   217

Appendices

 1   Children's drawings of a gathering   251

 2   Response to prepared drawings   261

 3   Prepared drawings and instructions   263

Bibliography   271

Index   279

List of figures

1   Map of South Pacific   26
2   Map of Fiji   27
3   Map of Lomaiviti   28
4   Typical house layout – Sawaieke   32
5   Layouts of other houses   38
6   People seated at family meals   60
7   Map of Sawaieke village   77
8   Typical seating pattern for *yaqona*-drinking   93
9   Ladies' seminar (1)   112
10 Ladies' seminar (2)   113
11 Ladies' *solevu*   115
12 Men drinking *yaqona* out of doors   118
13 Floorplan of Sawaieke church   132
14 Village meeting (1)   148
15 Village meeting (2)   152
16 Village meeting (3)   156
17 Country Council (1)   159
18 Country Council (2)   161
19 Provincial Council   164
20 Distribution of drawing types by age and sex   201

List of tables

1	The chiefly clans	70
2	The commoner clans	70
3	Tributary relations across villages	79
4	Relations between 'land' and 'sea'	82
5	Relations between 'people' and 'chiefs'	83
6	Patterns of opposition for *cake/ra* in drawings	200
7	Rank/seniority distinctions (i)	205
8	Rank/seniority distinctions (ii)	206
9	Rank/seniority distinctions (iii)	207
10	Summary of means	213
11	Summary of significance levels	213

Preface

From July 1981 to February 1983 I lived in Fiji, eighteen months of the time being spent in the chiefly village of Sawaieke on the island of Gau. There I carried out the field research described in this book (a revision of my doctoral thesis); the research was funded by a grant from the Social Science Research Council. I also had financial support from the Horniman Trust; this allowed me to take my son with me to Fiji and so was very gratefully received.

In writing this preface I feel myself overwhelmed by the number of people to whom I owe gratitude and to whom I can never sufficiently express it.

I have to begin with thanks to Ms Taufa Vakatale, who was Deputy High Commissioner for Fiji in London in 1981, for her friendship and generous support. She supervised my first stumbling efforts to learn Fijian, helped me choose a fieldwork site and, then and later, answered numerous questions. I have also to thank Jo and Meli Waqa for their hospitality in Suva; Jo also helped me outfit myself for the village and gave me the secure feeling that I could always call on her in a crisis. Ratu Isoa Damudamu Tokalauvere and his wife Apolonia were unfailing in their kindness and hospitality to myself and my son, both in Sawaieke and Suva.

In the village of Sawaieke, Takalaigau, Ratu Marika Uluinadawa, his wife Radini Takalaigau and his sister Adi Ateca Tui always made me pleasantly welcome to their homes. My teacher, Tunitoga, Savenaca Waqa, was invariably patient and generous with his time and never took amiss any of my foolish questions. Ratu Marika Tokalauvere and his sister Adi Mulonivalu looked after me well and the children of the house made my son welcome and watched over him. Serupepeli Vuetanavanua put in much hard work in transcribing tapes during the last weeks of my stay and helped me with translation. I must mention too some of those who in their friendly tolerance of my mistakes made me feel welcome: Ratu Sefanaia Laua Lewanavanua, his wife Adi Makareta and all his family; Sakiusa Damudamu Vererusa and his wife, Salote, whose advice was always kindly given; and Marika Tagicakibau and his wife Mere, who between them taught me how to joke. There are many more in Sawaieke to whom I owe a debt of gratitude and whom I cannot mention by name lest the list become endless. However, I cannot forget the teachers and all the children at Sawaieke District School; the teachers for their welcome to me and the children for their willingness to carry out the tasks that I assigned. Not only did the children provide me with material I needed, but during my time in the school they never took advantage of my status as a novice 'teacher' and were always gentle, well-behaved and eager to help.

I have also to thank my teachers and colleagues at the London School of Economics, with particular thanks being due to my supervisor, Professor Maurice Bloch, whose support and criticism have been invaluable, and to my colleagues in the Thesis Writing Seminar whose humour, tolerance and critical faculties could always be relied on. Ms Sereima Lomaloma, a student at the LSE in 1984/5, read an early draft of parts of the thesis and discussed many points with me and I am grateful for her comments and her friendship; as I am to Maria Phylactou, with whom I have more recently discussed various matters. I remember too my friend Susan Hiller, who started me on this long journey by making it impossible for me *not* to take up my studies as an undergraduate.

There remain to be thanked my husband, Amikam Toren, and my son, Manuel. Their understanding and generosity of spirit have always made the going less rough. I owe them both much more than I can say.

Christina Toren

Preliminary notes

Note 1: The pronunciation of Fijian words requires that the letters below be pronounced as follows:

> *b* as *mb* in number
> *c* as *th* in that
> *d* as *nd* in under
> *g* as *ng* in song
> *q* as *ng* in longer

I have also made use of the following standard abbreviations:

> B for brother
> D for daughter
> E for elder
> F for father
> M for mother
> S for son
> Z for sister

Note 2: I have throughout used the term 'sex' or 'across sex' to discriminate descriptively between men and women, boys and girls. I use the term 'gender' when I am referring to differences across sex as these are constituted in terms of a culture-specific history.

Note 3: For reasons of space I have had to exclude a number of appendices of raw data; these are contained in my Phd thesis — examined in 1986 and now in the University of London Library, Senate House, and in the Library of the London School of Economics.

Note 4: The diagrams on pp. 60, 93, 112, 113, 114, 118, 132, 148, 152, 156, 159 and 161 show the relative position of the persons represented on the above/below axis of the space depicted and do not show the way the people are facing.

1 Introduction

Hierarchy and balanced reciprocity as spatial relations

What is the significance of the spatial categories in whose terms Fijian villagers express social relations? What is the nature of the process by which their significance is constructed over time? And what may be the implications of this process for a sociological analysis and for cognitive theory in psychology and anthropology? Expressed in the most general terms, these are the questions I attempt to answer here; they are questions that arose inevitably out of data collected during my fieldwork in the chiefly village of Sawaieke, on the island of Gau, Lomaiviti (central Fiji). There social relations find their most obvious expression in people's disposition in space.

In what follows I deal with two different orientations in space; one is bound up with tribute and redistribution and is constituted as a relation between *i cake*, 'above', and *i ra*, 'below'. All horizontal spaces within buildings inside the village and certain contexts out of doors can be mapped on to an axis whose poles are given as 'above' and 'below'. Whenever people gather to drink *yaqona* (*piper methysticum*, kava), to eat, to discuss village affairs, to worship, to celebrate or to mourn – that is to say, on virtually all social occasions – those of higher social status 'sit above', and those of lower social status 'sit below'. Here the above/below axis usually refers to a single plane; no one is seated literally above or below anyone else. The other spatial construct that concerns me here is bound up with balanced reciprocity in exchange and is given by *veiqaravi*, literally 'facing each other'. The term describes the orientation of houses to one another in any village, but *veiqaravi* may also refer to attendance upon chiefs in *yaqona*-drinking or upon God in worship. I argue that hierarchical above/below entails a transformation of *veiqaravi* such that balanced reciprocity across households is transformed into tribute to chiefs.

Hierarchy has long been a subject of debate among anthropologists of the region (see e.g. Goldman, 1955; Sahlins, 1958, 1976; Nayacakalou, 1975; Ortner, 1981). The problem has been to find out whether or not it constitutes an analytical category, one that operates according to similar principles throughout Austronesia. Analyzing *what* the Fijian idea of hierarchy might be and *how* it is brought into being, both at the level of the group and of the person, is my concern here.

I set out to do my fieldwork with a general interest in the way culture-specific notions are constituted: historically in relation to society, but also in relation to microhistorical processes of cognition in persons. I wanted to discover something of the way processes at the level of the group enter into cognitive processes, and in so doing to understand something of how people come to be at one and the same time products and producers of those same unique – but none the less changing – group processes. It seemed to me that, because of its conspicuous intrusion into day-to-day life, the above/below axis provided a proper focus for an investigation into these problems.

The behaviour of villagers where I worked was striking in respect of spatial relations. At virtually all times their body postures, their disposition within a space, and their general comportment were apparently predicated on their understanding of how the above/ below axis governed the disposition of all persons present according to their relative status. This all-pervasive concern with the disposition of people within any given space – indoors or outdoors – and the taken-for-granted nature of people's behavioural responses provoked investigation.

What does it mean that we find expressed in terms of above/below a number of hierarchical relationships that we might consider different from one another? As will become plain in succeeding chapters, Fijians enter into several different forms of hierarchical relations in the course of daily life – but are these 'different hierarchies' in fact analytically different? Whatever the nature of the hierarchy that is physically manifest on the above/below axis, it inevitably refers back to the spatial construct, which thus itself becomes defined by these hierarchical relations – an observation which suggests that we may not be justified in distinguishing between the variety of hierarchical relations as different in kind.

I should perhaps point out here that I am *not* trying to establish congruence between Fijian social relations and the spaces in which they are constituted. This is to posit a relation of identity between what have been distinguished as different domains of analysis, and thus to imply that both have recourse to an overarching and logically interrelated set of principles that neatly embraces both (cf. Winch, 1958, 1970: 3–6). I avoid this problem by trying to understand how spatial constructs inform people's notions of social relations, and how this process is manifested in people's cognitions over time. In so doing, I attempt to reconcile the requirements of an analytical stance with the subjective cognitions of Fijian villagers. As will become plain, in this Fijian context there is no neat congruence between spatial constructs and ideas about social relations, but rather a series of overlapping sets of constructs in each of these two cognitive domains.

I said above that *veiqaravi*, 'facing each other', is a spatial construct that has itself to be analyzed if we are to understand above/below. Here I wish to emphasize that I am discussing these terms in so far as they describe the orientation of *people* to one another in space; they also have other referents. Thus *cake/ra* – above/below – also describes the relation between objects on different planes, a usage that does not preclude its use in distinguishing between people on a single plane. Indeed, as we shall see, in some sense the latter usage rests on an awareness of the logic of 'above' and 'below' as describing the relation between different planes. The significance of each of these conventional usages is cognitively constructed with reference to different properties of the environment, but there are nevertheless points where these properties actually coincide: thus, when a chief sits in a chair that is placed in the area called above, he is literally *and* figuratively above all others present. So it seems best to think of above/below as denoting a conceptual continuum whose extremes refer to a distinction between objects on different planes and to a distinction between people on the same plane. I shall show later how this notion of a conceptual continuum is suggested by the data from Fijian children which reveal the process by which they construct for themselves the meaning of above/below.

Above/below describes the space within the house, church and village hall, but it has rather different implications in each of them; this is so whether we compare those domains with each other or look at changes in any one of them over time. In respect of kin relations, religious office, and traditional or central governmental political offices, there have been historical shifts in what constitutes their conceptual and empirical properties. Nevertheless, be it in house, church or village hall, hierarchy is manifested on the above/below axis. So, to understand the interconnections between space and hierarchy one must examine both the various notions of hierarchy and the various ways they come to be made manifest in space.

There are a number of ways to undertake this task: one can describe and analyse behaviour within a broad sociocultural context; or one can investigate in certain persons the process of cognitive construction of the meaning of above/below; or one can search the historical record for possible causal links in the direction of change in social relations over time. Taken alone, none of these approaches seems adequate; here I have combined the first two with a limited amount of historical data in an attempt to achieve a fuller understanding of the significance of Fijian spatial constructs in everyday life.

This multidisciplinary approach entails certain difficulties, not least of which is that my data in respect of any one of them cannot be as meticulous or as extensive as they should be had I adopted any single perspective. I cannot claim that the present work constitutes a full ethnography of the area, an in-depth psychological study of spatial constructs, or an account of their historical development. Rather, via an investigation into certain aspects of the cognitive construction of above/below, I try to show how culture and history can be incorporated into a model of cognitive development in persons.

It is important to emphasize at the outset that I am *not* attempting here to show how a Fijian 'learns' aspects of his or her 'culture'. This would be to imply that a set of cultural concepts exists independent of the people whose behaviour at once constitutes and expresses them. 'Culture' is a useful term for us as anthropologists, but in so far as it refers to a 'system of meanings' it can only be an abstraction. Meaning does not reside anywhere 'out there'. Meaning is manifest in behaviour, in objects, in the land, etc., only in so far as living persons make it so. In saying this I do not posit the existence of an 'asocial individual' – far from it. Rather, my work rests on the assumption that human sociality is innate. I hold that human cognition is inherently social – meaning cannot be made in isolation, it requires others in order to be brought into being. We cannot even conceive of human beings without at the same time situating them in some history – real or imagined – and history is, of course, the artifact of our sociality. But if meaning is made by persons, how is it that the meaning of notions such as God, good breeding or taboo – or in this case, of above/below – is made to appear, or indeed to become, consensual?

I try to show here that consensus – whether 'real' or 'apparent' – is the inevitable outcome of the way interpersonal processes at the level of the group inform cognitive development. In talking of 'cognitive development' I do *not* imply a neatly defined process or set of processes that ends at some point in adolescence; nor do I assume that there are no innate cognitions. Rather, I take cognitive development to be a series of constructive processes that continue throughout the course of life, their culture-specific products to be founded upon innate discriminations and elaborated, brought into being, in relations with others who are themselves making culture-specific meanings out of their own experience. So I take cognitive development to encompass all of a person's experience, to be as it were a kind of 'microhistory' that situates each one of us within a certain sociocultural history.

This position implies a radical cultural relativism, in that it would seem to say that each person embodies a culture unto him- or herself. Certainly, persons embody aspects of a culture, but what constitutes 'a culture' is itself the abstracted product of the manifold products of persons in social relations with one another and does not even come into existence except in books like this one. This is not to invalidate the present work; rather, I shall show how meaning is always the product of particular minds, even while it is being cognitively constructed in relation to the meanings made by others, and how coming to understand this process itself makes possible a valid analysis of 'cultural meanings' at the level of the group.

A preliminary discussion of models of cognition

An undergraduate training in psychology fuelled my interest in cognition, but left me dissatisfied with its 'asocial' models (cf. Schweder, 1984) and its research methods. Some time in early 1979, I decided it might help to become an anthropologist and so I shifted disciplines. My scepticism of psychology had been first aroused by work on intelligence and then by cross-cultural studies of cognition –

often in a Piagetian mould – which almost invariably showed that, with respect to concepts of number, space, time, volume, etc., non-European subjects suffered from so-called deficits.

This finding seemed to me to be an artifact of Piaget's characterization of the subject, who supposedly acts *directly* on his or her physical environment and constructs knowledge out of this activity in a way that is virtually unmediated by others. Given that humans are biologically social animals, this seemed an untenable assumption. When Piaget did attempt to deal with cross-cultural differences and to revise his general stage theory in their light, he attributed differences across different peoples to their social environment (see Piaget, 1972). However, he never tried to investigate how culture and history might enter into cognitive development – a problem that was posed by his contemporary, Vygotsky, and examined by him and his followers largely in terms of the relation between language and thought (see Vygotsky, 1978: 19–30, 1986; Greenfield and Bruner, 1969 in Bruner, 1980: 368–91). Bruner's experimental work has focused on language as the locus of both 'culture' and developmental shifts (see Bruner, 1987). The problem here is that Bruner seems to assume that 'culture' is immanent in what the child learns and primarily in language; *how* it comes to be so would appear to be a matter for anthropologists. But the 'how' and the 'what' of cognitive development are intimately bound up together; neither element can be taken for granted, and each demands investigation in terms of the other.

The problem of the Piagetian model lies not only in its 'asocial' subject but in its ethnocentric assumption that the ends of cognition are known – an assumption that is common also to the work of Vygotsky and Bruner, and indeed of most other psychologists and even of some anthropologists. Thus Bruner, in his early work, takes it for granted that at the level of the group, technological development is the mark of 'intellectual maturity' and some societies are 'less demanding intellectually' (1980: 391). That this still very prevalent assumption may be set aside as invalid is demonstrated in, for example, Mimica's (1988) remarkable work on the counting system of the Iqwaye, a Papua New Guinea people.

Bourdieu's (1977) work offers an anthropological perspective on the problem of how culture enters into cognition; his 'theory of practice' does not lose sight of the human subject nor, like most others, implicitly ascribe *sui generis* properties to 'culture', or reify it in 'collective representations' or 'ideology'. But there is a profound problem too at the heart of Bourdieu's theory of practice, where an over-accommodation to culture makes *his* subject virtually a prisoner of history. The logical end of Bourdieu's argument is as ethnocentric as that of the various psychologists. To take the most obvious example, Piaget assumed that a cognitive developmental model derived from data on middle-class Western European children was universally valid and thus condemned everyone else to cognitive deficits; but Bourdieu similarly condemned them by incidentally predicating any ability to *challenge* cultural constructs on the historical conjunction of the members of one culture with those of another.

These logical implications of Piaget's and Bourdieu's theories may in part be traced to their focus on different domains of cognitive activity. Piaget concentrated on cognitive processes engaged with *invariant* physical properties of the environment, for example cognitive processes that culminate in the conservation of volume. Bourdieu, on the other hand, sought to understand cognitive processes concerned with social relations (for example the notion of honour) and so focused on highly *variable* sociocultural properties of the environment. This distinction may ultimately prove to be a useless one, for sociocultural processes enter into the way one conceives of invariant properties of the physical environment. However, it is demonstrable that everywhere people are capable of what Piaget calls 'concrete operations'; the anthropologist has only to locate the domain where they are embedded – a point I take up again below.

Piaget can be criticized for a too arid constructivism, but his theory is – at base – biological and processual; his starting point is the child in interaction with the world. So certain aspects of Piagetian theory can be retained and made to allow for the fact that language is basic to humans, that learning is an emotional as well as an intellectual experience and that, because brains are embodied, much of what we learn is inscribed in and made manifest in our bodies rather than in words. So, in respect of the cognitive construction of knowledge, I take Piagetian theory as the starting point for an eclectic approach that is especially influenced by Vološinov's (1929, 1986) notions of the nature of language and the interface between structure and process, by certain of Vygotsky's ideas concerning the way language enters into cognitive developmental processes, and by certain problems posed by Bourdieu's theory of practice. Vološinov's approach to language is especially useful in that he did not (*contra* Saussure) assume that meaning lay in the form of an utterance, but rather that meaning must always be constituted anew; so one has always to understand the *novelty* of an utterance rather than merely to recognize its identity to another utterance of the same form (ibid.: 68). I do not take the now fashionable theory of Vygotsky as my starting point – partly because it does not, of itself, hold all the answers, but also because it has allowed anthropologists to continue to privilege concepts in language over those that are not articulated and thus failed to force a genuinely multidisciplinary approach to cognition.

In trying to understand the significance of above/below for Fijians, both at the level of the group and of the particular person, I begin by assuming that its 'meaning' is not acquired ready-made, enshrined in a 'collective representation', but has rather to be constructed anew by each person over time. I use the word 'constructed' here because it is the term which best describes how the process of forming concepts over time looks to an analyst of that process; it is *not* meant to imply for anyone in the throes of that process that a 'goal' is known at the outset or that the process itself is a conscious and transparent one. Indeed, as I show in the final chapter, it is crucially important that the process is opaque to one who undergoes it. I assume too that any general account of cognition has to allow at once for its universal aspects and for cultural and personal differences.

One of the most important features of Piaget's 'genetic epistem-ology' is the methodological stance it entails. Piaget's colleague, Inhelder, has pointed out that 'that which is knowable and that which changes during the genesis of knowledge is *the relation between the knowing subject and the object known*' (Inhelder, 1962, quoted in Furth, 1969: 24). It is not fortuitous that this lucid statement of the Piagetian position ignores the fact that the genesis of knowledge takes place in a socially constituted environment. By contrast, I start with the assumption that this 'relationship' can *never* be unmediated and that the nature of the mediating process is given by the fact that humans are biologically social animals. In other words, the most salient object for the developing human being is inevitably another human; what and how the child comes to know is mediated by virtue of the child's being, from the very beginning, actively *in* relations with others (cf. Trevarthen, 1988).

Even with respect to constructs predicated on invariant properties of the material environment – constructs of space, time, volume, number, and so on – one cannot assume a direct, unmediated interaction between the child and its material environment. So, to understand the process by which a person constructs concepts, one must also be able to situate that person within social processes taking place at the level of the group. Thus, my 'knowing subject' is always a 'social' subject whose coming to know the world is mediated by others – themselves still in the process of constructing their own knowledge of that world.

I retain from the Piagetian approach the idea of construction over time by 'the knowing subject' and of the 'scheme' that is its product. Cognitive development is taken to involve the gradual construction of generalized concepts, which nevertheless permit progressively finer discriminations and are articulated with one another in ways that allow (but do not *necessitate*) an ever-increasing independence of thought from its concrete referents. This type of process is, I shall argue, amply demonstrated with respect to children's construction of the 'meaning' of above/below described in Chapters 8 and 9.

However, I do *not* suggest that the constructive process be described in terms of Piaget's general stage theory where, for instance, the stage of concrete operations culminates in the construction of a general principle of conservation that is independent of specific conservational problems. A child who is able to 'conserve' volume understands that a given quantity of liquid remains the same whether it is placed in a vessel that is short and broad or tall and thin; the general stage theory requires that the child understands the *principle* of conservation and is able to apply it across all possible instances such that length, quantity, volume, and so on are all conserved. The attainment of this understanding is, for classical Piagetian theory, a necessary precursor to the next stage, that of formal operations. However, there is wide variation across culture with respect to the course of development for any construct so far investigated – a predictable finding from an anthropological perspective, and one entailed by the assumption that our construction of knowledge is mediated by other people. These cross-cultural variations led Harris and Heelas (1979) to propose the notion of 'local constructivism'; so they save the idea of stages while dispensing with those aspects of Piaget's general stage theory that rule out cultural differences. They view cognitive development as having a constructive, stage-like character, but as occurring simultaneously in a number of relatively autonomous 'cognitive valleys' (ibid.: 219). In other words, they take cognitive development to be in some respects domain-specific – a notion that allows for differences across cultures.

I wish to argue further for a theory of cognitive construction which allows for significant personal differences, so I introduce here the idea of 'modulated construction'. This is intended to convey the idea that cognitive activity is modulated at once by the nature of the cognitive domain on which it bears, by factors such as age and sex, *and* by the fact that the cognitions of any one person within a group with a common cultural heritage can never be quite the same as those of any other. 'Modulated construction' allows for those nuances of thought and behaviour that make any person at once a product of the history of his or her sociocultural group and of his or her own personal history.

Any process of cognitive construction requires two key Piagetian notions: assimilation and accommodation.

> Every act of intelligence, however rudimentary and concrete, presupposes an interpretation of something in external reality, that is an assimilation of that something to some kind of meaning system in the subject's cognitive organization. ... If intellectual adaptation is always and essentially an assimilatory act, it is no less an accommodatory one. In even the most elemental cognition there has to be some coming to grips with the special properties of the thing apprehended ... (Flavell, 1963: 48)

Via these complementary processes, cognition is organized in ever more complex and highly differentiated 'schemes', whose inherent quality is that 'once constituted, they apply themselves again and again to assimilable aspects of the environment' (ibid.: 55). Schemes both underlie the production of behaviour (including thought and language) and are the product of it.

The cognitive process of scheme construction also requires 'equilibration'; this 'self-regulated mechanism' (Piaget, 1968, 1972: 62) works to produce a cognitive equilibrium. For example, a child who is able to conserve volume realizes that when one pours a given quantity of liquid from a short wide vessel into a tall thin one, the quantity of liquid does not itself change. Now the child's accommodation to the perceptual information given by the short wide vessel and the tall thin one come to be balanced by a simultaneous realization that the liquid now contained in the tall thin vessel is the *same* liquid that was first seen in the short broad one. In this simultaneous and complementary assimilation and accommodation the two processes shift from a previously unbalanced 'equilibration' to a balanced 'equilibrium' in which the mental operations themselves have become reversible.

Piaget's description of equilibration implies that, because it is an endogenous (that is, self-regulated) process, it is immune from environmental influence (ibid.: 68). But this fails to recognize that what is assimilated and accommodated and finally equilibrated is information which, even if it is not peculiar to a culture, is inevitably informed by it. Indeed, that 'reflective abstraction' (ibid.: 19) which is dependent upon 'the ability to evoke what is not actually perceived' (ibid.: 64) is also engaged with cultural constructs.

Given that all cognitive activity entails active seeking after knowledge, it is inevitable that salient information in the environment leads to assimilation and accommodation. I take this view of the nature of cognition from Neisser (1976), where he rejects the premises of his previous information-processing approach (Neisser, 1967) which implies the subject to be a passive 'receiver'. When the knowledge that is sought (often unconsciously) concerns the behaviour of other people who are highly salient to the person, the notion of the gradual construction of schemes appropriate to understanding their behaviour and to producing actions in accordance with it becomes even more compelling. Here I suggest that equilibration may itself require a 'push' from the environment, and that this is especially the case for constructs such as above/below which are concerned with social relations.

The point here is that the construction of such a scheme may be supposed to require the simultaneous cognitive manipulation of information pertaining to various domains of social interaction.

Moreover, the information derived from these different domains may be contradictory. To a certain extent accommodation – 'the process whereby the schemes of assimilation themselves become modified in being applied to a diversity of objects' (Piaget, 1968, 1972: 63) – is sufficient to allow for the reorganization of existing schemes. But it cannot allow for reorganization of a number of different schemes into a complex whole. A cognitive construct of such complexity may require that certain information be given priority over other, perhaps equally salient, information, and here the notion of equilibration is surely important. However, it seems to me that this kind of equilibration demands a push from the environment, one that would govern the endogenous selection of those schemes that have to be assimilated to one another, so that the person achieves an accommodation to the environment that accords with his or her experience of it.

This kind of cognitive activity does not, I argue, have to be conscious. One may suppose a reorganization of existing schemes to be triggered by, for instance, a subliminal awareness of some fact to which no previous accommodation has been made. Whether or not equilibration is an entirely endogenous 'self-regulation' that takes place willy-nilly will be further discussed in the final chapter.

In his discussion of Lévi-Strauss's structuralism, Piaget points out that from his own perspective, 'only self-regulating transformational systems are structures' (Piaget, 1968: 113). Thus while certain cognitive processes are constructive in their nature, this does *not* imply that they give rise to a fixed structure. As I shall show later, my own data suggest that while complex cognitive schemes like above/below may be characterized as having a definite shape, they are simultaneously labile in nature, open to further transformation in respect of their component parts and the relation between them. The problem here is to recognize – as Piaget never really did – that the self who is regulating the 'transformational system' is always the locus of a number of social relations. So the abstract logic in whose terms Piaget characterizes psychological structures cannot provide a satisfactory account of either the structures themselves, or the processes by which they were brought into being.

The advantage to be gained by accepting the notion of modulated construction that I argue for here is that it allows for both cultural and personal differences in cognition at the same time as proposing a constructive process that is at base universal in so far as all human beings have to adapt to certain invariant properties of the environment and thus to construct notions of space, time, number, volume, etc., that are able adequately to describe, and to allow for manipulation of, those invariant properties. The notion of modulated construction and the labile scheme that is its product will perhaps prove too vague to satisfy psychologists; however, I would ask the reader to bear in mind that, limited though it is, my project here is a complex one, for it attempts to reveal at least some aspects of *how* culture and history actually enter into the cognitive development of persons who are themselves making that culture, that history.

Modulated construction dispenses both with Piaget's asocial individual and with his general stage theory and retains the core of his notion of mind as 'the as yet unfinished product of continual self-construction' (1968: 114) – this self-construction being mediated by virtue of the fact that it inevitably bears upon social products; humans cannot perceive, feel, think or act without invoking their own historically specific forms of sociality. This perspective allows for the transformations that occur in history and in the cognitive development of persons situated in history. This is *not* to imply that historical transformations are of the same kind as those entailed by changes in cognition; rather, as I shall show in my final chapter, the actual process of cognitive construction itself has certain implications for the nature of historical transformation.

I would argue further that modulated construction has a psychological validity that is lacking in Bourdieu's theory of practice In his view, everyday life presents a Kabyle child with other people's 'endlessly redundant' actions; the child imitates this multitude of actions and from its own countless imitations derives cognitive schemes that 'are able to pass from practice to practice without going through discourse or consciousness'. The Kabyle child 'has no difficulty in grasping the *rationale* of what are clearly series and in making it his own in the form of a principle generating conduct organized in accordance with the same rationale' (Bourdieu, 1977: 87–8).

As a cognitive theory, this is clearly inadequate; but certainly, conceptual thought of great complexity does not require speech. Some cognitive abilities – for example that of discriminating a category of living kinds and within it, humans – appear to be present from birth. Smith, Sera and Gattuso (1988) refer to a number of studies of children's pre-speech abilities. Like others before them, they criticize Piaget for failing to recognize the extent of children's early cognitive abilities, and while they argue for domain specificity, they retain the notion of qualitative changes (i.e. stages) within cognitive domains. Among other findings they refer to children's ability at six to eight months to match a number of objects to the same number of sounds – an ability which must underlie (if it does not denote) counting. Other studies show, for example, that infants at thirty weeks can form a category of female faces (Cohen and Strauss, 1979); and Bowerman (1980) argues that children form categories before they acquire the terms that 'name' them (compare Luong, 1986).

However, perhaps even more impressive than these examples is the fact that cognitive construction of what Piaget called a concrete operational scheme does *not* require that a person be able to articulate his or her knowledge – even though other people's linguistic behaviour may have been important for the construction process. Piaget himself requires of fully developed 'concrete operational schemes' that the person be able to articulate correctly the concept that underlies his or her actions. However, the ethnographic record shows clear evidence of complex concrete operations in the absence of standardized systems of measurement and articulate reasoning. Audrey Richards's (1939) ethnography of the Bemba describes activities such as house-building and grain storage, and an analysis of her account shows the activities themselves to be dependent on concrete operational concepts of length, quantity and time (Toren, 1980). These are evident in the use of a strip of bark fibre to compare the length of two poles, etc. (Richards, 1939: 204) and in the way women estimated how long stores of millet would last (taking into account the number of people to be fed) in terms of how long another crop might take to ripen (ibid.: 88–9). Bemba notions can have been constructed only with reference to invariant properties of the physical environment via processes similar to those described by Piaget *et al.* for Europeans – and this in the absence of any standardized systems of measurement or any explanations that were to Richards's satisfaction.

Given that concrete operational schemes could thus *perhaps* be said to 'pass from practice to practice without going through discourse or consciousness', a notion of cognitive construction offers a better solution to Bourdieu's problem of how the 'rationale' is attained than does his explicit appeal to Hull's 'common element' theory of concept attainment (see Hull, 1920; Bourdieu, 1977: 88) and his implicit appeal to the more sophisticated behaviourism of G. H. Mead (1934; see also Gell, 1985). Moreover, his notion of the dispositions that make up the habitus are close to being Piagetian schemes; thus the 'habitus' is described as 'systems of durable transposable dispositions, structured structures predisposed to act as structuring structures' (Bourdieu, 1977: 72). The idea of construction is clearly important here and is, incidentally, in direct conflict with Hull's approach. Bourdieu paraphrases Marx, but might just as well be paraphrasing Piaget when he says that 'the theory of practice as practice insists, against positivist materialism, that the objects of knowledge are *constructed*, and against idealist intellectualism, that the principle of this construction is practical activity oriented towards practical functions' (ibid.: 96).

In Piaget's view, as in Bourdieu's theory of practice, 'the knowing subject' constitutes 'practical activity as an object of observation and analysis' (Bourdieu, 1977: 2) *in consciousness* only in so far as this practical activity has become objectified for him or her in discourse. But the discourse in which a cognitive construct is embedded does not generally include discussion of the conditions of its cognitive construction. This means that the cognitive activity I call 'modulated construction' should be able to allow for what Bourdieu has called the 'doxic' function of symbolic practice whereby 'the natural and social world appears self-evident' (ibid.: 164). It is 'doxa' that precludes questioning of traditional practice, making it seem 'natural' and therefore taken for granted.

The value of Bourdieu's work is that he attempts to understand how cognitive development may give rise to symbolic constructs at the same time as he investigates their meaning both for subject and for analyst. So he is able to show how the subject's meaning cannot be the same as the analyst's, since the latter has to take account of history in order to understand the conditions that make possible the meaning held by the subject:

It is because subjects do not, strictly speaking, know what they are doing that what they do has more meaning than they know. ...

That part of practices which remains obscure in the eyes of their own producers is the aspect by which they are objectively adjusted to other practices and to the structures of which the principle of their production is itself the product. (Bourdieu, 1977: 79)

Perhaps the main problem with Bourdieu's habitus (i.e. the mature 'cognitive system') is that while he talks of it as 'constructed', he has also characterized it in terms that make it virtually impervious to change – that is, to any change except that generated by forces exogenous to the group within which the habitus is formed. Bourdieu says of the habitus that it is 'as remote from a creation of unpredictable novelty as it is from a simple mechanical reproduction of the initial conditionings' (ibid.: 95). Thus he does not allow for the possibilities that may follow from cognitive differences that are given by 'a unique integration' of each person's habitus (ibid.: 87). I argue that this uniqueness can itself provide the conditions necessary for calling what is taken for granted into question – that is, for the transformation of 'doxa' into 'orthodoxy' (ibid.: 164–71).

'Creations of unpredictable novelty' cannot be commonplace or even highly likely, but some allowance has to be made, first for the creative elaboration of constructs by particular persons even in the absence of extracultural stimulation, and secondly for the possibility that this elaboration could have consequences for the nature of social processes at the level of the group. The cognitive organization of human beings is such that they seek after knowledge; they are not passively *conditioned* by their environment. Piaget demonstrated this finding exhaustively, but it is also basic to current cognitive psychology and psycholinguistics; thus studies of children's acquisition of language show that they *construct* classifications and the grammar of their language rather than merely imitate the linguistic behaviour of adults (see Cohen and Strauss, 1979; Luong 1986; compare Strauss, 1979; Bowerman, 1977, 1980; Mervis and Rosch, 1981). My point here is that the combined effect of personal differences in cognition and the *active* seeking after knowledge that is basic to it could allow at least some persons to go beyond the apparent 'limits to thought' that Bourdieu calls 'doxa'.

'Modulated construction' derives from my attempt to reconcile in theoretical terms certain anthropological and psychological perspectives on cognition. In the attempt I have raised a number of questions. Perhaps the foremost of these is the matter of exactly *how* processes at the level of the group enter into cognitive processes in particular persons; in what follows I try to reveal as much of this process as my data will allow in respect of above/below. There is also the matter of historical transformation and how this is effected; can the process of cognitive construction in particular persons throw additional light on historical transformations? Given that above/below is an aspect of Fijian hierarchy, in what sense can it be understood as implicated in its constitution? I shall try to answer these questions in the course of this book; at the same time I hope to provide sufficient evidence to show that the notion of modulated construction is convincing. At the very least, I think I may argue that my data do demonstrate the social processes whereby a hierarchical notion is simultaneously constructed in the cognitions of particular persons over time and manifest in the behavioural interaction between people in groups.

A summary of contents and methods

The book is effectively divided into two parts, according to the nature of the data with which it deals. In Chapters 2–7, data from participant observation are analyzed to show how indigenous spatial constructs are manifest in certain key social contexts and tied to specific relations of exchange. I try to show how notions of hierarchy are played out against notions of equality in terms of the relations between people in space – the social relations concerned being those between kin, between men and women, and between households at the level of the clan. As we shall see, the crucial outcome of this interplay of notions consists in the apparent dominance of hierarchy over equality in social relations. An examination of everyday ritual occasions in the house, the village hall and the church, and in certain contexts out of doors, shows that people's use of space makes hierarchical relations appear to be the essence of 'the way according to the land'. However, when we look at precisely *how* above/below is manifested in the house, the village hall, and the church it becomes apparent that somewhat different forms of hierarchy are constituted there. These differences point to inherent complexities in the notion of above/below, which may be supposed to present a problem to persons who are constructing its 'meaning'. Thus Chapters 2–7 describe social processes at the level of the group within and through which people constitute hierarchy; they prepare the way for an attempt to investigate the developmental process by which a person constructs over time the 'meaning' of above/below.

Chapters 8 and 9 use psychological techniques as well as participant observation to investigate the way children come to make relations in space isomorphic with hierarchical relations. This entails an account in Chapter 8 of the typical style of interaction between adults and children, one that fosters in the developing child an acute awareness of seniority, constituted in terms of what it means to be *madua,* 'shy' or 'ashamed'. Children's essays on the subject of being 'grown up' reveal their ideas about gender and rank. Chapter 10 describes data derived from children's drawings of *yaqona*-drinking, and their commentary upon them, together with their responses to prepared drawings of meals, *yaqona*-drinking and meetings. The responses to these tasks are analyzed to discover what children take to be the significance of above/below; the analysis reveals a three-way interaction between notions of rank, seniority and gender that is largely derived from the images children form of everyday ritual contexts; however, the precise nature of this interaction varies across contexts and according to age and sex.

Finally, Chapter 10 discusses the significance, in this Fijian context, of a conflation of social relations and space in the light of the process of its cognitive construction, together with its wider implications for the cognitive theory discussed above. The sensitivity of the above/below axis to fine hierarchical distinctions makes it a perfect vehicle for the constitution and expression of images of collective social relations as hierarchy; moreover, it allows for an effective assertion of a single, overarching principle of hierarchy – as if social relations within the collective were in all domains the same. Analysis of the ethnography in the light of data on children's cognitive construction of above/below shows how everyday ritual behaviour is crucial to children's construction of a flexible hierarchical scheme in whose terms they represent for themselves relations between people. The apparent congruence between the household as a microcosm of the community and the community as the household writ large is constituted in everyday ritual where tributary relations are made to contain – and so seem to overcome –

the egalitarianism implicit in relations of balanced reciprocity. Indeed, given that balanced reciprocity is the foundation of the subsistence economy, it is only in and through ritualized behaviour that hierarchy can be made to appear self-evident.

Chapter 10 includes discussion of the implications of the data for the nature of certain historical changes in Fiji in the nineteenth and twentieth centuries, and argues that these changes were in part prefigured in the nature of above/below as cognitive construct. It shows too that 'hierarchy' cannot be conceived of as an analytical principle, even with respect to Fiji itself, since conceptions of how it works differ as a function not only of the age, but also of the sex, of any given person. There remains the challenge of formulating a model of cognition that is able at once to accommodate differences in the constructive process *and* to account for the production and comprehension of a particular person's behaviour in the course of any given interaction. Given the data derived from the combination of methods and theoretical perspectives used here, it is suggested that cognition is best treated by focusing on the developing person as the locus of a complex of historical and social processes that find their expression in lifelong cognitive development, and in the cognitive interactions made possible by the course of this development.

A brief introduction to Fijian history, and to the country and the village of Sawaieke

Fiji was colonized in the early part of the nineteenth century – Captain Bligh being credited with the first systematic recording of some of the islands in 1789 (see Figures 1 and 2 for maps of the South Pacific and Fiji). Missionary activity, especially by members of the Wesleyan (now Methodist) Missionary Society, was extensive from 1835 onwards (Henderson, 1931: 142; Clammer, 1976: 12). They found a highly developed culture, for some material features of which they had high praise, but were appalled by widespread and apparently routine cannibalism and by such practices as the strangulation of wives to accompany a dead chief to the other world (Williams, 1858, 1982: 60–89, 200; Calvert, 1858: 31; Waterhouse, 1866: 45, 197–201, 309; see also Seeman, 1862: 180; Diapea, 1928;

Clunie, 1977: 35–42). By all accounts missionary success was conspicuous – perhaps through their deliberate policy of establishing a widespread literacy whose objects were religious texts – and was assured when Cakobau converted in 1854 (Clammer, 1976: 56–70). Calvert (1858: 401), quoted in Geddes (1948: 334), claimed 54,000 conversions to Christianity by 1856 – that is, one-third of the population (compare Burton, 1910: 127).

Cakobau was paramount chief of a large area of central and eastern Fiji, and his conversion prompted mass conversions by his subjects. Cakobau had been aided in his rise to power by King George of Tonga and his kinsman Ma'afu, who had originally set out to conquer Fiji but were unable to subdue Cakobau, and Christian Tongan influence was of great importance in the history of Fiji in this period (Derrick, 1946: 55; Lessin, 1971: 9). However, the links between Tonga and Fiji were extensive before the nineteenth century and their reciprocal influence on one another is to be seen in social organization, ritual and myth.

At the period of European colonization Fiji was made up of some large confederations or kingdoms (in south-east Viti Levu, Lau and Vanua Levu) with much smaller chiefdoms in most parts of Viti Levu, in the leeward islands and in interior Vanua Levu (Derrick, 1946: 53). Derrick has it that while wars were frequent, they were 'small affairs' (ibid.: 24) conducted according to certain rules; with the advent of Europeans and new weapons, war took on a grander scale and increased in frequency (ibid.: 48–52; also Erskine, 1853: 159). Others argue that the introduction of the musket had little to do with intensified warfare (France, 1969: 21–2) and that consolidation of large and complex political hierarchies had long predated regular contact with Europeans (Sayes, 1984).

Whatever the facts, it does seem that the history of Fiji up to the 1850s was one of alternating diplomacy and warfare between the larger confederations, with each of them striving for a paramount position (Derrick, 1946: 53–63), a situation which reached its peak in the 1840s (ibid.: 75–89). Internecine warfare dramatically reduced in the late 1850s, and after some vicissitudes contingent upon the claims of rival colonists and sporadic warfare directed against them and the missionaries, Fiji was ceded to Britain in 1874. However, the chiefs of the larger confederations continued to exert political influence under Britain's 'indirect rule'. A study of Fijian leadership by Nayacakalou (1975), carried out in the early 1960s, shows how dependent was the colonial administration on traditional structures (see also Geddes, 1948: 169–73). At the time of my fieldwork, many important chiefs held positions of power in central government or in the Council of Chiefs, which advises the government on matters concerning the Fijian population.

From the late 1870s until 1916 Indians were brought to Fiji by the British as indentured labourers to work sugar plantations established by the colonists. A recent census showed their descendants as forming more than half the population of Fiji – given as just over 634,000. The Fiji–Indian population was concentrated in the sugar-growing and urban areas on the two largest islands and was not a significant proportion of the population on most smaller islands. In 1970 Fiji gained its independence from Britain while still retaining strong links with that country, the British Queen being acknowledged as Queen of Fiji and the democratic constitutional government being based on the Westminster model.

The politics of democracy and the sociocultural differences between the two populations inevitably entailed some confrontation, as did certain features of the constitution such as those concerning land rights. Nevertheless, until the military *coups* of 1987, the history of Fiji since independence had been marked by a largely peaceful coexistence of the two groups (see Norton, 1977; Mamak, 1978; Mamak and Ali, 1979). The *coups* restored to government many of the most prominent members of the predominantly Fijian Alliance Party, which had lost the 1987 election to a coalition between the National Federation Party, the party of the vast majority of Fiji Indians, and the Labour Party. Undoubtedly there are profound repercussions in this for both Fiji-Indians and indigenous Fijians (see, for example, Kaplan, 1988), among which are the probable entrenchment of practices and ideas that constitute tradition for indigenous Fijians. These are, in part, the subject of this book, whose ethnographic present refers to a time before the *coups* – the twenty-month period of my fieldwork, from July 1981 to February 1983.

Landholdings, as established by the Lands Commissions of 1912 onwards, are largely in the hands of indigenous Fijians. By law they are not able to alienate land which is held in the name of the clan and reverts to the state only when there are no descendants in the male line who may claim it. The Fijian population of the smaller islands, including Gau, has a mixed economy based on subsistence gardening, the keeping of a small number of livestock (pigs, cows, chickens and sometimes goats), and the occasional production of cash crops and copra. There was no Fiji-Indian community on Gau and at the time of my fieldwork there were perhaps six Fiji-Indians living there.

Gau is one of the islands of Lomaiviti (see Figure 3), situated between Bau (whose chief, Cakobau, exerted such influence in the early days of colonization) and the Lau group (another important chiefdom, whose paramount chief is Ratu Sir Kamisese Mara, the Prime Minister). Eight of the sixteen villages in Gau owe allegiance to Bau, but this is not the case for the other eight villages that form the country [*vanua*] of Sawaieke. Sawaieke people assert the historical independence of their chiefdom; however, there as elsewhere in Gau, Bauan influence has been strong. Villagers speak Bauan – the language of the Bible and other religious texts, today recognized as 'standard Fijian'; however, a few words peculiar to Gau are still in common use. Many other – perhaps most – Fijians still speak the language peculiar to their own area (see Capell and Lester, 1941; Roth, 1953: xix; and compare Cook, 1975: 173; Geraghty, 1983).

Gau is the fifth largest of the 332 islands of Fiji, about 140 square kilometres in area (Derrick, 1951: 287). It lies 60 kilometres east of Suva, the capital city of Fiji situated on the island of Viti Levu, and may be reached by boat or plane – there are three flights to the island by twelve- or sixteen-seat passenger planes every week in good weather. Virtually all villagers have relatives in Suva, Lautoka or one or several other urban areas and enjoy a holiday or even an extended stay of many months with their relatives in these areas. Similarly, urban dwellers tend to retain strong links with their natal village and return there for the Christmas season or to fulfil traditional ritual obligations. The villagers of Gau cannot therefore be said to be quite cut off from urban life, and by the age of ten most children have paid a visit to the big city.

The centre of Gau is mountainous and heavily forested; all villages are situated on the coast. Remains of earlier villages are to be seen in the lower hills, near what is now gardening land, and I was told that more ancient village sites may be found on hilltops further inland.

Sawaieke is the chiefly village for the eight villages that constitute Sawaieke country [*vanua*]. The recent Gau census shows the villages varying in size: 6 houses in Yadua and 41 in Nawaikama, with the other villages having between 20 and 30 houses on average. The population for Sawaieke country is shown as 1,242 and for Gau island as 3,119; the chiefly village of Sawaieke is listed as having 39 houses and a population of 227. My own census – completed some months later and updated shortly before I left – shows a total of 46 houses for Sawaieke village (41 inside the village proper and 5 on gardening land adjoining the village) and a population of 257. The discrepancy between the two censuses arises partly because it is likely that some houses outside the village proper were overlooked, and partly because a large number of young men were away working on another island when the Gau census was taken that year.

Fijian villages may not, to the untutored eye, appear especially traditional. On the mainland of Viti Levu the villages I visited consisted entirely of houses made of wood or concrete breeze blocks, usually lit by electricity. On Gau the villages varied in appearance; in some most houses were built of local materials with a roof of corrugated iron or, in some cases, of thatch. European-style houses are considered a sign of prosperity and in Sawaieke village over half the houses were made of wood or concrete breeze blocks, the rest being built of local materials and all of them having corrugated iron roofs. Most villages had a piped water supply or, where this was not possible, vast rainwater tanks. The water for Sawaieke village was piped from a pure spring source in the hills above the village – one standpipe being available for every three or four houses. Most villages also had electricity generators that were used to light the church and the village hall on Sundays and on the occasion of large gatherings in the village hall.

The economic policies of central government include the support of 'self-help' projects. If a village community, wishes to institute a business or a development project, the money raised by their own efforts is matched by government aid. So it was that Sawaieke became the first village in Gau to have electric light made available to all its houses, the electric lines being laid and the lights lit for the first time a few days before I left the village to return to England in February 1983. Until that time houses were lit by benzene and kerosene lamps.

Typical village design is such that houses are grouped round the *rara* or village green, on one side of which stands the church, with the village hall on another. Given the variety of materials used in house-building, villages tend to have a rather ramshackle but still attractive appearance, with large areas of grass crisscrossed by the paths worn by bare feet and here and there coconut palms, huge mango trees, vivid flowering shrubs and other plants. Daily life is a mixture of the routine work of house and garden, the relaxation to be found in an afternoon or evening of chat around the *yaqona* bowl, and the important demands of *na cakacaka vakavanua* – traditional ritual obligations (literally 'work in the manner of the land').

Primary schooling is free and compulsory and children attend their local school, which stands on its own land perhaps half a kilometre from the village; on average there is one primary school for every two villages. Children between the ages of twelve and sixteen or so whose parents can pay the fees may attend Gau's single junior secondary school; this takes in weekly boarders from all villages except the one closest to it. A full high-school education can be had only if the parents can afford to send their children to school outside Gau.

The atmosphere of village life is generally relaxed, despite the hard work that goes into gardening and house-building, fishing, mat-making and housework, to say nothing of the constant attention given to ceremonious and polite behaviour which all villagers observe in relation to others. This polite behaviour finds expression in day-to-day interaction; what constitutes a proper expression of the hierarchical relations that obtain between kin is exemplified by their disposition in space; it is the nature of these relations and of their manifestation in space that I discuss in that next chapter.

A note on the generality of research results

I lived in Sawaieke village on the island of Gau, Lomaiviti, for eighteen of the twenty months of my fieldwork, making visits to other villages in the 'country' [*vanua*] of Sawaieke with occasional visits to other countries for meetings, funerals and other purposes in company with Sawaieke villagers. The detailed data presented in this book refer either to the village of Sawaieke, or to the country (i.e. to all eight villages) of Sawaieke when this is specified in the text.

Given the salient differences in social relations to be found in northern Fiji (Quain, 1948: 244–5) and the sparseness of existing ethnographic accounts of space in Fiji, I do not wish to claim that my findings would extend to take in the northern and western areas. This said, I do suggest that the generality of my thesis would hold for central and eastern Fiji; however, the reader must bear in mind that some details of social relations, of ritual, of polite behaviour and so on, vary from one place to another in Fiji, as does language. The Fijian language as reported here is Bauan. I have to emphasize that none of my excursions abroad, either to Suva or, in company with Gau villagers, to Ovalau (an island in Lomaiviti), or to Bau for the Council of Chiefs in 1982, gave me any reason to suppose that the essence of my findings would not hold for other Fijian contexts, at least in central and eastern Fiji. In Suva, in those houses I visited whose owners had been born in Gau, the polite behaviour imposed by awareness of spatial constructs was certainly attenuated, but it had by no means disappeared. That all urban visitors to the village behaved with perfect propriety and seemed to know what was expected of them (even in the case of those young people whose experience was largely confined to the urban context) argued for the generality of an understanding of the nature of relations between people in space. Of course, the owners of those town houses where I visited had retained close links with the village and presumably reared their children to observe village values. I did on occasion hear people above middle age lamenting a certain lack of respect in the behaviour of the urban young – the evidence for this being found in their failure to observe the behavioural constraints imposed by above/below; however, I never observed any similar behaviour myself in any context except in those who were 'too young to know better'. In what follows, it should become apparent that there is a striking continuity of traditional modes of behaviour and traditional values in a situation whose history is one of radical and far-reaching change.

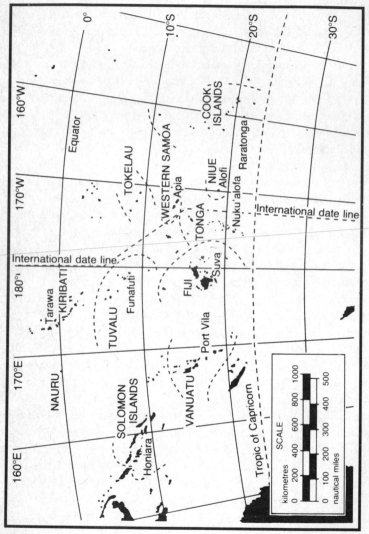

Figure 1 Map of South Pacific

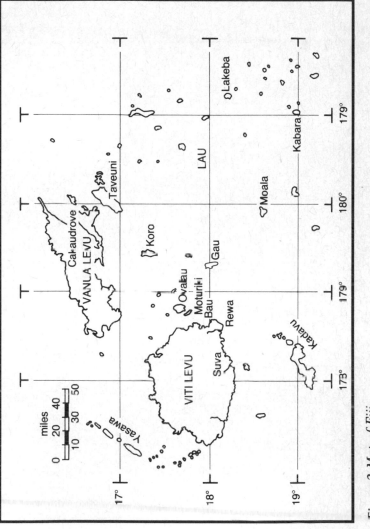

Figure 2 *Map of Fiji*

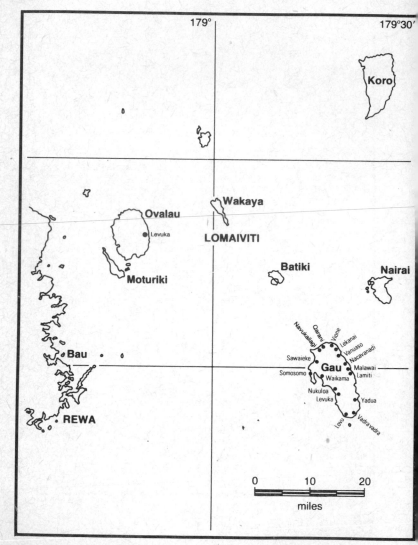

Figure 3 Map of Lomaiviti

2 Kinship and hierarchy within the household

Fijian tradition evinces a dynamic continuity whereby traditional values are constituted anew and objectified in material culture (see Toren, 1988). These values find their focus in kinship and exchange relations and their form in spatial constructs. In this chapter I describe relations that are *vakaveiwekani*, 'in the manner of kinship'. Hierarchy and equality are both manifest in relations between kin, but hierarchical relations are focused inside the household, with relations of equality being typically outside it. The house itself is the locus of hierarchical relations, so I begin with a description of house space and the behaviour that is proper to people in that space.

Design and use of house space

A number of ethnographers have noted the importance of the Fijian house for social relations and have given some brief account of its layout and the use of space within it; these accounts largely accord with my own data for Gau (see Hocart, 1929: 9–10; Lester, 1940: 277; Thompson, 1940: 64, 170; Quain, 1948: 82–3; Sahlins, 1962: 106; Belshaw, 1964: 6–8; Hooper, 1982: 31–3). Sahlins (1976: 23–46) attempts a more extended analysis which I discuss later.

The typical Sawaieke house is one large, rectangular room, 20–25 feet long and 10–12 feet wide. Until recently all houses, I was told, were built on a *yavu* or foundation of earth, but today *yavu* are less in evidence than they used to be and the new concrete houses are usually without them – even if their owners are chiefs. Formerly the relative height of the *yavu* – mostly less than 1 metre but sometimes up to 2 metres – signified the relative rank of its owners. Roth (1953: 18) notes that a public health regulation of 1885 made it mandatory for every house to be built on a raised foundation, but that resistance was encountered in enforcing it: 'the people's houses used to be built with no raised site whatever . . . the people . . . lived, both literally and figuratively, at a lower level than their chief' (compare Thompson,

1940: 160; Sahlins, 1962: 318). One concrete house in Sawaieke *did* have a *yavu*; some 2 metres in height, it was by far the most prominent *yavu* in the village and belonged to a family who numbered two previous paramount chiefs among their recent ancestors.

That *yavu* may still be important for chiefs' houses is apparent in Book 1 of Fijian school readers. This shows two drawings of houses. The first has no *yavu*: 'This is a Fijian house. It is a big house and looks good.' The second house has a definite *yavu* with a little stairway leading up to the entrance: 'This is a Fijian house. It is the house of a chief. It has a high *yavu*. The elders built it.'

Yavu are owned and bequeathed in the agnatic line; the name of a *yavu* belonging to the senior line of a clan or lineage may not be changed: a new house takes its name from the *yavu*. House sites are private to the owners; one must not play there or even walk across them. While I was in Sawaieke, several *yavu* on one side of the village were levelled by bulldozer. The *yavu* owners in Suva and elsewhere had apparently agreed to this, but for one old man it was a tragedy. On the appointed day he was outside, impotently threatening the bulldozer and weeping: 'Now the *yavu* belonging to our ancestors will disappear'. His behaviour amused many; some older people sympathized, others said, 'He doesn't understand about development; it's good that the village be made clean'. The levelled *yavu* remained the property of their owners, not to be built on without permission; but after a few months they ceased to retain their distinctness from the space around them, and the footpaths worn by bare feet no longer always skirted the boundaries where *yavu* had been, but sometimes went across them. Nevertheless people still remarked admiringly on the height of existing *yavu* even if they thought little of levelling those that were undistinguished.

The respect accorded the remaining *yavu* in the village and the sorrow of the old man above suggest a continuing conceptual link between village house sites and *yavu tabu* ('forbidden, or sacred, *yavu*'). These stand on clan or lineage gardening land and are still held to be sacred as the home of the ancestors – *na qase e liu*, literally, 'the old ones before' (compare Milner, 1948: 10). The term for clan – *yavusa* – itself refers to the house site, while the specific honorific title accorded a clan or lineage and used to refer to it in all ceremonial speeches is the name of its *yavu tabu*. One who steps on a *yavu tabu* may incur ancestral wrath, but people are sceptical about this and some say that nothing happens if one violates the taboo; however, mothers still attribute a child's illness to the eating of fruit taken from a tree growing on a *yavu tabu*.

When I asked what makes a *yavu tabu* taboo, people would mostly shrug and say *Esi!* (a verbal shrug that amounts to something like 'Who knows?'). However, one young man said that 'it concerns something our ancestors put there', but he was unable or perhaps reluctant to say what that might be. In pre- and early colonial times bodies were buried in the *yavu* of houses – a common practice in various parts of Oceania (see for example Firth, 1936, 1957: 76–82, 1970d: 388). However, it is not clear that this was the case for all the Fijian dead. Williams (1858, 1982: 191) talks of the burial of children in the *yavu* 'at the best end of the houses of several Chiefs' and in Capell's dictionary there is a reference to the *sautabu* as 'a chief's graveyard; in olden times his grave in the house foundation' (Capell, 1941: 186; see also Waterhouse, 1866: 43; Hocart, 1912: 448, 1929: 182; Thompson, 1940: 222; Peck, 1982: 152 fn.). Today the dead are laid out in the house before burial; thus Hocart (1929: 178) notes that 'lying in state is . . . 'lying above' or 'at the upper end' [*koto i cake*].'

There is no fencing or other demarcation of property beyond the walls of the house, but the area belonging to it extends some distance – this in relation to density of housing in the immediate area. So it is polite, if one trespasses off a recognised path, informally to ask the householder's permission should one see him or her; one might say: 'Allow me perhaps to make a short cut here', and the owner answers, 'Yes, fine', and the trespasser replies: 'Thanks, I'll be off then'. If, on a hot afternoon, one is seated outside on a mat, it is placed nearer one's own than one's neighbour's house; to take a mat and sit on it under someone else's tree is not good form.

A typical village house has four doors symmetrically placed in the centre of each side (see Figure 4). Wooden houses often have three doors – the 'end door' being omitted – and concrete houses may have only two. The 'door of the cooking irons' [*darava i sue*] is the common entrance. This door marks the lowest part of the space that is *i ra*, below. Everything to do with meals is relegated to this area; one must not bring food into the house by any door other than the common entrance, nor indeed use the other doors at all unless one is classed

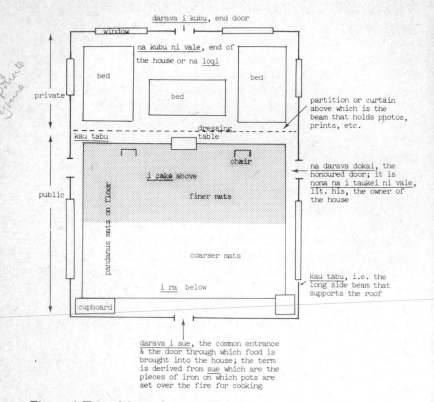

Figure 4 Typical house layout – Sawaieke

as an owner [*i taukei*] of the house or of high enough status for their use to be a prerogative of that status, or unless one is specifically invited to enter by the honoured door.

The honoured door [*darava dokai*] usually, but not always, faces the sea and is also called the 'sea door'; the door directly opposite it and facing inland may be called the 'land door'. The taboos on the use of these doors may once have been connected with *na kau tabu* – the 'sacred' or 'forbidden beams' that support the roof on both long sides of the house. In pre- and early colonial days the distinction between the sides of the house entered into traditional obligations in house-building. Hocart quotes an informant as saying, 'The side of the house towards the sea was called the noble side ... and with it went the east end, or if the house were perpendicular to the seashore, the east side was the noble one and with it went the sea end' (1929: 126). But there is no indication in either Hocart or Thompson (1940) that this division governed seating arrangements *inside* the house, as Sahlins suggests (1976: 34). As we shall see later, it is more probably connected with the orientation of houses to one other in the layout of the village and with exchange relations of balanced reciprocity between 'seapeople' and 'landspeople'.

To some extent *all* doorways are tabooed: one must never sit on a threshold in such a way that one's body is inside the house and one's legs and feet outside; nor may one wear shoes inside the house – they must be removed outside or immediately inside the entrance and to one side of it. If the fourth door, the 'end door' [*darava i kubu*], exists, it may never be used by anyone except the house owners. I heard children being scolded by old women for using this door in their own house: it was only for 'the elders' – in this case the children's parents – and forbidden to the young.

The end door leads out of *na kubu ni vale*, 'the end of the house', sometimes called the *loqi*. This is a private sleeping area, off-limits to any person other than the house owners, or guests who are sleeping in the house. It is also 'the space where everything good is kept'. Clothes, linen and valuables are stored there in wooden chests. Beds may be shared, or people sleep on individual sleeping mats on the floor; in this case they lie in the open area *i cake* – above. The private area is separated from the rest of the house by curtains (drawn only at night) or in some houses by a plywood partition.

The crossbeam that runs above the curtain, or above and to the fore of it, joining the two long beams, marks the upper limit *i cake* – above – of the public area of the house. On the crossbeam hang photographs of kin, awards for bravery, community service or perhaps skill in sewing, and brilliant reproductions of da Vinci's 'Last Supper', the prodigal son downcast among the swine, and Christ on the cross. There are also photographs of the English royal family – faded prints of George VI, or the Queen at the time of her engagement to Prince Philip, or magazine cutouts of Charles and Diana (cf. Lester, 1938). Photographs, awards and prints are all neatly framed and may be added to when a family member returns from a visit to Suva with a new studio portrait of self or kin taken against a backdrop of the English countryside, the Swiss Alps or some such other exotic place. The collection may be referred to as 'things of family history' [*ka ni tukutuku vakamatavuvale*].

Towards the top of the public, open area of the house there may be a couple of chairs, a chest of drawers with a mirror, and sometimes a table. The table is used to put things on but not to sit at: I saw this only once in eighteen months. Chairs are used only by the house's owners; such behaviour would be highly presumptuous in a guest. But if one is seated in a chair when someone arrives, it is proper to move to a place on the floor so as to be on a level with the guest. Only old and high-ranking men may retain a chair when a guest is present, and then only if the visit is likely to be brief and involves one or two younger people of lower rank. Indeed, it is rare to see chairs used at all.

The lowest part of the house *i ra* – below – is nearest the common entrance. When this door is open, one knows that people are 'at home' and will not be disturbed if one enters the house. But one does not walk directly up the path to the house, up the steps (if they exist) and enter. Instead, one approaches as it were indirectly. Modesty of demeanour, an unwillingness to presume upon one's welcome, is apparent in the slow gait adopted, the frequent dawdlings and halts when in sight of the house and close to it, and the way in which, finally, one puts one's head round the door frame or coughs discreetly to indicate one's presence. The occupants then encourage one to enter: 'Here, do come in!' – and the visitor enters, removes his or her shoes if wearing any, and sits down to one side of the common entrance and within a couple of feet of it. One's seated posture is important; in contemporary Gau women sit cross-legged like men, but on very formal occasions they sit in a 'ladylike manner' [*vakamarama*], their legs drawn back under the body and to one side.

One sits immediately on entry into a house because it is impolite to remain standing when others are seated. If one has to pass people who are seated, one adopts the manner called *lolou*: one bends from the waist, ducks one's head down and walks in a stooping posture, all the while murmuring an apology: *tulou, tulou*. Not until one has passed those who are seated may one stand upright again. Women and children may walk on their knees when in company inside a house, especially when passing among men. Unless one is an older man of high rank, one almost always approaches a seated chief on one's knees. The corollary of these postural acknowledgements of status in terms of vertical orientation is that it is *very* rude to touch someone on the head. So one asks permission of others present if one has to stand up or reach above their heads. One apologizes on reaching for the object and when the action is completed and one is seated again, claps softly three times to thank the company for their forbearance. The clap, or *cobo*, is performed with the palms crossed and slightly cupped to give a soft, hollow sound. The *cobo* is a feature of Fijian politeness and is used to express thanks in all kinds of situations, but especially in ceremonial performances and in the drinking of *yaqona*.

The noticeable differences in the extent to which people incline from the vertical when walking *lolou* tend to correlate with their status relative to those in the same company. A high chief walks *lolou* only in the company of men of similar or higher status from other areas; a clan chief or an elder shows only a slight inclination from the vertical to women and lower-status men, and a noticeable (i.e. respectful) postural deference to his peers. Married men and young men may walk on their knees for a high chief, bend low from their waists for clan chiefs and older men, incline politely to their peers, and simply duck their heads with a slight forward inclination from the shoulders for women. Only for the very few women accorded high status do they incline forward from the waist. Women, on the other hand, nearly always adopt the full *lolou* position when passing among their peers and people senior to them who are seated, are likely to walk on their knees inside a building, and seem less likely to make subtle changes in their own body posture with reference to the relative status of those with whom they are in company.

So. The visitor enters the house and seats him- or herself on the mat near the common entrance, but unless the visitor is a child, every effort is made by the house's occupants to get him or her to move up, to sit in a higher position. The visitor, however, knows what is fitting. One who is of high status will shortly move to a more honoured position. Indeed, he or she may have entered by 'the honoured door' – straight into a position above – but one would do this only if of much higher status than the house's occupants. A lower-status guest consents to move only a couple of feet from the common entrance, and if the guest ranks somewhere in the middle he or she moves, by degrees to a rightful place. This is never achieved without some urging by the house's occupants and demurral on the part of the visitor, the length of the exchange usually depending on the participants' comparative status. For both lower- and higher-status visitors the exchange tends not to last very long; for a middle-status person whose rights are less clearly defined it may be rather prolonged and be renewed several times over the course of the visit. The exchange goes something like this:

Owner: Here, here. Sit above.
Visitor: Thanks, thanks. [Meaning 'no'.]
Owner: Sobo! [indicating disapproval of the speaker's refusal and a desire to hear no more of it.] Sit above!
Visitor: Thank you, no. This suits me.
Owner [persuasively]: Please do sit above. Alas, it's no good; you are sitting in a poor position. Go and sit above.

Finally the visitor moves, and only when he or she is settled is the reason for the visit touched upon.

If the occupants of the house are drinking *yaqona* when a guest arrives, those present who may speak to the newcomer will urge that person to move until he or she is seated suitably relative to others, and in a large gathering this type of exchange takes place often. In polite recognition of the other's worth, one may urge the other to sit above oneself. This behaviour occurs in all situations, from the most informal to the most grand and solemn (when it takes the form of significant gestures and facial expressions and inaudible mouthings of the invitation to move) and in all buildings, from temporary shelters to churches.

This glance at polite behaviour is intended to convey something of the all-pervasive importance of people's disposition within any given space. True politeness means behaving as if the other is of higher status than oneself, so one should comport oneself in a modest and unassuming fashion compounded with a dash of shyness or quiet dignity according to age. Hence the constant attempts to place others on a higher level and to deprecate the necessity for having to assume a higher position oneself, not because one *wants* to but because others have insisted upon it.

But this humility may be only apparent and if – in a large gathering, for example – invitations and repeated urgings to 'sit above' are neglected, one may simply take it upon oneself to move up the room to a position more calculated to show one's standing in the community. This is particularly true of one who is in fact manoeuvring for recognition that is rather greater than that which would normally be accorded him or her in respect of rank by birth and age. One must be seen to be of high status, and there is no clearer manifestation of this than one's seating position in any gathering.

When at home, men sit in the public area above. If both a man and his wife or a woman and her brothers are present, she is always seated closer to the common entrance than they are. This is true too for a woman and her grown-up sons unless she be of high rank in her own right, and very old. The lower part of the house is associated with domestic hubbub and, more particularly, with cooking. This is evident in the use of space in villagers' homes in the capital, where the kitchen is inside the house rather than separate from it, as it is in the village. These small terrace houses or flats are on two floors, an indoor stairway leading to the upper room, and there is only one entrance from the street. In these homes the part of the sitting room that is below is farthest from the entrance and nearest to the kitchen (Figure 5a). When I asked why *i cake* – above – and *i ra* – below – denote areas of a room or of the typical village house, I was told by both men and women that the area below is near the kitchen and generally occupied by women. It is with respect to food provision and cooking that women's labour is devalued by comparison with that of men, both within the household on an everyday basis and in the ritual presentation of foods.

Gender is a significant factor in the construction of differential status on the above/below axis; however, the interaction of gender with rank and seniority is not, as we shall see in later chapters, straightforward. Nevertheless, with respect to the use of house space it is women who customarily sit below, and it seems to be their association with this area that allows it to be so called. The proximity of the space below to the kitchen and the common entrance is of less importance than the customary seating position of women. This is clear when one examines layouts that do not conform to the norm.

In Suva apartments (Figure 5a) the common entrance is at the high end of the room; in Figure 5b the kitchen is adjacent to the area of the sitting room above; while in Figure 5c the above/below axis is out of alignment with the norm for having the private area above. The house in Figure 5b is unusual in being divided into rooms; that in Figure 5c is very small and built on a slope that does not allow easy access to a third door. In all cases practical considerations have led to

ie mechanical in terms where physical design do not lend meaning?

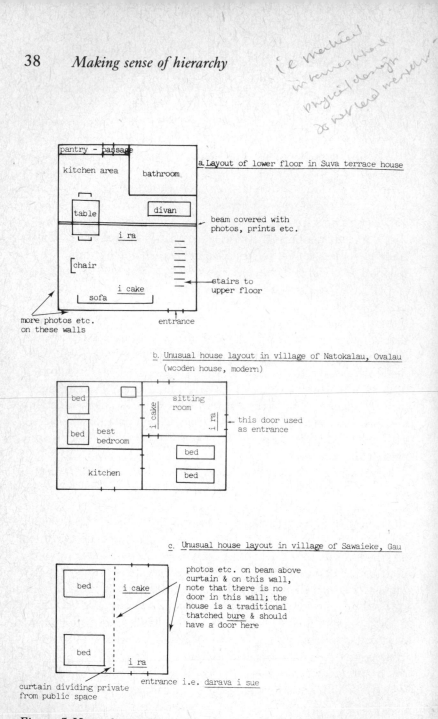

a. Layout of lower floor in Suva terrace house

b. Unusual house layout in village of Natokalau, Ovalau (wooden house, modern)

c. Unusual house layout in village of Sawaieke, Gau

Figure 5 House layouts in Suva, Ovalau and Sawaieke

a break with conventional design, but no matter – one always knows which area is below; it is the place where the women sit.

Particular hierarchical relations between kin are marked by behaviours which themselves enter into the valuation of the space within the house or other building in the village. I describe these relations and behaviours in detail later on. Here I only remark that, within the household, the senior member sits above the junior member of the same sex (though this is not necessarily so for women seated at meals). Across sex relative position is complicated, since if the senior party is a woman she is usually, but not always, seated below her male junior. As we shall see, gender poses something of a problem for hierarchy within the household.

The household: its composition and division of labour

Sawaieke people use two terms for the 'people of the house': *lewe ni vale* or *matavuvale; vuvale* derives from *vu*, 'source' or 'root' and *vale*, 'house'. They eat together daily and share in the products of each other's labour; they have access to all parts of the house and may sleep there. Given the sexual division of labour and the fact that young men may *not* sleep the night at home (especially if they have sisters whom they must avoid) but rather with their peers in a kitchen or otherwise unused building, eating together is the most salient marker of household membership. Indeed sharing food is itself definitive of kinship.

At the peak of its developmental cycle a household includes three generations: a man and his wife in their fifties, their older, unmarried children who are not at work in an urban area or away at school, their younger children and at least one married son with his wife and perhaps a baby. It may include an aged parent, an unmarried, widowed or divorced sister of the male household head, and perhaps an illegitimate child or two. There may be ten to twelve members in such a household; average membership is about eight, with a very few households consisting of only an elderly couple.

Neolocality on marriage – whereby a young married couple move as soon as possible to a house of their own in the man's village – is encouraged by both church and central government; so fully extended households do not seem to last for more than a few years or so. The relative autonomy of the neolocal nuclear household in the first stage of its developmental cycle does not preclude submission to the authority of the senior man in the older generation. It is he who calls lineage meetings (in Sawaieke village, the smallest social division beyond the household) to discuss matters of common concern to all its members, and it is his decisions that govern the action taken. Given that lineage houses are usually grouped together, a young married woman may also be at the beck and call of her mother-in-law.

The senior man in each household may assign his sons or other male household members specific tasks such as the preparation of copra, the tending of animals, or the digging of a new garden plot; or he may leave them to carry on work in their own gardens. In general, men clear land, plant and weed gardens, prepare copra and do all heavier jobs such as house-building, roadworks, and so on. Some men fish with line or spear; they focus on species larger than those usually caught by women.

However, it it women who must provide fish for the family several times a week; they go net-fishing [*qoli*] in large groups every Saturday, and otherwise fish singly or in small groups with line and bait [*siwa*]. Within the household, the senior woman may oversee the labour of younger women and of children when they are not at school. Women's labour is more unremitting than men's. They do the daily housework of cooking, cleaning and washing – all heavy tasks in a large household – and often have to tend to babies and pre-school children while going about their work. They must also prepare pandanus and weave it into mats. A wide variety of coarse and fine mats are used for floor and bed covers and are important items for ceremonial exchange. Women also sew many of their own and their children's clothes, make baskets and brooms for household use, and often have to collect and bring home dried firewood for cooking.

In a large household, women in their thirties may be aided by their band of young children, who are adept at washing up, running messages, gathering firewood, peeling cassava, and so on. Adolescents between the ages of twelve and sixteen are not very visible in terms of day-to-day labour: they are mostly away at Gau's Junior Secondary School or at high school elsewhere. Children's labour is discussed later; here I wish just to point out that a woman with a very young family may have a hard time meeting all her obligations unless she has the aid of one of her husband's sisters who is junior to her in age.

In general women's labour is as highly valued as men's and their mat-making and other skills are openly admired by men. Thus the sense in which gender is a differentiating factor in hierarchical relations cannot be said to rest on a *general* devaluation of women's labour.

Hierarchy and gender in kin relations

To a casual observer of social relations in Fiji, it seems that men have a social and political status that is vastly superior to women's. On the whole, wives are submissive to their husbands, sisters to their brothers, and in their talk men tend to represent women as their inferiors. Women themselves assert the superiority of husbands and elder brothers within the household and do not quarrel with these men's right of command.

This is not to say that all men are superior to all women. Status within the household is *said* to be in terms of seniority, so some older women rank above younger men. Here I am opposed to Nayacakalou's view that: 'as descent is patrilineal, marriage patrilocal and the lineage group exogamous, the female members of the sibling group need not come into considerations of seniority at all ...' (1955: 47). In conversation men *do* assert the importance of seniority even across sex, and this despite the fact that their behaviour often contradicts their speech; and women are adamant that the seniority of a woman who is the eldest of a sibling group should be observed, even while they maintain in general that men should lead. The interaction between gender and seniority is complex (compare Geddes, 1948: 199); so, for example, the senior status of older women over young men is evident only in the extent to which the women are accorded 'respect' [*vakarokoroko*] and their orders obeyed. Young men often ignore the requests of old women who stand to them as classificatory mothers or mothers-in-law, or else mock and tease them. Only if they are close kin (for example mother or elder sister within the household) is it usual for young men to show much respect for older women. If, however, an older woman is of high rank by birth and/or marriage, she is treated respectfully by younger men.

Nayacakalou's (1955) model of Fijian kinship stresses patrilineal descent – properly so with respect to rank (to be further discussed in Chapter 5). However, given the importance of connections through women, it seems more accurate to describe Fijian kinship as reckoned bilaterally (see Sahlins, 1962: 168). In talking about differential rank people emphasize descent through the father; but if they wish to establish an impeccable claim, they take pains to mention the chiefly rank of the mother. Similarly, in disparaging a claim to chiefly rank they will remark that, after all, the claimant's mother was 'just a commoner' [*tamata ga*]. But it is not only for reasons of rank that ties through women are important. Women often marry out, into other villages or other islands, but even when she marries within her own village a woman is understood to marry into her husband's house. In all cases, matrilateral links are ritually elaborated in the *vasu* relation between a child and its mother's natal lineage.

This relation is said to allow the *vasu* (i.e. a man's sister's child) the freedom of his or her mother's father's and mother's brothers' houses: the *vasu* may rely on them for unquestioning hospitality and may take anything desired without asking for it. The relation may obtain across lineage or within or across clans within a given village, and was relatively common in Sawaieke village, where there is about 45 per cent village endogamy. However, the relationship more often obtains between ego and the mother's lineage in another village. The relationship is explicitly recognized as important, and people say that it is through women that 'the path of kinship' is created because, as I was told, they 'carry the blood of posterity' [*kauta na dra ni kawa*] (compare Sahlins, 1962: 168; see Hocart, 1915b, 1929: 40; Thompson, 1940: 62ff.; Belshaw, 1964: 32; Hooper, 1982: 196ff.).

Within the village, *vasu* rarely exploit their privileges but the bond is normally a close one, in part because the children of mother's brother are cross-cousins to ego (i.e. the *vasu*) and this relation in the junior generation is likely to be an intimate one. The *vasu* relation cannot be equated to that of *veivugoni* – parents-in-law and children-in-law – despite the fact that the *vasu* refers to mother's brothers as 'father-in-law'. The *vasu* relation is established for the eldest child of a marriage in the ceremony of *kau mata ni gone*, 'carrying the face of the child', in which the ritual exchange of goods must favour the maternal kin. One is *vasu* to one's mother's lineage, and this includes men who are one's grandfathers, fathers-in-law and cross-cousins (compare Walter, 1979: 369–70).

Kinship terminology is Dravidian – distinguishing cross and parallel relatives in ego's generation and in the first ascending and descending generations. Terminology and marriage preferences in Sawaieke country largely accord with descriptions given by Nayacakalou (1955) for Tokatoka Tailevu, by Sahlins (1962: 147ff.) for Moala, and by Hocart (1929: 33–42), Thompson (1940: 53–65) and Hooper (1982: 20–23) for Lau (see also Capell and Lester, 1945; Quain, 1948: 244–97; Groves, 1963; Scheffler, 1971; Walter, 1975).

All relationships except that between cross-cousins are character-ized by a certain degree of respect and avoidance. For true and classificatory siblings of opposite sex [*veiganeni*] avoidance becomes more marked as children grow older, and once they reach sexual maturity is characterized by the description *veitabui*, 'forbidden to each other'. It is said of such relationships, 'they cannot speak to each other'. Relations between same-sex siblings [*veitacini*] may be friendly and relaxed, especially when classificatory, but here the seniority distinction means that relations rarely attain the degree of ease possible between cross cousins.

The relationship across sex between parents-in-law and children-in-law is one of marked avoidance. A daughter-in-law speaks to her husband's father only if she is addressed by him, and he will address her only if strictly necessary. The relationship between a son-in-law and his wife's mother is perhaps somewhat more relaxed, but again the senior party must be shown great respect; she is addressed by her son-in-law only if this is unavoidable. A man is rather more at ease with his father's sister, especially if they live at close quarters; but this is not the case for a woman and her mother's brother. These 'in-law' relationships are called *veivugoni*; they include wife's father and mother, husband's father and mother, father's sisters, mother's brothers, a woman's brothers' children, a man's sisters' children, and the husbands and wives of one's children. Relations within sex may be fairly easy when they are classificatory, but again the younger party may not address the older party on terms of equality, and the relationship – especially between men – becomes more strained and marked by avoidance as the parties grow older. *Veivugoni* are *veitabui* – 'forbidden to each other' – as are siblings and indeed all categories of relative other than cross-cousin.

However, young unmarried people of marriageable age (late teens and older) sometimes ignore the incest taboo on relations with classificatory *veivugoni* of their own age. I knew of at least three cases where sexual relations flouted the conventions in this respect. Again, young unmarried people in their late teens and early twenties may be quite friendly and relaxed with people of their own sex and age to whom they stand as *veivugoni*.

It seemed that it was only on marriage that relations between *veivugoni* of the same age settled into a fairly rigid pattern of avoidance, both across and within sex. This may be connected with the fact that marriage marks adulthood. Children know something about avoidance, but do not begin to practise it with any regularity until they are in their mid-teens. In other words, adults may not begin to impose a *tabu* on social intercourse with children until they are past puberty. This is especially true of within-sex relationships; thus a boy might be a great favourite with one or two of his *vugo* (his classificatory mother's brothers) but at some time in his adolescence they would tell him that they were *veitabui*, 'forbidden to each other', and instruct the boy to cease to address them.

Relations between true and classificatory *veiganeni* (siblings) and true and classificatory *veivugoni* across sex and across generation are most clearly marked by avoidance. 'There are also emotional elements in these relationships – men feel great "respect" for their sisters, and they are "afraid" of their parents-in-law' (Arno, 1976b: 74). Respect is expected of the junior generation for relations between *veitinani* – true and classificatory mother and child – and *veitamani* – true and classificatory father and child. This is especially so if the partners to the relationship are adults or near-adults of similar age and opposite sex (cf. Ravuvu, 1971). They are subject to the incest taboo.

In the incestuous [*veitabui*] relationships, terms of address are not reciprocal even where terms of reference are. All these relationships are hierarchical; seniority gives the older party superior social status. However, classificatory brothers of the same age may address each other as *kemudrau* – 'you two', use of the dual plural denoting a respectful familiarity; and women call each other by name. Where there is a large age difference between true and classificatory siblings the younger party rarely ventures to address the older party at all, while the latter may continue using familiar terms within sex.

All intergenerational relations – consanguineal or affinal – accord authority to the senior party; mother's brother as well as father and father's sister as well as mother are owed unquestioning respect and obedience. Any offence against a close senior relative may bring sickness or misfortune upon the offender, whose actions anger God and the ancestors (cf. Arno, 1976a, 51). Gender *is* an issue here because, as I noted above, it is only to close female kin and women of chiefly birth that young men in particular can be relied upon to show proper respect. Nevertheless, *close* senior kin are bound to be accorded respect and obedience irrespective of sex; thus gender does not pose the same problem here as it does for relations within generation – for example those classified as siblings. Relations between siblings are also strongly hierarchical and, as we shall see in Chapter 8, the idea of seniority as basic to social relations is impressed upon a growing child in all his or her interactions with older persons.

Within the household the senior generation treats siblings as if the relation between them mirrors that between generations. Here gender becomes a complicating factor: an eldest child who is a girl is dignified by the appellation *ulu matua* (literally 'mature head') and allowed some authority over her younger siblings, but she is rarely, if ever, given the status of an eldest child who is a boy. It is instructive to compare the Fijian relation between brother and sister with that obtaining in Tonga and Samoa, where the sister has higher ritual rank than her brother while he has executive authority; the sister's curse is a powerful sanction. In both Samoa and Tonga a woman's close kin recognize her personal status independently of that of her husband and without reference to him (see Rogers, 1977 and Bott, 1981, 1982: 162 for Tonga; Mead, M. 1930: 122–3 and Shore, 1976, 1982: 228–30 for Samoa).

Fijian terms of reference for siblings always distinguish 'older' from 'younger' within sex; a male or female ego refers to older same-sex siblings as *tuakaqu*, to younger same-sex siblings as *taciqu*. For cross-sex siblings the concern with seniority means that one is usually told who is the older by a qualifying statement, but for either a male or female ego a sibling of the opposite sex is *ganequ*. So for cross-sex siblings there is no automatic marking of relative seniority in the term of reference itself, and only the gender distinction is acknowledged (cf. Firth, 1970c). This is interesting because in terms of actual behaviour – by contrast to discourse – relative seniority across sex is as likely to be ignored as it is to be acknowledged. So an older sister sometimes has to conform to the wishes of an adult younger brother – the notion that men should lead and women follow here overriding the notion that those who are older may command those who are younger. However, if she is the eldest of a set of siblings a woman should be consulted by her younger brothers and her judgement deferred to (cf. Arno, 1976b: 73).

Nayacakalou (1955: 47, 1978: 15) takes a Fijian man's view in his unqualified assertion that male status within the kinship group is always higher than female status; Calvert (1858: 299) says that sisters should be subservient to brothers; but Geddes notes that his chiefly informant told him the opposite was the case, which Geddes attributes to a strong Tongan influence in Bau (1948: 191 fn.). I show later that this apparent contradiction is inherent in the interaction between seniority and gender.

A woman is subservient to her true father, elder brothers and/or husband. These men may command her, and it is her place to obey. She is affectionately subservient to real and classificatory fathers, practises avoidance and is subservient to real and classificatory elder brothers and often to younger brothers if they are adults and close to her in age; she defers and is subservient to her husband.

Unless she lives with her husband a woman is subject to the control of her father and brother. An unmarried, separated or widowed woman may be disciplined by her brother for insubordination – the following instances provide typical examples: a man of twenty-one slapped his nineteen year-old sister hard on the face when he caught her smoking, this being said by young men to be a male prerogative and unseemly for young women; a man in his early sixties beat and turned out of his house his slightly younger widowed sister for failing to take part in a ceremonial exchange with kin in another village and thus, he said, 'shaming' him; a man of twenty-six threatened to beat and turn out of the house his thirty-year-old sister, who was married but separated from her husband, because she expressed a desire to ignore a kinship obligation and her behaviour would, her brother felt, have put him to public shame – she gave in to his threats and produced the mats required of her. This incident entailed an argument concerning their respective authority – to be discussed further in Chapter 10. 'Shame' or 'shyness' [*madua*] is a behavioural marker of submission, and I shall have more to say about it later. However, note that the examples of male behaviour given here are not expressions of their own shame (though they are said to be so) but rather a means of inducing shame or shyness in their female relatives by forcing them to demonstrate submission.

Any habitual occupant of a house is an 'owner', but it is men who have authoritative ownership of immoveable property and so a woman is at the mercy of husband, brother or father. People may deplore a man's behaviour in turning his sister out, but it is rare for anyone to question his right to do so (cf. Chapelle, 1978: 74–7). Married women are never considered to be full owners in their marital home, especially where the marriage is exogamous to the village. A childless widow or one whose grown-up children have left home often returns to her natal village, where she can always find shelter with one relative or another. She has more rights in her natal than in her married home, though these do not go so far as authoritative ownership. Rather, she is there on her brother's sufferance.

Women do not have any legal rights in land, which is held by the clan or lineage with usufruct rights passing in the male line. Effectively a woman has the right to take coconuts, fruit and green vegetables from the gardens of her husband or brother, but again she can do this only on sufferance and since, in Gau, women do not garden very much and do not grow the root vegetables that form the staple crops, a woman is dependent upon a male for this food for herself and her children. France (1969: 17) says that before the Lands Commissions women were often granted rights in land on marriage in the ceremony of *i covicovi ni draudrau*, translated by Capell (1941: 38) as 'land given by a bride's *mataqali* [lineage] as her dowry, reverting to donors at the death of the woman's children' (compare Roth, 1953: 72). In Sawaieke land was formerly sometimes (rarely) given with a woman on marriage; it was called 'the plucking of the *lou* leaves' [*i betibeti ni lou* or *i covicovi ni lou*]; it was intended for her children, but also for her own use in case of problems with her marital kin.

Given the strict avoidance rule and the fact that women marry out, relations between an adult brother and sister are far less likely to come under public scrutiny than those between husband and wife. Thus it is in the marriage relationship that hierarchy across sex between adults of the same generation is most obvious. There is no problem here as to precisely how gender and seniority interact, as there is between brother and sister; in marriage it is axiomatic that the husband has authority over his wife, and the issue of relative seniority is entirely irrelevant. This is not to say that women cannot exert influence over their husbands in respect of important decisions and, as far as I could gather, a wife's influence was likely to be impressive. This was recognized by male Methodist preachers; thus women were sometimes exhorted to make use of the good feelings aroused in the privacy of the marital bed, to urge men to give up drinking and to take on tasks that would further develop [*vakatoroi-caketaka*, literally 'make to move upwards'] their family's standard of living.

Both men and women often emphasized in conversation that a wife should respect her husband's wishes and follow his lead; the man is household head [*liuliu ni matavuvale*]. A wife should defer to her husband, respond at once to his needs and even anticipate them. This deference is, as we shall see in Chapter 3, particularly evident in the way she attends upon him at meals. Husband and wife avoid each other in public, but the respect behaviour this entails largely devolves upon the wife; a husband *may* address orders to his wife in public, but she must wait until they are alone to speak to him or, in case of urgency, send a discreet message to him by one of their junior kin. In very relaxed public situations (perhaps around the *yaqona* bowl in their own house) a wife of long standing will address remarks to her husband, but this is an unusual rather than an ordinary occurrence. Geddes (1948: 189–91) notes that Deuba woman use the term *Ratu* (usually a prerogative of chiefs) in address to their husbands, but that there is no reciprocal term for wives; he also says that women must be cautious in interrupting their husbands.

A woman's behaviour reflects upon a man's, but the same does not hold vice versa. A woman *may* leave her husband for repeated infidelity, but on the whole, and despite the fact that her jealousy may be understood, a man's adultery is not entirely unexpected. I heard of many instances of adultery by married men with unmarried women, but no cases of adultery by married women. If it does occur, the women involved must go to extraordinary pains to conceal it. Such an offence by a woman would call down on her the most violent censure by kin and affines alike. Thompson (1940: 58) says of Lau that 'adultery ... usually causes only temporary friction. Fidelity to one's spouse is not really expected.' This could be said to be true for men in Sawaieke, but it is certainly not true for their wives.

It will be apparent from all the foregoing that hierarchical relations between kin within the household are given by an interaction between gender and age seniority. However, attitudes may differ regarding the precise nature of this interaction with respect to hierarchy between siblings. Only within the marriage relationship is it axiomatic that males have authority over females of the same generation, whatever the relative seniority of husband and wife. How this authority is derived from a transformation of the equal relations between cross-cousins is the subject of the next chapter.

3 Transforming equality into hierarchy

Relations within the household are the focus for hierarchical kin relations and for behaviour 'according to kinship'. The term for kin – *veiwekani* – has as its widest reference the entire Fijian population, so in everyday usage it includes kin by marriage as well as by consanguinity, fellow villagers, fellow members of Sawaieke country, or the inhabitants of Gau. The relation between cross-cousins is the only kin relation that is *not* hierarchical and *not* incestuous; it is typically extradomestic. The equality of cross-cousins challenges the hierarchy within the household; the relationship and its transformation in marriage are described below.

Equality in relations between kin

Equality is inscribed in joking relationships. These obtain between people of certain areas who stand to each other as *veitabani*, literally 'of the same branch', and those who are *tauvu*, literally 'of the same root'. For *veitabani* the founding ancestors, or *vu* of the two groups are said to have been cross-cousins; for *tauvu* the people are said to have worshipped the same ancestor god. The conduct of these relations between people of different areas is modelled on that for cross-cousins (see Hocart, 1913a, 1952: 43–9).

An equality that is indifferent to age, rank and gender marks the cross-cousin relationship. The relationship is 'serious', important – but its essence is familiarity (cf. Groves, 1963: 280). Unlike other kin relations, terms of address are reciprocal within and across sex: men call each other *tavale* (cousin), *kemuni* ('you many') or use names; women call each other *dauve* (cousin) or use names. Men and women address each other as *kemuni* or by name; if they are parents, they may use a teknonym: 'mother of so-and-so' or 'father of so-and-so' (using the eldest child's name). The relation between cross-cousins within sex is as important for friendship, fun and confidential relations as, across sex, it is important for passionate desire, sex and marriage; across sex one may refer to a cross-cousin as *na watiqu*, 'my spouse', irrespective of whether one is married or not (cf. Quain, 1948: 262–80).

A man's *tavale* (male cross-cousin) and a woman's *dauve* (female cross-cousin) are the category in which fast friends are found, friends who can refuse each other nothing and rely on each other for psychological support. One should never refuse a request from a cross-cousin, be it for money, labour, or anything else. Exchange relations between cross-cousins are those of perfectly balanced, if delayed, reciprocity. However, relations between a man and his wife's brothers or a woman and her husband's sisters can become strained, particularly between women. Women are not more quarrelsome than men, but residence being virilocal, a woman may have to live at close quarters with her sisters-in-law; by contrast, adult men do not have to live under the same roof nor work along-side their brothers-in-law (cf. Sahlins, 1962: 138). The relation-ship is open to exploitation: a woman may take a thing from her brother's wife without asking and married women may feel themselves hardly done by in this respect. A man may feel that his sister is not being well treated by her husband. But in general relations between *veitavaleni* (male cross-cousins), *veidauveni* (female cross-cousins) and *veidavolani* (male and female cross-cousins, literally 'those who lie down together') are marked by equality, cordiality and friendly competition and intimacy. They may also argue without arousing the strong criticism that follows arguments between those who stand as close kin in any of the hierarchical relations governed by the incest taboo (cf. Quain, 1948: 265).

Relations of equality between cross-cousins across sex [*veidavolani*] contradict the notion that men should lead. For instance, a young woman is afraid to smoke in front of her real or classificatory brother (who may be only a little older than herself) because she will be beaten. But she can smoke with impunity in front of her male cross-cousin [*davola*] and even demand cigarettes of him; she can talk rudely or cheekily, make sly innuendos about his sexual adequacy, punch him playfully on the side of the head and generally act as if the two of them are equals. The significance of this behaviour is neatly conveyed by Nayacakalou's observation that in Tokatoka (Tailevu, Viti Levu): 'the familiarity and joking between cross-cousins of opposite sex are so intimate that some people even argue against cross-cousin marriage on the ground that the wife will be difficult to control' (1955: 48). As we shall see below, the relationship between *veidavolani* poses a very real problem for the hierarchical marriage relationship.

Marriage: the transformation of equality into hierarchy

A person's spouse is by definition a cross-cousin – this being the only marriageable category of kin; and it is usually cross-cousins who engage in pre-marital affairs. However, a girl's sexuality should be 'taken care of' [*maroroi*] and until marriage should be under the control of her brothers and father. The corollary of this is that a young man gains status by illegitimate parenthood, and a girl loses it. Female virginity is highly valued, if rarely a fact on marriage. Every young man wants to marry a virgin, and if the marriage is one arranged by their elders, and the young couple are not known to have slept together, and the girl has asserted herself to be 'truly a girl', then the absence of virginity in the bride brings public shame on her kin. The cavity of the cooked pig presented with taro to her kin after consummation of the marriage is left open rather than filled with leaves, as it would be had she been a virgin (cf. Brewster, 1922: 197; Lester, 1940: 283; Quain, 1948: 339; note that the wedding ceremony described by Sahlins [1962: 179–82] is substantially similar to that for Gau; see also Hooper, 1982: 76–82, 96–100).

In the matter of sexual relations in general, the man's sexuality is said to be 'stronger' than the woman's. But if a young man ventures into an affair with a woman who is much older than he is – say by seven to ten years – he is likely to fall victim to a mysterious illness called *dogai*. This is said to be caused by the overpowering nature of the older woman's sexuality and causes the young man to sit gazing into space all day, neglecting his work in the gardens; he loses his appetite and small things look large to him, so that he ducks if he sees a mosquito or other small insect flying towards him. The young man does not know he is ill, but at last his malady is discovered by one of his senior female kin who both understands the illness and knows the herbal remedy to use in its cure (cf. Thomson, 1908, 1968: 24; Brewster, 1922: 198).

The overpowering sexuality of older women militates against

marriages where the wife is significantly older than her husband; this suggests that seniority in a wife may pose a threat to her husband's assumption of authority. Seniority itself denotes authority, and if a husband is to be seen to be in command, then his wife should not be much older than he is himself. The threat to young men from older women's sexuality is one aspect of the questionable status of *cauravou* – 'young men', the most junior of male status categories. Are they indeed above and thus superior to females in general? As we shall see later, viewed as a status group over against other ranks of men, young men may be said to be on a par with (married) women.

A crucial change takes place in the relationship between *veidavolani* at the point where the partners to it become involved in a sexual liaison. Once she has had sex with a man, a woman's 'equal rights' begin to be undermined. That is to say, when the relationship becomes serious and looks like being of long duration then the man begins to assert himself: she should give up smoking because he does not like to see it, she should not flirt with other men, she should give up dancing, she should pay him more respect and be obedient to his wishes. On marriage, these assertions may overnight become 'laws', and woe betide the woman who ignores them. Young men also assert a man's right to command [*lewa*] or to lead [*liuliu*], and the first year of marriage can appear to the outsider as a battle for control as the woman is required to give up any previously held notions of autonomy (cf. Thompson, 1940: 58).

Even if no kinship relation can be discovered between them, the parties to any marriage are presumed cross-cousins; so any in-marrying woman learns to address her neighbours in terms that would be appropriate had she been known to be actual cross-cousin to her husband (cf. Sahlins, 1962: 160ff.; Belshaw, 1964: 29). It is during the first years of marriage that a woman is most often beaten by her husband, sometimes for very trivial offences, such as not providing him with sufficiently hot tea at breakfast. As the relationship settles into a pattern of masculine domination and female subordination, beatings occur more rarely. However, women do not necessarily submit without protest to violent behaviour by men, and repeated beatings may result in a woman's running off to her father's house and refusing to return to the marital home without assurances from her husband's senior kin that he will cease to use violence against her; in some cases she refuses to return at all.

Jealousy is reported as the cause of most violence, and both men and women take it to be an extenuating circumstance. Once a woman accepts an offer of marriage she is well advised to give up dancing at once and to refrain from too spirited an exchange of jokes with other male cross-cousins. Should she fail to do so, any violence on the man's part is thought to be understandable.

What emerges from this discussion of the relation between male and female cross-cousins is that marriage transforms a relation between equals into a hierarchical relation. The process begins with the ceremonial exchanges that take place on betrothal and marriage. In each exchange the 'side of the man' [*yasa ni tagane*] must give more than the 'side of the woman' [*yasa ni yalewa*]. Thus Sahlins says for Moala that 'At the marriage of the woman ... the husband's side would have given somewhat more in feasts and goods than they received ...' (1976: 31). For a Nakoroka wedding, Quain says, 'it is proper that a man should be a little stronger in giving than a woman'; 'it is right that the bride's people should be lavishly entertained'; and 'despite the competitive nature of the exchange, woman has never been known to "win"' (1948: 332, 334, 333).

Taken together, these remarks *could* imply that 'wife-takers' are 'superior', as Sahlins (1976: 26) maintains. However, my own data suggest that this is not so. The man's side was never said to be superior; rather it was said of these exchanges that the man's side must 'win' because if they do *not* give more they will be 'ashamed'. This suggests that the woman herself is part of what is given by 'the side of the woman' and that the greater amount of goods from the man's side is to compensate the woman's kin for their loss. The corollary of this is that the woman's kin are ashamed if the girl is not a virgin – because the previously balanced exchange is negated. For my purposes here, what is most significant is that the woman's status as 'object' in the marriage exchanges constitutes a distinct denial of the exchange relations that ideally exist between cross-cousins. In marriage exchanges the woman ceases to be a party to a balanced and reciprocal exchange between equals (that is, between cross-cousins) and is transformed into an object of exchange (cf. Brewster, 1922: 197).

Any couple, married or unmarried, who have a sexual liaison are said to be 'ashamed to look at each other in daylight', and any shyness or avoidance behaviour between cross-cousins across sex is often taken to be a sure sign that they are having sex together (cf. Waterhouse, 1866: 309; Lester, 1940: 280). Thus husband and wife practise avoidance in public: they do not sit side by side, joke or dance together. This shift in behaviour is also apparent in the language of love. The term for mutual sexual love and desire is *veidomoni*, and it virtually always refers to passionate love affairs before or outside marriage. By contrast *veilomani*, meaning 'mutual love, caring or pity', is the term used to describe one's feelings for parents, children and other close kin including husband or wife. A man may admit without shame to 'caring for' his wife, but if he is thought to feel passionate sexual love for her he becomes faintly ludicrous and may be the object of jokes behind his back. His legitimate desire for her makes her 'his to eat' [*na kena*] but as far as I know, this term is not reciprocal. These shifts in behaviour enter into the transformation of equality into hierarchy – both *veilomani* and avoidance relations being definitive of hierarchical kinship relations both across and within generations.

Marriage also creates avoidance between *veidakuni* – between a male ego and his wife's sisters or a female ego and her husband's brothers. Within sex, brothers-in-law and sisters-in-law retain their cross-cousin familiarity. Nayacakalou (1955: 49) remarks that between *veidakuni* in Gau there is 'an extremely strict avoidance relationship'. However, while avoidance is generally the rule between *veidakuni* in Sawaieke, there were times when I heard a person address his or her *daku* with some familiarity; so I could not describe the avoidance as 'strict' The relationship appears to obtain only between ego and his or her spouse's real sisters or brothers and not to extend to the spouse's classificatory sisters or brothers; however, *veidakuni* do not generally joke with each other; neither are they in the habit of familiar talk.

The transformation of the equality of *veidavolani* (cross-cousins of opposite sex) into the hierarchy of marriage is further underlined by the strict avoidance behaviour prescribed for relations between ego and his or her parents-in-law, particularly across sex. The authority of those classified as parent-in-law is already given *before* marriage, but it is after marriage that its most salient effect is seen in the subservience of the daughter-in-law to her husband's mother. The element that remains as a residue of the easy relation between cross-cousins is inscribed in the *vasu* relation between the children of the marriage and their mother's lineage, which includes their mother's brothers (i.e. their fathers-in-law); that is, the relation whereby the junior relative or *vasu* may take anything from the senior relative. But this is offset by a strict *tabu* on familiar day-to-day interaction and thus combines the licence allowed to affines (cross cousins) with the observance of hierarchy that is prescribed for kin relations between generations. The *vasu* relationship is formally established at any time from infancy onwards by the ceremony of *kau mata ni gone* (literally 'carrying the face of the child') when the child or adolescent is taken by the father's kin to be presented to the mother's kin (see Hooper, 1982: 199–218). The ritual exchange of goods must favour the mother's kin.

The relation of equality between cross-cousins is typically conceived of as being across households; similarly, joking relations for *tauvu* and *veitabani* obtain across chiefdoms. By contrast, hierarchical kin relations are most obviously manifest *within* the household and *inside* the chiefdom [*vanua*]. The cross-cousin relationship demonstrates an equality that is as salient to Fijians as is hierarchy. It constitutes a problem on marriage when an equal relation between cross-cousins across sex has to be transformed into a hierarchical one. This transformation is possible partly because cross-cousin relations are subsumed by 'kinship' and partly because it is axiomatic that a man has authority over his wife. Thus a potential challenge is effectively undermined.

I remarked above that the products of women's labour are in general valued as highly as men's. However, this is *not* the case for the provision and cooking of food. This specific devaluation of women's labour enters into the constitution of hierarchy within the household. This is manifest on a daily basis in people's seating positions relative to one another in the space of the house. The differential values placed on exchange relations involved in food provision are the basic rationale for a man's unambiguous authority over his wife.

Meals and food provision

Families may take their meals in the kitchen or in the house, but the long rectangular cloth is always placed on the mat to accord with the above/below axis of the house or other building. It is never placed in any other way. So household members can take their places according to the interaction between gender and seniority. Figure 6a shows that males usually sit above, with the senior man above, at the top of the cloth, and females at the bottom, with Mother seated at the pole below.

Meals are further ritualized by prayer. Indeed, I never ate a meal in the village that was not preceded by a prayer from one of the household members. This is as true for morning or afternoon tea (taken on special occasions) and for picnics at the beach [*vakatakakana*] as it is for meals inside the house or for communal meals in the village hall. The more important a communal occasion, the longer the grace that precedes the *kana vata* (literally 'eating together'). At home, the grace preceding Sunday dinner is always a more lengthy and solemn one than that for other days.

Meals are a public activity; only when it is very cold or windy are they taken behind closed doors. Any passer-by can see household members at the cloth, and it is 'according to kinship' [*vakaveiwekani*] to invite all passers-by to eat. If senior household members cannot, because of an avoidance rule, call to the person, then someone younger will be prompted to do so. This polite behaviour is so important that a deliberate failure to invite someone to eat violates the very meaning of kinship; and this is so even though the invitation is conventionally refused. One should watch for passers-by and ask them in even if one has finished eating and there is no food left to offer; the fact that one is still seated at the cloth is reason enough to call 'come and eat' [*mai kana*). If a person is so close to the house as to be able to *see* that there is no food left, it is polite to remark that *keitou sa kana oti*, 'we have already eaten'. The invitation is a compelling obligation of kinship – itself in part constituted in certain relations of exchange; the open doors and the compulsory invitations to eat mean that, in an ideal sense, one *never* eats alone.

The significance of 'eating together' is evident in the ethnographic record; Hocart (1952: 22) defines the lineage [*mataqali*] as 'an assessment unit for feasts'; in Lau sub-lineages [*i tokatoka*] are called *bati ni lovo*, 'sides of the earth oven'. Brewster (1922: 67) notes that he came across court records of 'convictions for selfishness, for not sharing food with one's friends and comrades and for stinginess'; these judgements apparently having been obtained in courts set up by early missionaries under their *lawa vakaTonga* ('law according to Tonga'). Brewster supposes such offences not to have been included in this system but to have been 'punishable by the old customary law' of Fiji. Sahlins (1962: 387) describes the installation of a chief, who is urged in a ceremonial speech: 'Do not eat in secrecy. Call the people to partake of your food.'

I shall say more about eating together and reciprocal food taboos in the next chapter; here I remind the reader that eating together marks out the household, and is at the same time a defining feature of kinship in the widest sense. Thus it is fitting that the nature of hierarchical relations between kin within the household should be physically manifest in the activity of eating together.

The choicest and largest portions of food are placed in dishes above – at the top of the cloth – so that one not only sits but eats according to one's status. It is rude to stretch above one's own position to take food from a central dish; one should eat only from the dishes directly in front of or 'below' one. However, those who are seated above are expected to leave a portion of what is there, so that when they have finished this may be passed to those seated below. Men are often absent from the evening meal, being off somewhere drinking *yaqona*. However, if men are present when the meal is served they eat first, usually along with the children, and the older women of the house serve them and either begin their meal when the senior man is halfway through, or wait until he has finished. If the husband or head of household is not present at the meal, then the best and largest portions of food are kept for him and the woman waits on him when he does come to eat.

It is a woman's duty to feed her man well, and often his food is of better quality than her own or the children's. He may be eating fish, green vegetables and root vegetables while the woman and children are eating only green and root vegetables. I never observed a woman to take advantage of her husband's absence to feast on fish (one of the most highly prized of all foods) unless the best portion had already been set aside for him. Children often assert that there are dishes they have never tasted – turtle, roast pig and other feast food – and even at Christmas there are dishes that never come within the children's reach.

Earlier on I remarked that seniority is said to govern status within the household: older brother is said to be senior to younger brother, father to son, mother to daughter, the eldest of a set of siblings to those born later. But it seems that, at least in terms of space, gender interacts with seniority in that females are rarely *seen* to have the same status as males or to be above them, even where this is confidently asserted to be the case. What villagers *said* was important for a person's status did not always coincide with behaviour. So, in saying that the eldest of a set of siblings is the 'leader' [*i liuliu*] of the rest who are bound 'to listen to him or her' [*vakarorogo vua*], Sawaieke villagers left gender out of the reckoning. They neglected to say that the word of a woman who is the eldest [*ulu matua*, literally 'mature head'] carries less weight than that of the eldest of her younger brothers who, unless *very* much younger, is effective head of household once the father and his true brothers are dead. The interaction between gender and seniority is apparent in seating positions at the cloth when meals are taken.

Figure 6a shows people seated at the cloth for the midday Sunday meal; this meal follows the mid-morning church service and is the one meal of the week for which all household members are routinely present. The food served is likely to be more lavish and varied than usual (the women having gone net-fishing the day before) and the grace is invariably a long one. For the meal represented in Figure 6a, Father's Eldest Brother was visiting from Suva and Father had made way for his brother to take up the position that may at other times have been Father's own. However, this topmost position is not always occupied and is usually so only when the senior man present may also claim to be head of family. An eldest brother is unlikely to sit in this position in the presence of younger brothers while their absent father is still alive. At the meal represented the sons of the family are seated in strict order of seniority. This is not always so, but while I did on occasion see a younger boy seated above his older brother, I never saw a younger seated above an *eldest* son. Moreover, as children get older, observance of seniority with respect to seating tends to become more strict. When we remember that the size and quality of the portions served to a household member accord with his or her status, the relationship between brothers as manifest at meals recalls that observed by Hocart nearly seventy years ago:

A man's own younger brother is called his 'after eater' [*kana e muri*] because he waits till his brother has finished in order to fall

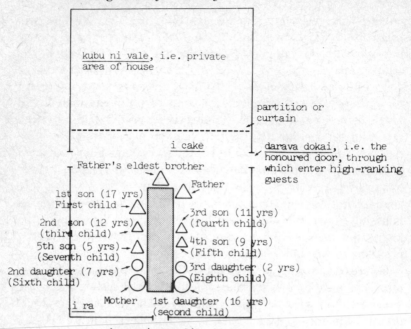

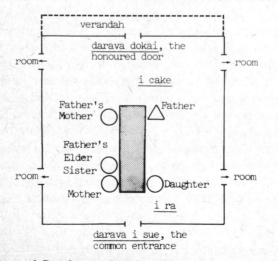

Figure 6 People seated at family meals

to. It is also the duty of the youngest to look after the food baskets, which used to be hung up at the lower end of the house … an opponent of inferior station will be silenced by the remark: 'Do not speak, you are he that sits by the food basket.' (Hocart, 1913b: 110)

Figure 6a shows that the relative seniority of daughters is not much acknowledged. The eldest daughter sits opposite her mother and helps to dish out the food. Here the two poles of the above/below axis are represented by Father's Eldest Brother and Mother/Eldest Daughter respectively; the senior man present is at the pole above and the senior woman at the pole below. However, while the position above is invariably taken by the senior man, the position below is not invariably taken by the senior woman. For instance, in a household where the aged mother of the male household head was still living, this lady (who was of a senior chiefly line) always sat relatively above, somewhat below her son and on the other side of the cloth (see Figure 6b). Here Father's Elder Sister – a widow some fifty years old, the first-born of her sibling set and formally of higher rank/seniority than her brother – did *not* sit in a very high position, though she *is* above her brother's wife (also a woman of chiefly birth) to whom she is senior, and she is not helping with the serving of food. This situation makes it clear that the pole below is not invariably occupied by the senior woman present.

In households of three generations' span, where Father's widowed Mother is living with her son's family, she may, if still contributing her labour to the cooking, etc., preside with her daughter-in-law over the dishing out of food. However, if her son is middle-aged with a grown-up family she is likely to leave this task to her daughter-in-law and take up a somewhat higher, though usually not very exalted, position at the cloth. In Figure 6b, Father's Mother's high position is more a tribute to her rank than to her seniority; many times I saw women almost as senior in age seated in relatively low positions at meals, even if they were seated above other women and girls and were themselves being served rather than serving.

From the foregoing it is clear, first, that seniority is not acknowledged independently of gender: a high-ranking Elder Sister sits well below her Younger Brother but above his similarly high-ranking wife. Secondly, seniority for females is not acknowledged independently of rank: an aged high-ranking lady sits above, nearer her high-ranking son, than does an aged woman of lower rank. Thirdly, the gender distinction operates in such a way that, within the household and irrespective of their age and rank, women are virtually always below men.

The seating arrangements at the cloth and the conduct of the meal are a concrete realization of hierarchy within the household – its membership defined by the act of eating together. Here we find a material expression of hierarchy constituted in an interaction between rank, seniority and gender and also in the reciprocal obligations that obtain between man and wife. On the above/below axis a father is superior to his sons, an elder brother to a younger brother and, most importantly, a man is unambiguously superior to his wife; it is she who occupies the pole below. In other words, whatever the seating position of a man with respect to other men at a family meal, his wife is always seated at the pole below. For example, if two brothers are eating together the elder will be seated above the younger, but their respective wives will *both* be seated opposite each other below, near the 'door of the cooking irons'.

The provision and cooking of food enter into the very constitution of the marriage relationship. Here the sexual division of labour is that men's gardening provides 'true food' [*kakana dina*] – the taro, cassava and yams that are the staple root crops. By definition there is no meal unless one of these foods is present. Men also raise the pigs which, when cooked and presented with root crops, make up the feast [*magiti*] that is presented to kin at weddings, funerals, and so on. Women provide their families with fish, but while it is a highly prized food, fish is just one of a number of accompaniments [*i coi*] and women's catches are not included in ritual presentations of food (see also Hooper, 1982: 250). Fishing style differs according to sex: men fish with spear [*coka*] or line and hook [*siwa*]; women with the net [*qoli*] or line and hook [*siwa*]; men tend to catch much larger, more impressive fish than do women. They use fish that women keep for eating to bait their hooks, and so they attract the larger species. Women *could* fish in this way, but do not consider it fitting.

For everyday meals women are expected to do all the cooking, but men cook on special occasions. Then the food (pig, root vegetables, special puddings, and so on) is cooked in the *lovo* or earth oven. The food cooked by men in the earth oven is considered by all to be much tastier than that cooked by women over the kitchen fire, and always forms a major part of the midday meal on Sunday and of any meals that are part of life-cycle ceremonies and so on. Many women say they do not know how to cook in the *lovo*, but this seems to be rather a matter of propriety than of actual knowledge. They also express horror at the idea of a man's cooking food for the family on any kind of everyday basis and talk in tones of righteous disapproval of any woman whose husband is known to spend much time in the kitchen. 'It is women's work only; it is not in the Fijian way for the man to cook.' The word for 'cook' in this quote is *vakasaqa* which, while it is used as a general term, refers specifically to 'boiling' as distinct from *vavi*, 'baked', which describes food cooked in the earth oven (cf. Hooper, 1982: 35). Only one man in Sawaieke village spent any time in *vakasaqa*; he was an affectionate husband and a man who took pleasure in cooking. However, his behaviour was not the subject of disapproval. It was his wife who was found wanting; she was 'lazy' and allowed him to spend time in an activity that was not 'manly'.

Sahlins (1976: 26–42) relates the sexual division of labour in Fiji to the complementary symbolism of 'sea' and 'land' by taking men to be associated with 'sea' and women with 'land' (ibid.: 26). He does acknowledge the way 'land' and 'sea' are connected in different ways with both men and women, but seems none the less finally to discount the complexity of the associations by nesting each set of sea/land oppositions within an overarching distinction given by 'nobles' and 'land' (i.e. 'the people'). I show later that this distinction cannot be taken to denote a clear superiority of 'nobles' over 'land'. *Contra* Sahlins, I would argue that one must fully accept that *both* sexes are associated with the land (for example men produce root crops, women produce mats from pandanus) and with the sea (for example fishing). This complex of associations denotes balanced reciprocity in the exchange of labour between *men and women*. I do not, as Sahlins appears to do, take 'sea' to be axiomatically superior to 'land' – a matter to be further discussed in Chapter 4.

The point here is that if one focuses on the relations between *husband and wife* in terms of exchange of foods, the contribution of the husband is valued above that of his wife and this relative value is apparent in what food is eaten, in how it is produced and cooked, and in the conduct of the meal itself within the space of the house. So it appears that it is specifically with respect to this exchange of foods within the household that balanced reciprocity in exchange relations between men and women is transformed into a hierarchical relation between particular husbands and wives, whereby the man both provides *and* redistributes 'true food' (and big fish) and his wife merely attends to it in her attendance upon him. Indeed, she is also his to eat; thus a man's legitimate desire for his wife's body is referred to by the expression 'he wants his own thing to eat' or 'he wants to eat what is his' (cf. Herr, 1981: 345; Quain, 1948: 322 fn. 32). In a similar vein a young man who regretted his marriage of only a few months' duration remarked: 'I have been eating cassava only every day – today it no longer tastes good to me.'

The dual salience of hierarchy and equality that is apparent when one compares the behaviour prescribed for ranked kin relations with that for cross-cousins is also apparent in relations between the chiefs and the people. Here the opposing meanings are manifest in the space of the village itself, where houses are *veiqaravi* (literally 'facing each other'). As I pointed out in Chapter 1, *veiqaravi* may denote either balanced reciprocity in exchange relations or hierarchical exchange in the form of tribute to chiefs. In the next chapter I show how both these meanings are made physically manifest in the orientation of houses to one another in the space of the village.

4 Hierarchy and equality beyond the household

In the two previous chapters I showed how hierarchical relations within the household are constituted, made concrete in the space of the house and physically manifest in people's positions at meals. These hierarchical relations are 'in the manner of kinship' [*vakaveiwekani*], but kinship subsumes affines as well as consanguines and so includes the relation between cross-cousins, the only kinship relation that posits equality and one that is typically *across* households. I also showed how, across sex, relations of equality between cross-cousins are transformed by marriage in such a way that a man is seen to have authority over his wife *within* the household.

This chapter deals with another domain of relationship – that which is 'in the manner of the land' [*vakavanua*] and manifest in relations across households and in the space of the village itself. Behaviour 'in the manner of the land' is by no means opposed to that 'in the manner of kinship'; but the two notions have different connotations and evoke different domains of reference and contexts of action. Relations 'in the manner of the land' may also be said to be hierarchical, but here again there are elements that posit equality. It is the balance between hierarchy and equality in this domain that I discuss below.

I begin with a brief outline of relations between social divisions beyond the household and within the village of Sawaieke. These divisions are those recognized today (see France, 1969: 102–48 for an account of the various Lands Commissions' investigations from 1880s onwards). I show below how the hierarchical ranking of these divisions is founded upon balanced reciprocity in exchange relations – which at once suggests the equality of corporate groups and the potential for its transformation into hierarchy. The second part of the chapter deals with the physical manifestation of this apparent paradox in the layout of the village.

Relations across groups

SOCIAL DIVISIONS

In the ideal model of Fijian social organization, households are grouped patrilineally. A sub-lineage [*i tokatoka*] ideally consists of a band of brothers whose households are ranked according to seniority, with eldest brother having authority over those who are younger. The sub-lineages within a lineage [*mataqali*] are ranked according to their order of descent with reference to the relation between eldest and succeeding brothers who were founding ancestors. The lineage is an exogamous, landowning group; the sub-lineage and clan are also sometimes landowning groups (see Fison, 1880; France, 1969: 118). At the highest level of inclusiveness is the clan [*yavusa*], all of whose members claim descent from a common ancestor or *vu* (literally 'root'). Several scholars have argued that this model is an artifact of colonial British acceptance of Bauan notions of descent and land tenure and is not valid for all areas of Fiji (e.g. Capell and Lester, 1941, 1945; Quain, 1948; Hocart, 1952; France, 1969; Clammer, 1973). In Sawaieke, for instance, group relations are never referred to the sub-lineage level, but always to lineage or clan level.

Mataqali – here translated as 'lineage' – may mean 'kind', as in *e mataqali ika cava na ika 'oya?*, 'what kind of fish is that?' and may refer to either lineage or clan. Context always makes the reference plain; as Sahlins says, 'the same set of people can be designated an *i tokatoka*, a *mataqali*, or a *yavusa* in different circumstances, and the same term might be employed in reference to different orders or kinds of kinship bodies' (1962: 238; see also Nation, 1978: 2–7; Walter, 1978: 357). In Sawaieke, people were often not sure whether the *mataqali* or the *yavusa* is the more inclusive level of social relations, and the fact that *mataqali* is the more commonly used term may have contributed to this finding. France (1969: 174) says that 'the classification of the Fijian population into social units impinges so slightly on their lives that, at the 1956 census, only 66 per cent of Fijians were able to state the *mataqali* and *yavusa* to which they belonged.' In my own experience young men (up to the age of twenty-five or so) and many women were unable to name their group affiliation for each level or confused it; adult men were always certain of their information. But unlike France, I do not take this as evidence that notions of clan and lineage are insignificant for Fijian social relations (cf. Nation, 1978: 7–8).

HIERARCHICAL RELATIONS WITHIN THE LINEAGE

The defining feature of the lineage is, as Hocart (1952: 22) pointed out, as an 'assessment unit for feasts'. So, when people present goods to kin outside their own clan – say at a wedding or funeral – these are first gathered together *vakamataqali*, 'according to lineage', and are then presented to senior men of the clan in one of their houses. When all the goods are gathered together, they are carried in procession to the house of a member of the receiving clan who are 'owners' of the business in hand [*i taukei ni oga*] and there presented. Similarly, the return presentation is made to the clan chiefs, who later divide up what they have received 'according to lineage'. The division is made in accordance with the relative status of a given lineage and the value of its original contribution. If the occasion is one within clan, then both initial and return presentations are 'according to lineage' (cf. Hooper, 1982: 8–16).

In contemporary Sawaieke, sub-lineage [*tokatoka*] membership does *not* differentiate groups within a lineage. In other words – and despite the fact that they may have distinct names – lineage and sub-lineage are coterminous; no lineage contains more than one sub-lineage and in most cases the given name of the latter is the same as that for the former. This situation may be in part attributable to errors by the Lands Commission in Gau in 1916; but since then it seems too that a number of sub-lineages have ceased to exist, either because there were no descendants in the male line or because they became so small that their remaining members were adopted by others. Epidemics of influenza and measles in which so many people died and so many were ill that there was no one to bury the dead are remembered by men in their seventies, and it seems likely that these epidemics contributed to this situation (see Roth, 1953: xvii). However, it may also be that my records are at fault in that they do not show sub-lineage and lineage membership for villagers who live in urban centres.

Whatever the case, the ranking of households within a lineage poses no problem since it follows the order given by the seniority of male siblings; the leader of the lineage [*i liuliu ni mataqali*] is a member of the senior generation and the eldest of the set of brothers in the senior household of that lineage. In a lineage gathering, this man sits in the central place above, with his younger brothers at some distance from him but above men of the next senior household who are junior to them in age. However, if senior men in the next-ranking household are *older* than the younger brothers of the lineage leader, they sit above these younger men. So, among men of the lineage, age seniority may be acknowledged irrespective of the fact that a man comes from a household that owes its descent to a younger brother – that is, to a genealogically junior line. The post of leader may be assumed by the senior man in a junior line if no male of suitable age (i.e. of the senior generation) is available in the senior line. However, when this man dies, the office of leader reverts to the male head of the line that is genealogically senior.

For offices such as that of lineage head women do not come into the reckoning at all; they may do so sometimes in other parts of Fiji but not, I was told, within living memory in Sawaieke. Nor was it likely they would ever do so (see Roth, 1953: 73; cf. Quain, 1948: 196). An interaction between gender and seniority is apparent in the disposition of people in space when members of the lineage are gathered together. Senior men are seated above, with young men in an intermediate position and the women of the group below; however, if the widowed mother or elder sister of the senior man is present she may – especially if she is of chiefly rank – be seated in a position that is relatively above (though not as high as his) in that she is separated off from the other women and above younger men. But this is not the norm and usually such a woman, even when she is the oldest living member of the lineage, sits with other women in the space below, though relatively above them.

Chiefly rank is of some importance here: a woman of high chiefly birth who is herself the eldest of a set of siblings is bound to be acknowledged as such by both her children and/or her younger siblings. This recognition becomes more visible when the persons involved are in the senior generation, because the senior man takes a prominent position above all in gatherings and is himself bound to show respect to his mother or elder sister. But on the whole chiefly rank is unlikely to be an issue within lineage; there may be an imbalance with respect to the rank of in-marrying women such that the wife of one brother outranks the others, but this is not necessarily a source of friction. The wives of brothers are called *veikaruani*; formerly a reference to the relation of junior wives in a polygamous marriage, today this is ideally a relation between equals even though seniority is, to some extent, still a factor. Moreover women, with the exception of senior, high-ranking women, are not apparently so concerned as are men with the niceties of their relative status.

RANKING OF LINEAGES WITHIN CLAN

The ranking of lineages within clan is, in contemporary Sawaieke, problematic. The composition of the clans in the village does not conform to Nayacakalou's ideal clan, in which 'there are five *mataqali*, the most senior of which provides the chiefs, and the others the chief's executives or henchmen, the heralds, the priests and the warriors respectively in order of seniority' (1955: 50 after Geddes, 1948: 97; cf. Thomson, 1908, 1968: 61). In Sawaieke, this type of relation obtains between clans rather than between lineages, and the traditional obligations are not quite those given by Nayacakalou. I shall have more to say about this below. For the moment, however, I wish to concentrate on relations between lineages within a given clan.

Tables 1 and 2 show the composition of the five clans of Sawaieke village. The component lineages of a particular clan may be distributed among a number of villages (cf. Geddes, 1948: 101; Sahlins, 1962: 225–7). In this case the senior family of the lineage from which a clan chief is chosen lives in Sawaieke village, sometimes along with senior families of the other component lineages; the remaining members of the component lineages which owe traditional obligations to the clan chief are resident elsewhere. This is true of Navure clan and Voda clan (also called Naividamu), whose membership within the village of Sawaieke is small. In the case of Voda and Koviko, where in Sawaieke village the clan is coterminous with the lineage, there can be no problem with respect to the relative ranking of the component households.

Where there is more than one lineage in a clan, the one providing clan chiefs ranks highest; however, problems can arise if the male head of the senior-ranking lineage is significantly younger than the male head of a junior lineage. In such a case members of the two

Table 1   *The chiefly clan*

yavusa clan	*mataqali* lineage	*i tokatoka* sub-lineage	*yaca ni vale* name of house
Nadawa	Naboginibola	Naboginibola	Tautu
		Naboginibola	Poa
		Naboginibola	Tuvunidrua
		Nagobinibola	Waqatalaca
		Naboginibola	Nacokula
		Naboginibola	Nakerebuli
		Naboginibola	?
		Naboginibola	Tamaleca
		Naboginibola	Natarokawa
	Tabaisa	Tabaisa	Tabaisa
		Tabaisa	Lomanibuca
		Tabaisa	Nacavuturaga
	Valebalavu	Valebalavu	Nakabuta
		Valebalavu	Valebalavu
		Valebalavu	Vunitavola
		Valebalavu	Vagadaci
	Naocomatana	Naocomatana	Vunibokoi
		Naocomatana	Naocomatana
		Naocomatana	Vunimakawa
		Naocomatana	Naiselesele
		Naocomatana	Naikasakasa
		Methodist Minister's house	Saioni

22 Nadawa houses (inc. Saioni), 2 new houses not included.

Table 2   *The commoner clans ('the people': na vanua)*

yavusa clan	*mataqali* lineage	*i tokatoka* sub-lineage	*yaca ni vale* name of house
	dau bulia na Takalaigau: 'those who install Takaligau'		
Sawaieke	Natuvakasuka	Natuvakasuka	Natuvakasuka
		Natuvakasuka	Naivikogau
		Natuvakasuka	Natuvatuva
	matanivanua: 'heralds'		
	Nadawa	Nadawa	Bole
		Nadawa	Naua
	bete: 'priests' (to Sawaieke clan)		
	Nalukuta	Bete	?
		Bete	Matanuku

(Nailavoci)	*Nadawaquruquru*	Nailavoci	Nadawaquruquru
		Nailavoci	Orevi
		Nailavoci	Nauluvatu
	Vusakaci	Lasekau	Waivuvu

11 Sawaieke clan houses inc. 2 outside village.

liga ni magiti, 'hand of the feast', landspeople
(to Nadawa clan)

Navure	*Naqaranikalou*	Naqaranikalou	Vatuwaqa
	Sisiwa	Sisiwa	Vakarewarewa
	Nadevodevo	Nadevodevo	Nadevodevo
	Navau	Navau	Waimaro
(Burei)	*Naduruvesi*	Naduruvesi	Duruvesi

5 Navure clan houses.

gone dau: 'fishermen', seapeople (to Nadawa clan)

Voda	*Voda*	Dakuisele	Taira
(Naividamu)		Dakuisele	Nabuabua
		Dakuisele	Tikovulagi

3 Voda clan houses.

bete: 'priests' OR bati: 'warriors' (to Nadawa clan)

Koviko	*Naivakavi*	Naivakavi	Tarakailamiti
		Naivakavi	Nacotube
		Naivakavi	Navolau

3 Koviko clan houses, inc. one outside village.

i.e. 23 houses belonging to *na vanua*, 'commoners'.
i.e. 28 houses associated with sea (Nadawa, Koviko, Voda).
i.e. 16 houses associated with land (Sawaieke, Navure).

lineages may fall out, since it may be thought that the older man goes too far in assuming rights that are not properly 'his'. So rank may pose a problem in its interaction with seniority across lineages and within clan – that is, among people who are somewhat more distantly related to one another than are the members of any given lineage, where the interaction between gender and relative seniority is the defining variable.

It was perhaps owing to the rather peculiar composition of clans in Sawaieke that people did not talk of the relative ranking of lineages within them in terms of traditional obligations. Only in the case of Sawaieke clan were these obligations relatively clear across component lineages (see Table 2), though not much observed today. The chiefly clan Nadawa, from which the paramount chief of Sawaieke country is chosen, contains four lineages which are not today differentiated from one another in terms of traditional obligations. I was told that a Takalaigau (i.e. a paramount chief of Sawaieke country) may be chosen from any one of these lineages. However, the records of the Lands Commission show that, within the memory of those people who gave evidence to the Commission in 1916, the office of paramount has been held by men from only three lineages: Tabaisa, Valebalavu and Naboginibola. In 1916 Takalaigau was Ratu Tomasi Tokalauvere of Tabaisa; I was told that he was succeeded by Ratu Ilaitia Lewanavanua, and then by Ratu Maika, both of Naboginibola; at the time of my fieldwork Ratu Marika Uluinadawa of Naboginibola had been named Takalaigau but was not yet formally installed. The heads of each of these three lineages were considered to be the highest-status men in Sawaieke country.

Seating arrangements at a communal meal [*kana vata*, literally 'eating together'] or a clan meeting reveal more complexity and subtlety in hierarchical relations between people than is apparent within a single lineage. In general, men in the senior generation of the component lineages sit above, with the clan chief (the leader of the chiefly lineage) in the top, central position. However, an older man of illegitimate birth (and therefore a member of the clan through his mother) sits lower than other men of his own age who are legitimate clan members. Senior ladies of the clan (for example the elder sister of the clan chief) are likely to be accorded relatively high seating positions; such ladies sit below the most senior men but above junior married men and young men. However, a senior lady does *not* take up such a position if her husband is alive and residing in the village, or if they are together paying a visit to her relatives there.

RANKING ACROSS CLANS

Traditional obligations between lineages are, in Sawaieke village, played out across clan. Nadawa is the chiefly clan and provides the paramount chief; Sawaieke clan 'makes the paramount chief'; Navure clan are 'landspeople' who once a year present *yaqona* and feast food to the paramount; and Voda clan are 'seapeople', obliged to present annually a large catch of fish. Koviko is said to be the clan of either priests [*bete*] or warriors [*bati*] and may indeed once have provided both to the high chief of Gau – a possibility suggested to me by Stephen Hooper in the light of his own data from Lau. People were unsure about the precise ritual functions of Koviko, perhaps because it was not recognized by all to be truly a clan. It was reconstituted in 1981/82 by splitting off from Voda clan the descendants of a Koviko man who had taken refuge with Voda some time in the 1920s or 1930s.

These traditional obligations do not *in themselves* denote hierarchical relations. Rather, they describe a set of reciprocal ritual obligations that are understood to balance each other. Here there is no clear principle of hierarchy such as that given by the relative seniority of brothers. Indeed, it appears to be the reciprocity of exchange relations both across clan – and, to a lesser extent, across lineage – that throws into question the precise nature of their relative ranking. The suggestion of equality across groups given by the notion of balanced reciprocity is of crucial importance, despite the fact that what any given person *says* implies that a particular form of hierarchy may be taken for granted.

What people say is that members of Nadawa clan are all 'chiefs' [*turaga*] in that they are all of chiefly descent, while the members of all other clans are commoners [*tamata*, literally 'people']. The descending rank order of clans is sometimes taken to be Nadawa, Koviko, Sawaieke, Navure and Voda – this being the order in which the component households are listed and read out every Sunday for the church *soli* (literally 'giving', the weekly donation to church funds). However, in conversation members of Sawaieke clan place themselves second and may even assert some of their members to be above some of those in Nadawa clan. Members of other clans supported this view of Sawaieke clan, so Koviko was placed either second or last depending upon an informant's point of view. Again, Voda informants said that their clan ranked above Navure.

As we shall see below, there is good reason for these conflicting views. On the one hand it seems that it is not hierarchical ranking that is at question, but the precise nature of that ranking; but it is also apparent that balanced reciprocity in exchange relations across groups in some sense challenges the notion of hierarchy itself.

Village layout and its significance

Ideally the houses of a given clan should be grouped together and members should co-operate with one another and give their help unstintingly on the occasion of some group effort. As with relations between kin, the relationship between clans is elaborated in spatial terms. Several ethnographers have noted that the space of a Fijian village is divided amongst the various groups in an ordered way, though they do not attempt any analysis of the symbolism of the space (see for example Thomson, 1908: 62; Hocart, 1929: 10).

The opposition between hierarchy and· equality that emerges when one compares the behaviour prescribed for ranked kin relations with that for cross-cousins is also played out in relations between the chiefs and the people. Indeed, these dual possibilities are made concrete in the space of the village; its layout denotes equality in reciprocal obligations across clans, whose houses are *veiqaravi* (literally 'facing each other'), and at the same time suggests the hierarchy of above/below in the relative height of the house foundations or *yavu* (cf. Hooper, 1982: 231).

Above/below [*cake/ra*] refers both to relative height and to different places on the same plane; *i cake* and *i ra* can also mean east and west. *I cake* signifies *na i cabecabe ni siga*, 'the rising of the sun'; and *i ra*, *na i dromudromu ni siga*, 'the sinking of the sun'. Today's Standard Fijian gives *tokalau* for 'east' as a point of the compass (Schutz and Komaitai, 1971: 244) – this usage being taught in schools. However, the expression 'to the east' occurs in statements like *e koto ki cake ko Nayau*, 'Nayau lies to the east' though *tokalau kei Gau*, 'east of Gau', is more common.

That *i cake* and *i ra* meaning 'east' and 'west' can simultaneously refer to a vertical orientation I infer from diagrams of directions of the winds, drawn for me by some Sawaieke men. These men made use of a grid where *i cake* and *i ra* named the poles of the vertical dimension and *ceva* ('south') and *vualiku* ('north') described those of the horizontal dimension. In other words, where we make north and south the poles of a vertical line and show north at the top and south at the bottom, with east and west at the right- and left-hand poles respectively of a horizontal line bisecting the vertical, these Fijian men, using the same grid, showed east as the topmost point of the vertical line, west as its bottommost point, with south and north being the right- and left-hand poles respectively of the horizontal line bisecting the vertical. I have only five of these diagrams, so I do not want to make too much of the 'east is above' inference; also, there were a number of discrepancies between them. These presumably arose from the grafting of European cardinal points on to indigenous categories for the winds (see Milner, 1968: 52–3).

Despite their concern with people's orientation in space with reference to *i cake* and *i ra* as 'above' and 'below', people in Sawaieke did not site their houses in accordance with *i cake* and *i ra* as east and west. The above/below axis of the house – where the public area furthest away from the entrance is above and the common entrance is below – does not coincide with the east/west axis, and appears to be largely independent of it.

I was told that people build their houses so as to present their least vulnerable area to the direction from which hurricane winds come. In villages on the west coast of Gau (excepting Somosomo) this meant that virtually all houses were built along a more or less north/south axis with the common entrance on either the north or south face of the house and the whole presenting a corner into the face of the wind that might come from the north-east [*na cagilaba mai na tokalau*] or south-east [*ceva*]. Of the nine villages I visited in Gau, only Somosomo's houses lay on the east/west axis so that common entrances faced west. I was told that the people of the village, which stands in a sheltered spot between two hills sloping down to the sea, liked the wind from the sea, and this was why they located their houses with the area *i ra* (below) facing *ki ra* (to the west). No other explanation was offered.

These rationalist explanations seem unsatisfactory. I argue instead that historically the orientation of houses had to do with relations between people as 'land' and 'sea' and that these associations survive in that 'the honoured door' is also conventionally *na darava e wai*, 'the sea door', the one that faces the sea. Hocart (1929: 9) records for Lakeba:

> With few exceptions, all the houses present their flanks to the beach. In Tumbou, a door is built at the west end, and along the north coast some houses, ... if not all, have their doors in this position. In Wathiwathi, where the beach runs south-west to north-east, the door is at the south-west end. ... Inferiors enter at

this door; superiors by a door which is usually in the side facing the sea.

Assuming the inferior door to be the common entrance, it seems that the houses' internal space above lay in the east, north-east, or north and the space below in the west, south-west or south. Clearly it is the orientation of the honoured door towards the sea that counts, for this door is more likely to be facing the sea than the common entrance is to be facing west. In other words, orientation with respect to points of the compass is irrelevant because what is important is that each house faces the same way, so that the 'land door' of one house faces the 'sea door' of another. This orientation holds for houses in Sawaieke village and for five out of the six Gau villages for which I have aerial photographs. With the exception of Somosomo village, houses have their long sides parallel to the sea front; and even in Somosomo the long sides of each house are parallel to those of the next. In general, the orientation of each house to another, and of the houses of one clan to the houses of another, is that of *veiqaravi*, literally 'facing each other'.

Veiqaravi signifies attendance on others: reciprocal ritual services across clans, attendance on chiefs (especially in *yaqona*-drinking), on God in collective worship, and the hospitality given to a party of men at work on behalf of a whole village (cf. Hashimoto, 1984); the term for witchcraft is *qaravi tevoro*, 'attending on devils', literally 'facing devils'. *Veiqaravi* is explicitly said to be *vakavanua*, 'in the manner of the land'. It figures in the mythical history of the formation of Sawaieke village, as follows:

> then they wanted to be nearer each other because if all the villages moved here it would make their attendance upon each other [*veiqaravi*, their ritual obligations to each other] easier. The owners of this village, of this land, were Sawaieke clan. ... They called to the people of the little villages that they should come here: 'Takalaigau, come here' – and they came; 'Tui Navure, come here' – and they came. And the Voda people also came here ...

Reference to Figure 7 reveals that houses in Sawaieke village are grouped roughly in terms of clan membership. Most Nadawa and Sawaieke clan houses lie on the central axis of the village, while

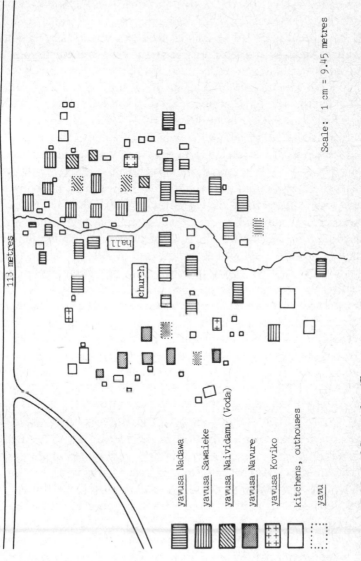

Scale: 1 cm = 9.45 metres

113 metres

hall

church

yavusa Nadawa

yavusa Sawaieke

yavusa Naividamu (Voda)

yavusa Navure

yavusa Koviko

kitchens, outhouses

yavu

Figure 7 Map of Sawaieke village

Navure and Voda houses are on the peripheries. Those Nadawa houses that lie on the north and south peripheries are new houses – built there, I was told, because there were no old Nadawa house foundations [*yavu*] on which to build new houses. Koviko houses were recognized as such (i.e. as belonging to a separate clan) during my stay in Sawaieke; they were previously classified as Voda houses.

That Nadawa and Sawaieke clan houses are contiguous and central is implied by the mythical history of the founding of the village – in which Nadawa clan are the first to be called to join 'the owners of this village'. Sawaieke clan is the original owner of the land on which the village is built, and it is its chief, Narai, whose prerogative it is to install and some say to select, Takalaigau – that senior man of Nadawa clan who becomes the paramount chief of Sawaieke country. Their relationship is further ratified in a myth that makes the first paramount a man from over the sea (Biu, son of a man from Gau who married elsewhere) who marries the daughter of a former Narai and is later installed by him as high chief. In the account I have Narai offers the head of a *saqa* (the fish that should be eaten only be chiefs) to the kin group led by Biu, and so challenges him to prove himself worthy of selection as the potential paramount chief. Only after he works for Narai, acts as his warrior and brings him men's bodies in tribute does Narai give Biu his daughter in marriage and, later, 'his high chief's comb'. The suggestion of bride service here – while it is not, to my knowledge, in force today – is further evidence for my argument against the superiority of wife-takers. Lester (1940: 284) quotes an article in *Na Mata*, 1899 (edited and isued by the Native Secretariat) as saying that when a betrothal takes place it is customary for a youth to dwell with his father-in-law for a period (possibly as long as two years); this was *na cakacaka ni tave ki vua na vugona*, work expected of the son-in-law. The myth of marriage between a stranger chief and a daughter of the land is prevalent in Fiji, and in the Sawaieke case clearly implies reciprocal obligations between 'the people' [*vanua*, literally 'land'] represented by Narai, and 'the chiefs' [*ko ira na turaga*] represented by Biu, the putative paramount.

Attendance on each other [*veiqaravi*], and thus by implication the layout of the village itself, appears to be dependent on two interacting sets of complementary relationships. These relationships are inscribed in food presentations and reciprocal food taboos; in essence they concern reciprocal obligations in exchange relations, those between chiefs [*ko ira na turaga*] and people [*na vanua*, literally 'the land'], and those between landspeople and seapeople. In Sawaieke village, members of Navure clan call themselves 'landspeople' while members of Voda clan are 'seapeople'; the more formal terms are, I was told, *liga ni magiti* (literally 'hand of the feast food' and *gonedau* ('fishermen').

The term 'chiefs' has a wide reference; conventionally *turaga* ('chief') is used politely for any married man (cf. Hocart, 1913c). In its more exclusive use *ko ira na turaga*, 'the chiefs', may refer to all members of the chiefly clan Nadawa or to the various clan chiefs considered as a group: *ko ira na malo*, 'the cloths'. This term is derived from the one for the paper mulberry tree out of which barkcloth is made; in former times the style of cloth worn by a chief was one of the signs of his rank (Capell, 1941: 133); a piece of

Table 3   *Tributary relations between the eight villages of Sawaieke country and the clan chiefs in Sawaieke village*

VANUA KO SAWAIEKE
Sawaieke Country

Village	---->	Traditional annual presentation	---->Sawaieke chief
Lovu Vadravadra Yadua	---->	*ika* & *uvi* (fish & yams)	--->Takalaigau, paramount, and chief of Nadawa clan
Nukuloa Levuka	---->	*dalo, magiti* & *yaqona* (taro, pig, kava, etc.)	---->Narai, chief of Sawaieke clan
Nawaikama	} --- >	*dalo* & *magiti*	---->Tui Navure, chief of Navure clan
Somosomo	}---->	*ika* (fish)	---->Tui Voda, chief of Naividamu clan (also called Voda)

<-------- { All the above chiefs are obliged to reciprocate with *tabua* (whale's teeth) and to give hospitality to visitors from 'their' village(s) when its members visit Sawaieke. They should also redistribute goods, food, etc.

barkcloth is still tied on the arm of a chief during his installation. Hocart (1952) tends to use *malo* for a lesser chief, not the paramount, but in Sawaieke the present Takalaigau used *malo* to refer to all the traditional chiefs of Sawaieke country, including himself. In this usage 'the chiefs', and most saliently their leader Takalaigau, are set apart from and above others. However, if we take 'the chiefs' to refer to members of the chiefly Nadawa clan, then they are not unambiguously above 'the people', and this is especially clear in the relation between the senior land chief, Narai (Sawaieke clan) and the senior chief of Nadawa clan. Should Narai be displeased with the conduct of a putative paramount, he may refuse to install him in office as Takalaigau (a matter I discuss further later).

With respect to the relationship between 'the chiefs' and 'the people', the people have obligations to wait upon their chiefs, to present them with first fruits (see Turner, J. W., 1984), to labour on their behalf if asked to do so, to pay them proper respect, and so on. This is particularly true for the people's traditional obligations to Takalaigau. He is chief of the chiefly Nadawa clan and thus paramount.

The chiefs too have obligations to the people: they must be fair and generous in reciprocating with presentations of whale's teeth [*tabua*] and redistributions of all food and other goods received, thus showing themselves worthy of the people's attendance upon them. So Hocart says:

> the whole *raison d'être* of a chief is the same as of a god of the land, abundance. . . . It is the same function as that of a god of the land who receives offerings that the land may flourish. In Ndreketi they appoint a 'cloth' [*malo*], a receiver of feasts, if food is scarce. A good cloth is not a virtuous chieftain, but one under whom 'the bananas will ripen and everything be plentiful'. (1952: 19)

The reciprocal obligations that obtain between the villages of Sawaieke country and the chief to whom they owe allegiance in Sawaieke village are shown in Table 3.

On the one hand, exchange relations between the chiefs and the people suggest balanced reciprocity – the chiefs rule only by consent of the people (cf. Nayacakalou, 1975: 115) and have reciprocal obligations towards them; on the other they suggest that all presentations take the form of tribute to chiefs (cf. Hocart, 1952: 27).

Reciprocal obligations between land and sea are similarly complex, but they clearly denote balanced reciprocity in exchange relations. At one level, within the category of 'the people', the relation is seen in the food taboos that come into effect when landspeople and seapeople are eating together. Those who are landspeople, members of Navure clan and others who are so classified throughout Sawaieke country, do not eat pig or certain freshwater products like prawns; those who are seapeople, members of Voda clan and others so classified, do not eat fish. So, when they eat together, seapeople symbolically make available the products of their labour to landspeople, who in return make available the products of animal husbandry. So, on any occasion that requires people to eat together [*kana vata*], the food that accompanies *kakana dina* (literally 'true food': cassava, taro, yams) has to include both pig and fish so that everyone present may eat well without violating food taboos that do not constrain them in the privacy of their own households.

Members of the remaining clans – Nadawa, Sawaieke, and Koviko – are also made to relate to one another in terms of either land or sea. Sawaieke clan is 'owner of this land' and its chief, Narai, is senior representative of *na vanua*, 'the land'. Koviko was until recently taken to be a lineage in Nadawa clan; when reconstituted as a clan, it was grouped along with members of Voda and Nadawa and so associated with the sea – the first Takalaigau being son of 'a chief from over the sea' (cf. Hocart, 1952: 27). The land/sea division may govern village-wide competitions, for example, a fund-raising venture [*soli*]. So, when raising money for their primary school, Sawaieke village divided into two competing groups: Koviko and Voda were allied with Nadawa clan, while Navure was allied to Sawaieke clan, and the names of the two groups – *Adi Burotukula* and *Senidawadawa* respectively – had associations with sea and land. *Adi Burotukula* refers to a mythical paradisal island that lies beneath the sea or floats upon it at the will of its spirit inhabitants (see Johnston, 1918: 72; Hocart, 1929: 195 ff.; and Thompson, 1940: 115 ff.), while *Senidawadawa* is a flower that villagers say smells sweet only when gathered in Sawaieke country, and especially in Sawaieke village itself.

Reciprocal obligations are thus embedded in an interaction between the constructs of 'sea-and-land' on the one hand and 'chiefs-and-people' on the other. Moreover, the interaction is such that one could make *either* the land/sea *or* the chiefs/people relation overarching, and embed the other in it (see Tables 4 and 5).

Table 4   *Relations between 'land' and 'sea'*

LAND [*vanua*]	<--->	SEA [*wai*]
Myth:		
Narai, ancestor of Sawaieke clan, offers a head of *saqa* to the group of men led by Biu, challenging him to eat of food that is only for chiefs.	<--->	Biu, ancestor of Nadawa clan, accepts Narai's challenge to show himself worthy of being selected as potential paramount; he presents Narai with the bodies of the dead – so demonstrating his *mana*.
The daugher of Narai, a 'woman of the land', is given in marriage to the putative high chief. Narai then gives him *nona i Seru ni Sau*, 'his high chief's comb'.	<--->	Biu, 'a chief from over the sea', is son of a Gau man, but born and raised elsewhere. He works for Narai, then marries his daughter. Biu becomes paramount.

Food taboos (when seapeople eat with landspeople):

Landspeople, Navure clan [*liga ni magiti*, 'hand of the feast food'] do not eat pig or freshwater fish.	<--->	Seapeople, Voda clan [*gonedau*, fisherpeople] do not eat fish.

Clan:

Sawaieke, Navure	Nadawa, Voda (i.e. Naividamu), Koviko.

The orientation of groups of houses to one another in the space of the village is also significant here. Figure 7 reveals that while Voda houses are at the periphery of the village, they also lie beside Sawaieke clan houses just as the sea is beside the land; then we have Sawaieke clan houses beside Nadawa houses just as 'the people' are alongside 'the chiefs'; and finally we have Nadawa houses beside Navure houses as the sea is beside the land, with Navure houses also situated on the periphery. The actual layout of houses is not

Table 5 *Relations between 'people' and 'chiefs'*

THE PEOPLE [*na vanua*]		THE CHIEFS [*ko ira na turaga*]
Sawaieke clan ---->	heralds, funeral rites, installation, etc.	---->Nadawa clan esp. the high chief, Takalaigau
Koviko clan ---->	priests and/or warriors	---->as above
Navure clan ---->	annual presentation of first fruits (pig, taro)	---->Takalaigau
Voda clan ---->	annual presentation of fish, turtle	---->Takalaigau

<---- { Takalaigau and other members of Nadawa clan reciprocate with presentations of whale's teeth plus redistribution of foods, goods, etc., received.

completely consistent with the ideal pattern, which looks something like this:

clan:	Navure	Nadawa	Sawaieke	Voda
	land	chiefs	people	sea
or	land	sea	land	sea
or	people	chiefs	chiefs	people

This may seem odd in that members of Sawaieke clan are listed as both 'people' and 'chiefs'. However, the position of Sawaieke clan, and especially of their chief, Narai, is such that from one point of view (that of the chiefs, i.e. of Nadawa clan) they are 'the people', while from their own point of view they are sufficiently exalted in their ritual status to be seen as *de facto* 'chiefs'; this is plain in the present Narai's observations on his ritual relationship to the present Takalaigau (see Chapter 5). In the myth/history of Sawaieke, Narai was once paramount; moreover, as I pointed out above, the relation between Narai and Takalaigau or between Sawaieke clan and Nadawa clan is best described as a tenuous balance rather than as a relation between inferiors and superiors.

Hierarchy and equality in the space of the village

Given the foregoing, it is apparent that the spatial significance of the layout of the village is twofold. If we look at it in terms of the relation between land and sea and the reciprocal obligations obtaining between clans, it appears that village-wide relations almost approximate to cross-cousin relations – they ignore rank and assume that people are different but equal. In contrast to this, if we take 'the chiefs' and 'the people' as the crucial relation – and especially when we remember the relative heights of the *yavu* on which some houses are built – we find that 'the chiefs' are put above the people in a hierarchical relation, which at the same time contains a challenge to hierarchy in the tenuous balance in relations between the paramount and the land chief.

So it seems that the relation between land and sea interacts with that between the chiefs and the people, and here too, as with kinship relations, there is an implicit opposition between balanced reciprocity and hierarchy. The typical cross-cousin relationship is across households and the core of hierarchical kin relations is within the household; so it is fitting that the predominant spatial construct governing the layout of houses relative to one other is that of *veiqaravi*, 'facing each other' – here denoting balanced reciprocity – rather than that of above/below, in whose terms are manifest the hierarchy within the household.

Given that the internal space of the house is governed by above/below, while its external orientation to other houses is that of 'facing' them, it is apparent that each house itself contains the opposition between hierarchy and equality. The *internal* ordering of the space denotes hierarchical relations, while *external* orientation of the 'land door' of one house towards the 'sea door' of the next denotes the balanced reciprocity that defines the relation between landspeople and seapeople. However, the 'honoured door' is also the 'sea door', and this recognizes a certain superiority in chiefs, whose prerogative it is to enter by that door. Nevertheless, there is also a *tabu* on entry by the 'land door' which, like the 'sea door', is situated under one of the *kau tabu* or 'sacred beams' that support the roof. The associations attached to the doors on the long sides of the house mediate between the balanced reciprocity that ideally underlies exchange relations between lineages, between clans and, most importantly, between cross-cousins, and the hierarchical relations that obtain *within* the household. In this connection the *tabu* that forbids one to sit or stand in any doorway becomes explicable: one is either inside a house and subject to household hierarchy or outside it and acknowledging the ideal equality of cross-cousins.

Many of the data outlined here and in previous chapters are identical to those given by Sahlins (1976: 24–46) for Moala; however, I have to differ with him on interpretation. Sahlins takes the distinction between 'the chiefs' [*turaga*] and 'the people' [*vanua*] to generate all other aspects of Fijian dualism – the underlying exchange relation being given by the superiority of wife-takers to wife-givers (ibid.: 26). His assumption of the historical existence of a 'two-section' system in Moala (ibid.: 24) is apparently derived from Groves's (1963) review article on Sahlin's *Moala*. Groves based his critical remarks on Hocart (1915a, 1952: 41–51), who had argued for the historical existence of 'the dual organization' in terms of two intermarrying moieties in Fiji (1929: 232 ff., 1936, 1970: 268–72). However, the evidence for this conclusion is problematic; Dravidian terminology in Fiji entails 'prescriptive cross-cousin marriage' only in the sense that one should marry someone whom one can call cross-cousin, and if one marries a person to whom no kinship link can be traced then that person is, by definition, cross-cousin. The two-section idea seems to have arisen because Hocart made land/sea symbolism more or less isomorphic with relations set up through marriage. This is possible *symbolically* because relations between 'land' and 'sea' are reciprocal and balanced, as are those between cross-cousins; but it does *not* entail that 'landspeople' marry 'seapeople' (however, see Quain, 1948: 244–5).

I showed earlier that wife-takers cannot be considered superior to wife-givers in Sawaieke country, and I would question whether in fact they are in Moala or in Lau, as Sahlins maintains. Sahlins appears to find the superiority of wife-takers over wife-givers in the origin myth whereby a 'woman of the land' is given in marriage to 'the chief from over the sea', and in the *vasu* relationship that thus obtains between the children of this marriage (who inherit their father's chiefly status) and 'the land' group, from whom 'the son of the chief' thus has the right to 'take anything he wants without asking for it'. He takes this set of relations to mean that any given male ego is superior in status to his Mother's Brother (1976: 30), even though he notes later that the exchange relations between them 'amount to the balancing of accounts that had first favoured the mother's brother' (ibid.: 31).

Sahlins has proposed a 'logical model of second cross-cousin marriage' which involves an oscillation between a four-part and a three-part marriage system: the quaternary component being given by the rule of second cross-cousin marriage and the ternary component by the fact that this rule prevents the duplication of alliances in successive generations and thus means that any given family stands as wife-takers to one set of in-laws and wife-givers to another. Leaving aside the fact that in contemporary Gau (and I suspect in Moala) the second cross-cousin marriage rule is no longer applied – marriages being allowed as well with first cousins – the 'rule' could not at any time have set up an even momentarily stable relation of hierarchy. Sahlins himself notes that 'the ternary system takes on a fugitive existence within an endemic contradiction between hierarchy and reciprocity' (1976: 31), since the exchange relations between the *vasu* and his mother's brother are ultimately those of balanced reciprocity.

However, I would go further than this and argue that *at no point* are wife-takers understood to be superior in status to wife-givers; this is not just because exchange relations are those of balanced reciprocity. Equally important here is the fact that a woman's brothers are cross-cousins to the man who marries her and thus stand to him in a relation of unambiguous equality; moreover, the man owes obedience and respect to his father-in-law, just as the son of his marriage (the *vasu*) will also owe unquestioning respect and deference to his mother's brothers, the avoidance relation between them being particularly strict – a fact that Sahlins does not take into account. As I showed in the last chapter, the crucial hierarchical relation established on marriage is that imparted by the authority of any given man over his wife. I shall argue later that it is *this* relation that is the pivot for Fijian hierarchy; for the moment I wish to discuss some other aspects of Sahlins's analysis, those having to do with land and sea as this relation is evidenced in space.

Sahlins acknowledges balanced reciprocity in exchange relations between landspeople and seapeople; however, he still takes the 'sea' element to be superior to that of 'land' – again presumably because he takes the distinction between the chiefs (associated with the sea) and the people (associated with the land) to be the fundamental one. So in his description of the Moalan house he makes the land/sea distinction that is given by the long sides of the house interact with the above/below axis in such a way that it governs the use of space *inside* the house. Here I hope I have demonstrated first that land and sea stand to each other as equals in an unambiguous exchange relation of balanced reciprocity; and secondly that the orientation of 'the land door' of one house to 'the sea door' of the next concerns relations that are *external* to the household. It does not govern seating arrangements within the house – these being given by the above/below axis.

The exterior plan of the house certainly 'mediates the relations between household and village and constitutes the relations of village production', but it is not 'the symbolic exoskeleton of family life' (Sahlins, 1976: 33). The house's exterior plan refers to relations of equality and balanced reciprocity between cross-cousins (i.e. between affines), these being at once constituted and expressed in the balanced exchanges over time between the sister's son and his mother's brother's group. However, once taken *inside* the house, the cross-cousin relation is transformed by marriage into a hierarchical relation whereby a man has authority over his wife.

Moreover, I cannot quite agree with Sahlins that family life is 'a miniature of the political community'; I would argue that the symbolism is rather more complex, for it is just as possible to assert that the political community is the household writ large. Village-wide relations involve continual play between notions of neighbourliness and reciprocity given by *veiqaravi* and the relation between cross-cousins, and the notion of one big household whose internal relations are ordered on the above/below axis. I mentioned earlier that *veiqaravi* is explicitly said to be 'in the manner of the land', and remarked that this is not necessarily opposed to what is 'in the manner of kinship'. Thus, despite the fact that the two notions have different connotations and evoke somewhat different domains of reference and contexts of action, they may be easily equated.

This type of equation is apparent in the notion of the village as 'a household'. Thus Nation (1978: 6) remarks that the 'corporate household is . . . both the basic unit with which larger social units are built and the model of their corporateness.' Hooper (1982: 34) says that 'a man is chief in his own house and this aphorism is supported by the fact that the respect shown to the chief of a village or kingdom is only a more refined version of the respect shown to a head of household.' The notion of the high chief as the head of one large household is found elsewhere in Polynesia (see, for example, Urbanowicz, 1975: 570–71 on politics as 'kinship writ large' in contemporary Tonga). In Sawaieke, the idea is often expressed in sermons and speeches and in discussions of property relations. In village and inter-village council meetings the putative paramount chief, Takalaigau, often referred to Sawaieke country (all eight villages) as *noda vuvale*, 'our household', and in this context *noda* as the inclusive form of 'our' clearly implied that as paramount chief he was head of this vast extended household.

Here what is 'in the manner of the land' (i.e. the relations between the various villages and the clans of which they are composed) is forced over against what is 'in the manner of kinship' in such a way that the two domains are made more or less identical. The prevalence of this explicit analogy – one that conflates kinship and 'the manner of the land' – effectively asserts that hierarchy dominates in social relations. This is because the primary reference of 'the household' is to domestic kinship, and this is by definition hierarchical. On the other hand, what is expressed in the interaction between the constructs given by land/sea and chiefs/people renders the chiefship a much more ambiguous source of hierarchy. Given the image of Sawaieke country as one big household, it is interesting to note that the relations between the two 'countries' [*vanua*] in Gau are joking relations; in other words, at any level of social intercourse that is conceived of as concerning *external* relations, joking, balanced reciprocity and equality come into effect.

On a day-to-day basis it is hierarchy rather than a balanced 'duality' that is the more stressed, if only because one has many more relations that are hierarchical than relations that are equal. Moreover, when people are gathered together for enjoyment or ceremony on any occasion that takes place inside a village building, the constraints imposed by above/below are such that hierarchy is seen to dominate and contain the implicit threat posed by the equality between cross-cousins, or between those who are 'different but equal' in terms of their obligations to each other in the context of what is considered the traditional polity.

The complexity of relations across groups lies in the fact that exchange relations between them are fundamentally those of balanced reciprocity, while at the same time they contain the suggestion that 'the people' pay tribute to 'the chiefs'. Here I would argue that the notion of equality that is given by balanced reciprocity in exchange relations is of the same crucial importance for relations across groups as is the equality of cross-cousins for relations between kin. In each case equality in social relations has at once to be recognized and 'contained' if hierarchical relations are to dominate. Just as relations of equality between cross-cousins have to be transformed on marriage so that the man is seen to have authority over his wife, so exchange relations between the chiefs and the people have to be rid of any connotations of equality and rendered clearly hierarchical. This transformation is achieved in a shift in the meaning of *veiqaravi* which, in the activity of *yaqona*-drinking, ceases to suggest 'attendance on each other' and comes to denote 'attendance upon chiefs' and the giving of tribute.

5 Containing equality – the yaqona ceremony

If hierarchy is to dominate social relations, then the challenge posed by balanced reciprocity in exchange relations across groups has to be contained. The equation of the household with the village or country is one aspect of the process by which this occurs. Given that differential status within the household is manifest on the above/below axis of the house's internal space, what we have now to examine is how above/below makes hierarchy appear fundamental to social interaction *beyond* the household and across lineage and clan.

The meal at home manifests the household in action, the statuses of its members and their reciprocal obligations – especially with respect to man and wife. At a higher level of inclusiveness, the gathering [*soqo*] in the village hall constitutes the village-wide 'household' – the community. The gathering is defined by the drinking of *yaqona*, and in this context social relations are mediated by 'the exchange of drink' rather than 'the exchange of food'.

Below I describe the type of jolly and less overtly formal gathering that takes place during the Christmas holidays, or fêtes men from outside the village who have been working there for some community purpose. Even when the fun is at its height all the etiquette attached to differential status is observed; this is exemplified in the way people make use of the space where the gathering takes place (cf. Geddes, 1948: 475; Johnston, 1918: 75).

The gathering

The late afternoon holds a sense of happy anticipation – one of the young women making garlands says there will definitely be dancing, a chiefly lady having already asked the chiefs for this favour. By 6 p.m. men are drinking *yaqona* in the village hall while women and girls are still busy cooking or feeding children. Young men begin to loiter in groups outside the hall, taking it in turn to pound *waka* –

yaqona root – so that there will be plenty ready for use. Inside, other young men are mixing and serving *yaqona*, and those who play guitar and sing are already seated in a small circle below the *tanoa*, the large bowl in which *yaqona* is mixed. Their songs are composed by one of their own number or taken from the radio. Men make their way to the hall, singly or in groups, their *sevusevu* – a presentation bundle of *yaqona* – being formally accepted by the assembled men and added to the common supply.

Dinner over, the women shower and dress in their best. They scent themselves with sweet-smelling coconut oil, tuck blossoms behind their ears and garland themselves with flowers. They take their handbags (homemade out of pandanus or bought in Suva) and fill them with certain necessaries: talcum powder, scent, cigarettes and chewing gum. Now they're ready to go. They call at each other's houses on the way to the hall so that they may enter as a group.

The indirect fashion of approach to a house is even more strongly marked if one is going to drink *yaqona* there or in the village hall. One may loiter outside, perhaps, and exchange a few words with the young men who are pounding *yaqona*, or stand to one side of the doorway to obtain a partial view of the interior; if it is dark one can stand outside the pool of light that issues through the door and get a good view of what is going on inside. Or, if the building is made of bamboo slats or other material that allows of chinks and crevices, one can go up to the walls, peer through the cracks and overhear the talk.

By these manoeuvres one finds out what is going on, whether one wants to and can easily join in, and where one may sit when one enters. It is quite usual, especially at night, to approach a house where people are drinking *yaqona* and find others ranged about outside in small groups or peering through cracks in the walls. Eventually they will probably enter the house and seat themselves in a suitable position. Women, girls and young men are more likely than men to be discovered 'peeping' [*iro*]. Men have a more direct manner of approach and entry to a building, though they too always loiter for a few moments on the path nearby or just outside. One often hears people say that they are just off to 'peep in at the village hall', or at so-and-so's house where people are drinking *yaqona* or stretching pandanus. Where only some relationships can be convivial and easy, one has to assure oneself that a few of one's mates are present in a gathering. Moreover, one has to check where and with whom one will be able to sit down.

Women do not like to enter a large gathering on their own and will not do so unless other women are already present. The first group usually consists of at least six to ten women – but they do not enter at once. Instead they stand for a while outside the hall, peeping in at the doorway and through cracks in the walls and urging one another to be first. The young and those of low rank hang back, waiting for higher-status women to take a position at the head of the group – 'Mother of Manasa, do take the lead.' 'No, no thank you, please take the lead yourself' – until at last they are arranged in suitable order and the leader sets off towards the entrance to the hall, followed by older women, with young, unmarried women in last place.

The leading woman pauses on the threshold and says: '*Bogi saka!*' ('Good evening, ladies and gentlemen'), and the assembled people answer: '*Bogi!*' as she walks to her place and sits down, followed by the other women. She has with her a bundle of *waka* (*yaqona* roots) – the *sevusevu* for all those who accompany her – and she pushes this across the floor to one of the young men seated near the *tanoa*. He passes it to a herald (*matanivanua*, a member of Nadawa lineage in Sawaieke clan) who claps his hands three times. A silence falls on all the people, and the herald makes the formal speech of acceptance on behalf of the chiefs.

This over, the music starts up again and *yaqona* begins going the rounds. The drink is made from the pounded root of the *yaqona* plant infused in water. A few handfuls are placed in a cloth and water is poured over it; the pounded root is squeezed and rubbed to extract its essence and water is added until the mixture reaches saturation point. The process is overseen by the senior member of the Sawaieke clan, who is present above the *tanoa*. At each round the young man behind the *tanoa* dips a small bowl into the *yaqona* and pours it into the coconut-shell drinking bowl held by a young man who is serving. People are served in order of status. The first 'three' bowls are`the important ones – that is, the first, third and fifth bowls; intermediate bowls are discounted because they are served to the chiefs' heralds, who do not rank after their chiefs. Top-status people are seated *i cake*, above the *tanoa*; and once they have drunk, the serving becomes general. Three or four young men take up drinking bowls and lend their aid, serving older people before their juniors. This type of

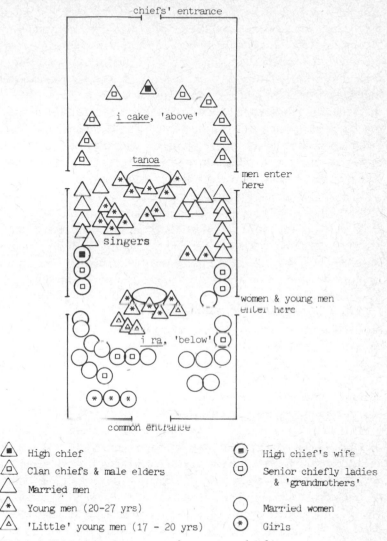

Figure 8 Typical seating pattern for yaqona-*drinking*

'general' serving takes place at a large *soqo*, but in a small one only one, or at most two, bowls are used and then status order for all people present is plainly apparent (see Figure 8 for seating at a large *soqo*).

People who are *veitabui*, subject to the incest taboo across sex or to avoidance rules within sex, do not sit near one another. The junior party gets up and moves down the space so the senior relative may be accommodated. This is most noticeable among men who are above the *tanoa*. A man moves to make way for his real or classificatory mother's brother, father or elder brother. There is an interaction here between age and rank. A chiefly married man moves so that his mother's brother (not perhaps as high-ranking by birth, and perhaps not much older) may sit on the same level as he is but at some distance away, at least a metre or so; a young man of chiefly birth moves so that his much older mother's brother is plainly seated higher than himself. Men classified as sons and younger brothers move a good deal below much older classificatory fathers and elder brothers. But if they are near in age, or the junior party is of high rank, they do not move far, if at all. Real sons and real younger brothers move to obviously lower places; they are definitely junior in status to their elders. Women make way for each other in a similar fashion, though they do not show as much concern for these matters as do men.

Cross-cousins do not move to make way for one another; rather, they are vociferous in urging an opposite number to sit above but close to them if they are friends of the same sex; across sex this urging is of the joking variety, as – except on occasions of great jollity where daring behaviour is countenanced in visitors from outside Sawaieke country – men and women do not sit close together.

A big gathering usually includes guests from other villages and they are to be honoured, joked with and shown as much attention as possible. During the interval between rounds of *yaqona*, and as soon as the first chords of the next song are struck on the guitars, some two or three of the newly arrived women get up together and sally up the room to penetrate the men's group. They walk *lolou* in a stooping posture: one carries sprigs of blossom, another lighted cigarettes, another a handful of sweets or a bottle of scent or talcum powder. Each one goes to a man – usually one of the guests – takes the garland [*salusalu*] from round her neck and puts it over his head, or pops a sweet or a lighted cigarette into his mouth, or sprays him with scent, or sprinkles his head with talcum powder, or tucks a flower [*i tekiteki*] behind his ear. One after the other a number of men receive these little attentions from two or three women acting together – each woman goes to the man or men whom she can 'speak to', to whom she does not stand in any relationship that is *veitabui* ('mutually forbidden'). If the woman is venturing above the *tanoa* she makes a slight detour to touch it with her hand as she passes – a sign of respect. Her attentions to the men being over, the woman returns giggling to her former place.

A man so honoured by female attention tends to make a little show of amazement – who, me? – but if the gathering is very lively he may take her action to initiate a joking public flirtation that lasts the rest of the evening and amuses everyone. When the next round of *yaqona* is served, he may get up, dispossess one of the servers of a bowl and, filling it to the very brim, serve it to the woman whose garland he wears. A bowl of *yaqona* must be drunk without pause. To serve someone a very large bowl is a challenge; it cannot properly be refused unless one has already drunk during that round, and to refuse is to be defeated [*druka*]. In making someone accept a brimful bowl of *yaqona* one gains a joking revenge. These encounters are often full of fun, especially if the man and woman so involved are good at the mandatory flirtatious or mock angry dialogue they entail.

The powdering and perfuming, the bedecking with flowers, the giving of cigarettes, chewing gum and sweets, the serving of brimful bowls of *yaqona* and the joking, are all part of *veisamei*, 'teasing each other', and may go on for hours, especially if the gathering and the music made by a changing group of five or so young men are very lively. *Veisamei* involves an element of competition: one wishes to outdo the other in getting him or her to accept large bowls of *yaqona* and one is 'defeated' if one does not drink or if one vomits because one has drunk too much. *Yaqona* is only mildly intoxicating and in large quantities makes one sleepy; it is sheer volume of liquid that induces vomiting (for a pharmacological analysis of *yaqona* see Buckley, Furgiule and O'Hara, 1967). *Veisamei* occurs within as well as across sex, but is considered more fun when both sexes are present and the teasing has a sexual element. Men too may tuck flowers behind women's ears or deck them with garlands, but it is usually women who initiate this exchange, and only women wield tins of talcum powder and bottles of scent – often with a vengeance, so that the man's features virtually disappear under a shower of powder.

All the while jokes are being called from one side of the room to the other and people are thanking each other. They thank each other for coming, for joking, for sitting there, for drinking *yaqona*, for smoking, for singing, and anything else that is conceivably or jokily appropriate. A man might call from one end of the room: 'Mother of Ropate, thank you very much for coming here!' and if she does not hear, a woman nearby tells her: 'Mother of Ropate, the Father of Kitione is thanking you.' And she then replies: 'Yes, thanks, Father of Kitione, thank you for drinking.' One must always acknowledge and thank in one's turn when thanks are made. At the very least one replies: 'Yes, thank you for the thanking', but if one can build a joke or a bit of sarcasm into one's reply so much the better, since this provides others present with an opportunity to laugh.

Joking [*veiwali*] and teasing each other [*veisamei*] are confined to those who are cross-cousins, and to people who are *veitabani* (literally 'of the same branch') and *tauvu* (literally 'of the same root'). These latter relations obtain between territories rather than between categories of kin. People who are *tauvu* have the same ancestor god: Sawaieke is *tauvu* with Bua, Cakaudrove and Macuata because in the distant past one of the ancestor gods came to Sawaieke from Dama in Bua, Vanua Levu. Today it is accepted that all of Vanua Levu is *tauvu* with all of Gau. A man from Bua would not be treated as 'more' *tauvu* than one from elsewhere in Vanua Levu. *Tauvu* are said to be 'just the same as native-born Gauans'; visiting *tauvu* have the freedom to act as they wish. The respective ancestors of *veitabani* are said to have been cross-cousins. The eight villages of Sawaieke country are (as a group) *veitabani* with the other villages on the island; at a higher level of inclusiveness Gau is *veitabani* with Kadavu and Nairai (cf. Deane, 1921: 60).

The relation between cross-cousins is the basis for all the enjoyment to be had from a gathering. The cross-cousin relationship is sharpened, made all the sweeter, by the challenge it poses to the hierarchy that is given in the conduct of avoidance relations and in the seating arrangements in any gathering. The significance of the cross-cousin relationship, of proper acknowledgement of avoidance relations, and of the constraints imposed by *cake/ra* are all neatly contained in the following story.

One night during the Christmas holiday season of 1982 I left the *yaqona*-drinking in the village hall and went home to bed. I could hear the songs of the young men, the laughter and voices of those remaining. Then there came a lull which, at my distance from the hall, appeared to be a total hush; some moments later it was broken by a great shout of laughter – so loud, so emphatically expressive of absolute hilarity, that I was almost persuaded to get up again and find out what was going on. Next day I was regaled several times with the following story, given in the words of the young woman of twenty-nine who first told it to me. To take the point the reader must know that the woman in the story, Mary, is a lady well over sixty who enjoys a joke and that the joker, Samuel, is a man in his thirties, cross-cousin to both Mary and Andrew, a married man of Samuel's own age against whom the joke was directed. Mary and Andrew, however, are classificatory *veiganeni*, 'brother and sister', so it is impossible for them to be in close proximity or to speak together. The relation between *veiganeni* is, of all *veitabui* relations, the one most strongly marked by avoidance and thus, by implication, the prototype of all possible incestuous relations. It should be remembered too that at the outset Mary would have been seated *i ra*, well below the *tanoa* and alongside other women. (In the story below, false names disguise the identity of the people involved.)

'Mary and Samuel are cross-cousins. Mary was joking with him [i.e. across the length of the hall] and then she said: "Samuel, go back to your own village. You're not a Sawaieke person; go back in the morning to N—." Then Samuel got hold of a big bowl and served *yaqona* to Mary – the bowl was brimful! Mary refused to drink it, so Samuel gave the bowl to the mother of Luisa. Then he took hold of Mary's arm and dragged her right up above [*ki cake sara*, i.e. above the *tanoa*]. Mary was still in a sitting position but he managed to pull her right up above so that she was seated beside Andrew. Mary and Andrew are forbidden to each other – they are brother and sister! We all laughed. Andrew was nodding, quite asleep, he didn't realise a thing. Then Samuel took Mary's hand and gave it into Andrew's hand. Then Andrew woke up suddenly like this [here the storyteller started back as if in violent surprise] and he wasn't able to say anything! Because he and Mary are forbidden to each other! How we laughed! Oh, Samuel is really an extraordinarily funny person. A true joker.'

It was Samuel's position as cross-cousin to both parties that made it possible for him to perpetrate this outrageous joke; one that would have been quite improper had Mary not been an old lady and far removed in age from her classificatory younger brother, Andrew. What aroused the delicious hilarity – and kept the story making the rounds of the village for days – was that Samuel managed simultaneously to violate the incest taboo, the hierarchical relations that obtain between kin, and the valuation of space that makes it impossible for a woman such as Mary to sit above the *tanoa* in a gathering that includes senior men of her own family. The startled hush and great shout of laughter, the description of Samuel as 'a true joker', and the breathless and delighted account of the incident are all expressive of what is ultimately represented by the relation between cross-cousins: the potential violation of the proper order. The sheer brilliance of Samuel's joke was that it turned that order upside down, threatened chaos, in a context that, as we shall see below, is paradigmatic of ranked and ordered kin relations. At its most extreme the relation between cross-cousins posits not mere equality but total anarchy as hierarchy's opposite term.

At some point in a big gathering there is a ceremonial exchange of *tabua* (whale's teeth; see Hooper, 1982: 84–134). They may be presented by the guests to the hosts to thank them for the occasion and by the hosts to the guests to thank them for coming. If the guests have been working in the village, they are draped with *i sulu* (lengths of fabric) by women as another form of thanks. This is in addition to ceremonies that will already have taken place in the late afternoon. *Tabua* are always exchanged between the highest-ranking men of each side, each of whom makes a brief acceptance speech and then passes the tooth to his herald for a longer acceptance speech.

If the *soqo* is held to be an occasion of great rejoicing, the chiefs will already have given leave to the women to 'stand up'. This means that dancing may take place – a rare and much-enjoyed pastime; rare both because dancing is closely akin to gross immorality in the tenets of Wesleyanism, and because it is in any case lacking in respect to stand up when the chiefs are present. So when the *taralala* 'spread like an epidemic' through Fiji in 1925, it was to the horror of both chiefs and Wesleyan missionaries (McNaught, 1982: 106). If dancing does take place it may not begin until quite late, perhaps after eleven or so. The highest-status men tend to leave shortly afterwards, as does the lay preacher so that he may not be seen to be condoning immorality.

Dancing always takes place below, near the big doors at the common entrance, and it is women who invite men. Young, unmarried women do most dancing, and sometimes old women join in too, to everyone's amusement. Young married women have to be circumspect in their behaviour – they may be beaten by their outraged husbands for 'standing up' or for joking too heartily. By early morning most older people have gone home to sleep, but provided the *yaqona* lasts, the girls still want to dance and the young men are keen on making music; then the gathering goes on until after six, breaking up only when the girls leave to put the kettle on the fire for breakfast tea. But if the *yaqona* is finished before this time, one of the young men informs the senior person present that this is so and asks if more *yaqona* should be prepared. When only a few people remain, and the young men have not taken it upon themselves to prepare more *yaqona*, this is accepted as a sign that the gathering should come to an end and the offer is refused. The *yaqona* attendants adjust their posture to take up the formally proper position around the *tanoa* and the senior person present nods and says: '*Cobo!*' ('Clap!'). The server behind the *tanoa* clasps his hands together, passes them in a fast circular movement above the *tanoa*, says: 'The chiefly *yaqona* is dry', and claps his crossed palms together loudly three times, as do the other servers in unison. This means that the gathering is over and one is expected to go home.

I have tried to give some idea of how, in a gathering, high good humour and liveliness are mixed with observance of formalities. One constantly invites newcomers to 'sit above', asks those nearby if one may get up to go outside or to dance, walks *lolou* so as not to offend by holding one's body erect, and urges one's neighbour to drink the proffered bowl of *yaqona* before oneself. These formalities may be read as disavowals of one's right to any high-status position and are performed whatever one's actual status. However, one is usually seated near people of similar status and so one's polite gestures do not refer to people who are much above or below oneself in hierarchical terms. A senior woman, for instance, would not invite a young married woman to drink before herself unless that woman was a very high-ranking guest and seated close by her.

Any gathering, be it large or small, is unthinkable without *yaqona*; it begins with the preparation of the drink and ends when there is no more to be drunk.

Yaqona ceremonies

The *yaqona* ceremony and the *sevusevu* associated with it are the central rituals of Fijian social life. They are performed on all occasions from the most minor, everyday affairs – such as a few men getting together for a chat around the *tanoa* – through all rituals attendant upon birth, marriage, circumcision and death, to the grand and lengthy ceremonial mounted to install a chief, or to welcome a high chief or other dignitary such as the Queen of England.

Yaqona ritual has often been described for Fiji, for example by Hooper (1982: 182–9) for Lau, Lester (1941) for Viti Levu, Fison (1904: 167–70) and Williams (1858: 141–6) for Bau. Kava is important elsewhere in the Pacific; its use is discussed by, for example, M. Mead (1930: 102–9), Holmes (1958) and Shore (1982: 240–45) for Samoa; Mariner (1827: 150–67), Collocott (1927), Gifford (1929: 156–70), Bott (1972) and Kaeppler (1985) for Tonga. Firth (1970a) relates Tongan and Tikopian myths of its origin; Hocart (1952: 127–8) gives a Fijian variant. James Turner's comparative analysis endorses the notion of kava ritual as sacrifice (Leach, 1972) and shows how kava-drinking allows direct access to ancestral power. He notes that in Fiji, Tonga, Samoa, Futuna and Uvea kava ritual shares certain features: status-ordered seating arrangements, formalized methods of preparation and serving, and the drinking itself ordered according to relative status (J. W. Turner, 1986).

My own analysis below tries to understand how the use of *yaqona* enters into Fijian daily life in such a way that people's disposition round the *tanoa* constitutes hierarchical relations. By analysing how *yaqona* ritual connects with certain other aspects of daily life, I show how it may be understood as a form of tribute and redistribution in which chiefs are seen to be effective [*mana*]. In *yaqona*-drinking, statuses across households are manifest on the above/below axis and in the order in which the drink is served. The significance of above/below and of *yaqona* are connected, so I begin by describing some uses of the plant.

A chief is installed when he drinks a bowl of *yaqona* served under the aegis of the chief of the clan which 'makes the chief'. Drinking this *yaqona* gives him the transcendent power that confirms and entrenches the political power that was his when he was only designated high chief, but not yet installed. Once he has drunk the chiefly *yaqona* his every command must be fulfilled, for illness falls on those who fail in their duty. A high chief does not will this punishment; it occurs because *e sa tu vei ira na sau*, 'the command (or prohibition) is his', – that is, has become intrinsic to him and mystically effective, so that his will is simply asserted; no dereliction of duty can be concealed from one who now has the powers of a god (see also Hocart, 1952: 93–9; Brewster, 1922: 20–21; Sahlins, 1962: 387, 1983; Hooper, 1982: 155–67).

The ability to create a high chief itself constitutes power – so much so that the question of *who* actually was the high chief of Gau was problematic for villagers in Sawaieke, since the man who held the title was not formally installed. This is apparent in the sentiments expressed by Narai, the chief of Sawaieke clan, in whose hands lay the power to install a high chief of Sawaieke country:

'The making of the chief is my task alone . . . that is a godly gift that is made to me . . . it is in the blood . . . that is the power [*pawa*, *mana*] that is mine. . . . But if the *yaqona* is given to him [Takalaigau] everything in the manner of the land is encompassed therein. It does not matter that the *yaqona* is given to him, I am still chief; but after I have given him the *yaqona* I shall address him as *saka* [sir], I shall act with great respect towards him. That is after I have given the *yaqona*, after I have made him drink. . . . After that I shall attend on him, everything he tells me I shall shoulder as a burden, nor shall I try to make myself great by refusing to follow him. Everything he wants done in this land will be told to me . . . I shall then order it to be done.' (Cf. Hooper, 1982: 169 f.)

Today the power of the high chief of a small country such as Sawaieke no longer extends very far and is perhaps best described as 'influence'; even if he is unscrupulous a high chief cannot extract very much from his people in the way of labour, money and goods partly because, unless he is formally installed in office, he is not thought to have any means of visiting retribution on those who fail to obey him. Moreover, villages are run on formally democratic lines, so a high chief's political influence tends to depend largely on the respect in which he is held by the community at large (cf. Sahlins, 1962: 303, 321, 325, 368).

Before British colonization and in the early days of the colony, chiefs had real economic and political power, including the power of life and death over their subjects. *Mana* (literally 'effectiveness') was bestowed on a high chief by the *kalou vu* or ancestor god who was the land's original 'owner'. The chief himself was not thought to be a direct descendant of the ancestral owner; he became *mana* by virtue of his installation as chief by those who were considered the jural owners of the country (cf. Sahlins, 1983: 79). Walter argues that because the chiefs are not descended from the land gods, their 'jural status with regard to land is anomalous' (1978–9: 7); this is not the case in Sawaieke, where the chiefly clan and its lineages have their own lands by right of descent. In myth and history, these lands were accorded them with the chiefship. But a high chief still depends for his *mana* on proper installation in office by those who are said to be the original owners of the chiefly village of Sawaieke. Today people say that a high chief's *mana* is not what it was, that this is because they are all Christians, and so the power of the ancestor gods has diminished because 'no one attends on them any more'.

I discuss political organization further in Chapter 8; here I only observe that it is in a context of marked diminution in the real politico-economic power of chiefs that *yaqona*-drinking has become of central importance. The current mode of drinking is said to be 'in the manner of the land' and eminently Fijian, in spite of people's awareness that historically women and young men were not permitted to drink *yaqona* at all. Women were excluded; young men merely prepared and served the drink to older men – those classified as *turaga*, specifically chiefs but also, politely, married men. There is said to have been a marked increase in frequency of drinking over the past sixty years or so, as well as in inclusiveness of persons involved.

A man becomes paramount by drinking a bowl of *yaqona* whose presentation manifests the power of the installing chief. When a chief installs a chief he is, in 'making him drink' [*vagunuvi koya*], at once disposing of *yaqona* as a chief does and creating his own ritual subordination; his act makes him junior in status to the man he installs, whose bidding he will now do. An act of chiefly tribute, this rare and highly significant ceremony takes its meaning from the everyday but equally significant *i sevusevu*. An *i sevusevu* precedes or accompanies the drinking of *yaqona*; it involves the presentation of a bundle of *yaqona* roots or, on grander occasions, an entire uprooted plant. In essence *sevusevu* is tribute to chiefs; it confers on those who present it the freedom of a place and entails obligations of hospitality, etc., from those who accept it (cf. Hooper, 1982: 182–7).

At its most simple the *sevusevu* involves only a brief, formal acceptance. A newcomer enters the space where the drinking is taking place and throws down a small bundle of dried roots beside the *tanoa*. In a few moments a silence falls on the assembly and one who is able to make formal acceptance of the *yaqona* places it on the floor where he can touch it, claps his hands three times and says: 'I am touching, sirs, the *i sevusevu*, the chiefly *i sevusevu*, the big *i sevusevu*. Ah, it is over, over.' He claps again and the others join in with their clapping, saying, 'Thanks, thanks' [*vinaka*], and the thing is finished.

This is an attenuated form of the most solemn ceremony which proceeds from the speeches accorded the presentation of an entire *yaqona* plant – say to a visiting high chief – to 'the chiefly *yaqona*' [*yaqona vakaturaga*], the mixing and serving of the first bowls; then the men who look after the *yaqona* are dressed in traditional leaf skirts and decorated according to rank with charcoal on the face and barkcloth sashes. The preparation of the drink is highly formalized: the gestures used to squeeze and strain the *yaqona* through a bundle of hibiscus fibres are orchestrated by a chant given out by other men, and the serving of the drink to the honoured high chief is itself 'danced' in a series of exquisitely slow and graceful gestures.

The rank relations exemplified in those of chief and commoner are manifest in the *i sevusevu*, where *yaqona* is the paradigmatic form of tribute. It was the *i sevusevu* that was evoked when Fiji's most famous chief, Cakobau, ceded the country to Britain's representative, Sir Arthur Gordon, in 1874: his 'formal act of submission ... consisted of the breaking off of a piece from a root of kava and placing it in Gordon's hand' (Legge, 1958: 206). Moreover, since every man is a chief in his own house, it is not surprising that the *i sevusevu* is an everyday occurrence. The *i sevusevu* requests the freedom of a place, so one takes an *i sevusevu* when going to visit another village or, within one's own village, when one wishes to join a group of people already drinking under a shady mango tree, or in a temporary shelter adjacent to an area where house-building is in progress, and so on. Similarly, if one wishes to ask someone a favour (the use of his land, perhaps, or the right to name a child) or to beg forgiveness for a fault committed (raising one's hand against one's father or wife, for example), one asks a senior man to present *yaqona* on one's behalf with a speech that asks the favour or begs forgiveness, and in the acceptance and the subsequent drinking the favour is granted or the fault buried.

To accuse someone of drinking *yaqona* alone is to accuse the person of witchcraft. Only one intent upon evil magic would prepare and drink *yaqona* alone behind closed doors. By pouring the first bowl as a libation to one's original ancestor god [*kalou vu*] and drinking the second oneself, one summons the god to one's aid and is tested by having to name a close relative as first victim to the god's death-dealing power. Once that person has died one is then able, in subsequent lonely *yaqona* sessions, to ask for aid in acquiring riches, sexual magnetism of an utterly irresistible kind, or whatever else one wants. In pouring out the first bowl as a libation to the god and drinking the second, one makes oneself like a chief's *matanivanua* or herald – traditionally his mouthpiece or executive – a position that used to entail material power. Only one death during my eighteen months in Sawaieke was said to be caused by *sova yaqona*, 'pouring libations of *yaqona*'; it occurred in a neighbouring village and whenever afterwards the accused man's name came up in conversation, someone would say darkly of him that he was *dau gunu yaqona duadua* 'always drinking *yaqona* by himself' (cf. Turner, J. W., 1986: 209).

One may also drink *yaqona* publicly to remove curses: illnesses said to be incurable because they result from witchcraft or other malign influences. To remove a curse, the *dau vagunu* (literally 'one who causes to drink') prepares *yaqona* and calls on the winds to beg the patient's ancestor god to remove the curse or overcome the malign influence; or he or she might pour a libation and ask the winds to intercede with his or her own ancestor god, who then does the curing. Sometimes the *dau vagunu* uses a Bible on which a whale's tooth is placed and calls on Jesus Christ as well as on the ancestor god. The *yaqona*, it seems, is always present.

The chiefly installation, the *i sevusevu*, the evil acts of the witch and the beneficial ones of the curer, suggest that *yaqona*-drinking is itself *mana*. So Turner writes, 'a person's *mana* can be nurtured or enchanced by the drinking of *yaqona*, for *yaqona* is itself *mana*' (1986: 209; cf. Firth, 1970a: 208). *Mana* is often glossed as 'spiritual power' but in fact means 'effectiveness' (Handy, 1927: 26–34; Capell, 1938;

Firth, 1967: 192; Hooper, 1982: 167–70). It may be the efficacy of *yaqona* in making one 'drunk', of a herb remedy in curing, of a clan chief who installs a high chief, or of the speech for *sevusevu* in which the formula *mana . . . e dina* (literally 'it is effective, it is true') is always repeated. So may the speechmaker's words (concerning, perhaps, peace between kin and continued prosperity) by their very pronunciation bring about the state to which they refer (cf. Hocart, 1914: 98).

Historically the notion of *mana* may have provided a key to above/below. *Mana* was from the ancestors; so the *mana* of curer or witch, and of the charms produced by magic or sorcery [*vakadraunikau*], was also from the ancestors. *Mana* as a form of transcendent power became inherent to an installed high chief. On the scale of human effectiveness, he was then the most *mana* and closest to the ancestors, so he could take the top central position above. The ancestors were above the chief, but he was the channel for the *mana* they dispensed downwards in *yaqona*-drinking along the above/below axis from ancestor to chief to commoner (cf. Firth, 1970a: 203, 212). The witch who 'drank *yaqona* on his own' initiated the flow of *mana* only to misdirect it to selfish ends; by contrast, the *mana* of a high chief was supposed to be for the good of his people in so far as it resulted in prosperity for all or victory in battle.

Today the salience of ancestral power has been much reduced by Wesleyanism. The ancestors still stand behind a paramount chief – indeed, the lowliest person has ancestors to call on – but they are said to be weak in face of the Christian God. Neither is magic what it once was, as is apparent in these half-serious, half-joking remarks from a man in his seventies to another old man and myself as we sat one afternoon round the *tanoa*: 'Magic is not so effective [*mana*] today, eh? In the past it was very effective and especially important in time of war. Magic might be useful today in the Falklands, eh, Mother of Manuel?'

Despite its relative loss of salience, it would seem to be the *mana* of *yaqona*-drinking that historically underlies its ritualization and even today subtly informs the notion of above/below. I show later that the position of the high chief defines the pole above and is itself ratified by association with transcendent power, but today this is not so much the *mana* of the ancestors as 'the strength of Jehovah, the high God'. Peck (1982: 134) quotes a Lovu (Gau) informant as describing the relation between the Christian God [*Kalou*] and ancestor gods [*kalou vu*] as follows: 'Na Kalou gave them [the ancestor gods] some *sau* [power] too, but they don't give the punishment before they let Na Kalou know about it. If Na Kalou doesn't give them the right they won't do it.' Further, Narai, quoted above, referred to his own power to install a high chief as 'a gift from God'; he used a borrowed term, *pawa*, and when I asked did this mean *mana*, he hesitated for a moment before giving his assent. I take this type of response – which I encountered several times – to indicate that *pawa* and *mana*, while subtly different from one another, may be merged in that their source is always, ultimately, a transcendent one (cf. Hooper, 1982: 172); the response may also be occasioned by a reluctance to use the term *mana*, which is today often associated with magic and witchcraft.

It should be clear from the description of the gathering above that drinking *yaqona* is not always a solemn undertaking. It is only so on solemn occasions; otherwise it means storytelling, laughter, singing and general enjoyment of the society of others. Also, *yaqona* is a drug that may induce mild euphoria in the drinker. Drinking *yaqona* is a social act in every sense of the word, and it is because it *is* the quintessential social act that drinking alone cannot be countenanced and is an idiom for the practice of witchcraft. The corollary of this is that most adult Fijians regard *yaqona*-drinking as obligatory.

If *yaqona*-drinking is in part constitutive of a notion of social order, to refuse to drink is an act of rudeness, a denial of social relations and a rejection of the status quo. So people drink *yaqona* even if they do not like it. An adult man, for instance, questioning me as to whether I *really* liked *yaqona*, revealed that he did not: 'I find it very difficult to drink *yaqona*; it tastes bad to me.' When I then asked him why he drank at all he said, 'I just drink a little, out of respect for those who are drinking.' One does not have to drink beyond one's capacity; but one should drink several bowls before one begins to say no. Thus one shows respect to the chiefs by whom, as it were, the *yaqona* is dispensed to the people. Neither may one pour away what remains of the drink when those assembled have had enough. Once prepared the *yaqona* must be drunk in the approved manner, bowl after bowl, until the *tanoa* is dry [*maca*]. Not everyone is so well-mannered as to remain until the end, but if one has to leave it is polite to ask permission of the highest-status person present: 'Father of so-and-so, perhaps I shall go; thank you very much for the *yaqona*'; he then replies, 'Thank you, Father of so-and-so, thank you for drinking, thank you for coming here.'

Yaqona-drinking is associated with transcendent power, so it is always hedged about by ceremony. It is prepared and drunk under the auspices of chiefs; if no actual chief is present the person of highest status must sit above the *tanoa* so that it 'faces the chiefs', even when the drinking is at its most informal. Moreover, there are approved modes of comporting oneself and only one who is ill-bred would fail to observe them: one must 'sit properly', with legs crossed, when actually drinking, clap before accepting the proferred bowl of *yaqona*, drain the bowl without pause and clap again politely after handing the bowl back to the server. Before stretching one's legs one should ask permission of one's immediate neighbours: 'I shall perhaps just stretch my legs, Mother of so-and-so' and 'Yes, good' comes the reply. To sit with one's knees raised is to sit at best 'like a European' and at worst 'like an Indian'; the position is immodest regardless of how one's dress might conceal the genitals and always gives rise to mirth from the onlookers. Similarly one must rise from a sitting position and sit down again with circumspection. If one is 'looking after the *yaqona*' [*qaravi yaqona*] one should not stretch one's legs, put one's hand on one's hip, smoke or in any other way violate the canons of good *yaqona*-tending manners. One who fails to observe these rules is said to be ill-bred [*kaisi*] and not to understand the custom of the land [*i tovo vakavanua*].

Transforming balanced reciprocity

Houses in a village are built *veiqaravi*, literally 'facing each other'. The term also denotes attendance on chiefs and refers too to *yaqona*-drinking: *qaravi turaga*, 'attending on chiefs' or 'facing the chiefs', is interchangeable with *qaravi yoqona*, 'looking after the *yaqona*' or 'facing *yaqona*'. I show below how balanced reciprocity in exchange relations across groups – a reciprocity that is given by the relations between cross-cousins and made concrete in the space of the village – is transformed in *yaqona*-drinking into a hierarchical rendering of tribute to chiefs.

In *yaqona*-drinking the primary reference of the term 'chiefs' is

not to members of the chiefly Nadawa clan but rather to *all* those
high-status men in the community who sit above in the gathering. In
Sawaieke, when a large gathering is in progress, those who sit above
are the clan chiefs, certain lineage chiefs (such as Tui Nailavoci) and
heralds (such as Tuinimata) and all those male members of the
various clans who are senior. Effectively this means that the oldest
and highest-ranking men in the community sit above, with
Takalaigau taking the top central position. Those who sit below the
tanoa and facing the chiefs, face upwards towards their senior male
kin. In order of status as given by their position on the above/below
a·is, they are the senior and junior married men, the young men and,
at the pole below, women. Those young men who look after the
yaqona are not above men who are senior to them; their apparently
higher position is negated by their serving others and by their other
peers' more lowly places.

So in *yaqona*-drinking people take their positions in terms of an
interaction between rank, seniority and gender – that is, in terms of
hierarchical kin relations. The image is that of one vast household,
the relations between them mediated by the exchange of drink.
Yaqona is a 'thing of the land' that is offered 'raw' to the chiefs in the
sevusevu and redistributed by them to the people in the form of drink
that cannot be further transformed but only accepted. So the
reciprocity of land and sea is recognized and contained in *yaqona*-
drinking, and apparently made subordinate to hierarchical relations
between kin. This is evident in the way land and sea are manifested
in the seating positions of people at every level of the above/below
axis and in the order of drinking itself.

Above the *tanoa*, sea is manifested in the persons of senior men
of chiefly birth and in the chiefs of seapeople clans, land in the chiefs
of landspeople clans and in senior heralds. The order of drinking is
as follows: Takalaigau, the paramount chief – sea; Narai, chief of
Sawaieke clan – land; Tui Koviko, chief of Koviko clan – sea; Tui
Navure, chief of landspeople; Tui Voda, chief of seapeople. Each
of these men is followed by a herald; for members of the chiefly
Nadawa clan the heralds are all members of Sawaieke clan. So the
reciprocity between land and sea is not negated by the order of
drinking; for if sea ranks higher than land when Takalaigau drinks
before Narai or when any senior man of Nadawa clan drinks before
his herald from Sawaieke clan, land ranks higher than sea when

Narai drinks before Tui Koviko or Tui Navure drinks before Tui Voda.

Thus *yaqona*-drinking does not violate the balanced and competitive exchange between land and sea, but now these relations are played out in a space defined by the above/below axis and the primary reference of 'facing each other' ceases to denote land and sea. Now it denotes the way those below the *tanoa* face those above it; the relationship is still mutual but now clearly hierarchical: it sets off a small group of senior and high-ranking men, those above the *tanoa*, against all others in the community. Those who 'face the *yaqona*' also 'face the chiefs'; so, when 'facing each other' [*veiqaravi*] denotes an official reception, the exchange relation becomes one of tribute to chiefs. The chiefs' acceptance and redistribution of tribute to their lower-status kin appears as *noblesse oblige*. In the context of marriage and the household the above/below axis is typically manifest in the family meal, where equality between cross-cousins is seen to be overcome. So, in the context of village-wide relations, hierarchical kinship is reasserted in *yaqona*-drinking, where people's behaviour is constrained by above/below, which thus seems to contain and subordinate relations of balanced reciprocity between land and sea, a relation itself implied by the equality of cross-cousins.

As we have seen, the relation between the people and their chiefs, is mediated by the exchange of *yaqona*; this mediation is physically manifest not only in the root and its transformation into drink, but in the *tanoa*. Its position on the above/below axis distinguishes chiefs – those who are above – from all others who are below.

Placing the chiefs

Within *any* space, the position of the *tanoa* apparently serves to define the space around it in such a way that it becomes both bounded and highly significant. *Tanoa* are made so that one side is seen to be that which 'faces the chiefs'. The bowl's diameter may be more than 30 centimetres or almost 80 centimetres and it is always round. It is mounted on four or six legs – two of which are joined at the top by a triangularly shaped piece of wood, whose apex points to the ground. In the apex, is a hole to which a rope of plaited *magimagi*, sennit, may be tied. Two white cowrie shells are attached to the other end of the rope, which (in any formal ceremony) is laid perpendicular to the apex of the triangle so that it leads in a direct line towards the highest-status person seated above. However, it is usually coiled beneath the *tanoa* or possibly not even attached, but whatever the occasion the apex of the triangle must face the highest-status of the men drinking *yaqona*, and this is so wherever, whenever and no matter how casually the drinking proceeds.

Once the *tanoa* has been positioned, the space around it is defined. Those who sit *i cake*, above the *tanoa*, are of higher status than those who sit *i ra*, below it. However, within this gross division one is seated above or below other people present, according to one's position relative to the top central position in which sits the top-status person present. The space beside and below the *tanoa* is there to be taken up; the space between the *tanoa* and those above it cannot be used and is always left free. So those of highest status are always separated off from those of lower status, and the latter may cluster together while the former never do. No one may sit with his or her back to the *tanoa* and the chiefs, and the open space between the *tanoa* and the line of chiefs is always noticeably large.

The position of the *tanoa* interacts with the seating position of chiefs to constitute the above and below of any given space. But this is not obvious when *yaqona* is drunk in a house or village hall, because in any enclosed space the place of the *tanoa* is more or less given by the above/below axis of that space: the side of the bowl that 'faces the chiefs' faces that part of the room called above. The place of chiefs, rather than that of the *tanoa*, is dominant; this is confirmed by observations made during a week-long seminar [*vuli*] held in Sawaieke for representatives of all the Women's Associations of Lomaiviti (central Fiji).

These women had gathered in Sawaieke to discuss the organization and duties of the Women's Associations and how they might best contribute to development. Some fifty women gathered every day in Sawaieke's village hall and occupied two-thirds or more of its available space, from the top end on down towards the common entrance. When, after lunch on the first day, some older village men entered the hall to drink *yaqona* there, they entered as a matter of politeness through the 'low' doors and had the *tanoa* set up to one side of them. They came to drink *yaqona* out of respect for the proceedings. It did not occur to me then that the men could be seated anywhere other than below, with the women above the men, but over the course of the next few days it became apparent that this was not so. In fact the women's position could be seen to be either irrelevant or actually below that of the men as the disposition of all the people in the hall changed according to what was going forward.

In the early afternoon of the first day's seminar, the disposition of people in the hall was as shown in Figure 9. Here it seems that women are seated above men – though this is undercut by the women's orientation: they are not facing *up* the hall. The woman who addresses them is not in the top central position of a high-status man; hers is a neutral position at the side of the hall. Later on, when the women split up into discussion groups and five or so women moved to occupy the free space at the bottom left of the hall, it became clear that the men's *yaqona* group occupied a space that was conceptually bounded, its focal point being the *tanoa*. The women were not encroaching on the *yaqona*-drinking: their manner of sitting marked them as cut off from the male group; far from having to 'face the chiefs', they were able to sit so that several had their backs to the men.

On each of the following days men came to drink *yaqona* in the hall and took either the bottom right-hand corner or the whole lower space, from the lower side doors to the common entrance. Just after lunch on the last day men again occupied the bottom right-hand corner, the seminar being due to recommence soon in the space above. Then it became known that the ladies from Narocake (a community of three villages, part of Sawaieke country) were coming to pay a formal visit [*veisiko*] to those gathered for the seminar. The leader of the Women's Associations (a woman of high rank in her own right, both the daughter of chiefs and the wife of a high chief) was hurriedly summoned with a few other women to observe the formalities. When this lady arrived she seated herself on a level with the chiefs but at a distance from them, near the lower left-hand door. The *veisiko* involved a formal presentation of goods, followed by a *sevusevu*; the disposition of the people in the hall is shown in Figure 10. The men did not move the *tanoa* to make it central to the whole group of women and men; the women were politely asked to drink, but were not expected to do so. Soon after the speeches were over one of the women asked permission for all of them to leave. All the women *left* the hall – even when they meant to move to the upper part

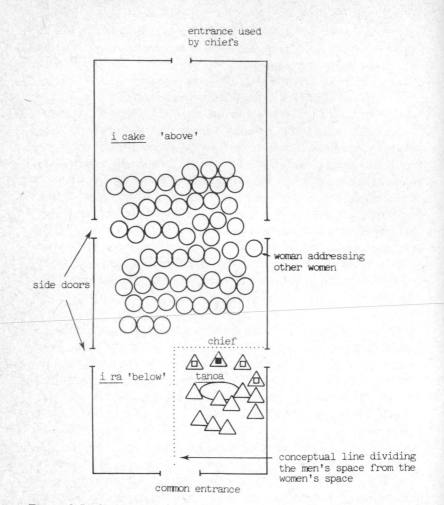

Figure 9 Ladies' seminar 1

of the room to join women already there. The leader of the Women's Associations and her herald went out through the lower left-hand side door and re-entered the hall by the top left-hand side door. Other women left by the common entrance, walked round the outside of the hall, and came in again by an upper side door. The women who came to *veisiko* exited by the common entrance and went back to the house that is their traditional host in Sawaieke.

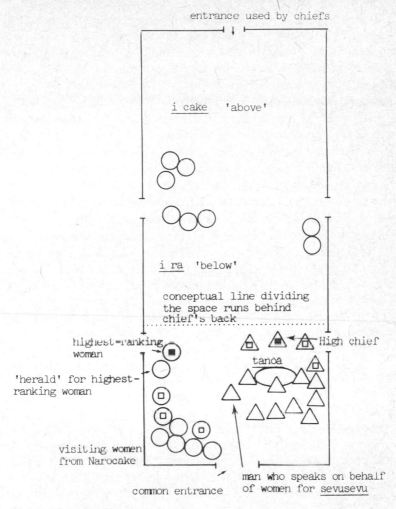

Figure 10 Ladies' seminar 2

So it is clear that the space of the men's *yaqona* group was conceptually separate. The space taken by the men had its own above and below given by the position of the *tanoa* and of the chiefs, and this was independent of the above and below of the village hall itself.

Further evidence for this is to be found in the way the given above and below of a space may be inverted. I saw this happen only once, again during the Women's Associations seminar. It came about as follows. An hour or two after the *veisiko* was over, another group of women came to make formal thanks to the leaders of the women's groups. Such thanks involve a presentation of goods, properly accompanied by *yaqona*-drinking. The leader of the Women's Associations was summoned and attended with her herald and again, once the formalities were over, the ladies were invited to join in the drinking. These women came from Nairai, a nearby island whose people are 'of the same branch' [*veitabani*] as the people of Gau. This is a joking relationship – one between equals – so the ladies accepted the invitation in high good humour and more or less instantly began to take the liberties allowed them. Two of them seated themselves above, beside the paramount chief, and other, equally spirited, women began joking exchanges heavy with sexual innuendo with various men. The occasion took on the atmosphere of a party. The men did not move the *tanoa* because the high chief had not moved his position; however, the women had penetrated the men's space and men who came later on were in some cases peremptorily ordered by women to come and sit by them – all this being entirely acceptable and predictable behaviour between *veitabani*. I left the group for an hour or so; on my return the high chief and the *tanoa* had changed positions so that they were now central to the whole group of men and women. The party went on into the early evening, when the women from Nairai left rather abruptly to join women who had come to *solevu* and were even then gathered outside the village hall with the goods they were to present.

A *solevu* is a vast ceremonial presentation of goods – in this case from the women visitors (considered as a group) to the 'owners' of the village where they were staying. The *solevu* reciprocated Sawaieke's hospitality, but the large number of women involved could not have been accommodated had they entered by the common door and had to sit below the *tanoa* and the chiefs. Neither could they have asked the men to move, as this would have been most impolite. The chiefs *could* have decided to move up the hall to their accustomed space, but this was not done – I suspect because it would have been undignified if it seemed that the men had previously been displaced by women, and also because *any* hasty action is considered unseemly and unfitting for chiefs. The problem was solved by the chiefs turning their backs on the *tanoa*. Then the disposition of the people in the village hall as shown in Figure 11.

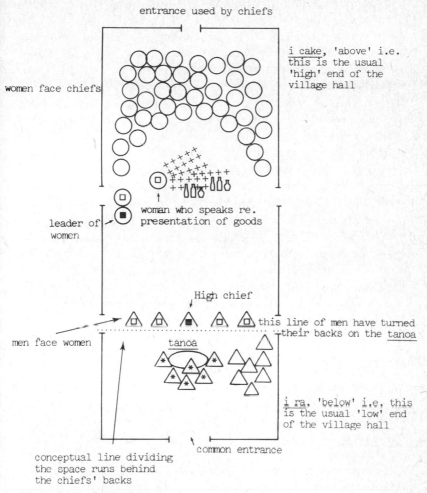

Figure 11 Ladies' solevu

I found this set of seating arrangements puzzling: who was seated above and who below? According to the usual above/below axis of the village hall itself the women were seated in the highest position, the chiefs somewhat lower and the men lowest of all. Later I made a diagram of these seating arrangements and showed it to a number of men and women, describing the situation it referred to. All said that the chiefs were seated above because they were chiefs and the women were seated below because they, as a group, always sit lower than men. But what about the men seated behind the chiefs – if the given order of the space has been inverted, were they not seated above the chiefs? No; they were below the *tanoa*, 'facing the *yaqona*' [*qaravi yaqona*]. These answers were unanimous, elicited from individuals in private conversation using questions that were as neutral and 'unloaded' as I could make them. In the end I always asked if it was not odd that in this situation the hall had two positions below, with the position above somewhere in between. All those questioned were aware of the incongruity and many found it amusing, but all insisted nevertheless that the chiefs were seated above and the women below. One young man, aged twenty-three, said to me: 'Look. The chiefs are seated above because they are chiefs. The women are seated below because they are women who are sitting with chiefs. The chiefs are present; it is nothing that the big doors [i.e. the common entrance] are here. The men here [pointing to those below the *tanoa*] are also seated below because of their looking after the *yaqona*.'

So, in this very unusual situation, the space at the chiefs' backs was ideally separate from them. They were no longer facing the space, and in so far as it ceased to be regarded by the chiefs it ceased to be. Not so for the men at the chiefs' backs; their place was below because they were *qaravi yaqona*, 'looking after the *yaqona*', or *qarava na turaga*, 'attending on the chiefs' (from *qara*, 'facing').

Clearly the chiefs' position dominates the interaction between them and the *tanoa* to define the space where *yaqona* is drunk. So when men drink *yaqona* out of doors the place occupied by the highest-status man is above: the *tanoa* is placed so that the wedge faces towards him. One orientates oneself according to one's status relative to that of others present and their position above or below the *tanoa*. Once men are seated and drinking, the space becomes bounded in terms of above/below. The invisible boundary is roughly rectangular – the top short side formed by the line of higher-status men, the bottom short side by the backs of the men who are seated below the *tanoa*. The space can be approached only from below; it is improper directly to penetrate the group from a point above the *tanoa* (except for the paramount chief and one or two other *very* high-status men). If one is coming from that direction one takes care to make a wide detour skirting the group of men, and finally to approach from the side below. Even if one is of high enough status to join those seated above the *tanoa* one should, in politeness, approach the group from a relatively low position, as shown in Figure 12.

The concern with the disposition of people drinking *yaqona* in any space, indoors or outdoors, is made concrete in all village buildings – be they temporary shelters [*vakatunuloa*], kitchens, houses, village hall or church. Here the above/below axis of the building governs the behaviour of people inside. However, in both house and church seating arrangements offer subtle variations on the focus, or on the image, of hierarchy that one finds in *yaqona*-drinking – matters to be further discussed later on.

The above analysis suggests that hierarchy in Sawaieke is constituted in part by reference to images people form of behaviour in particular contexts. Here I have focused on *yaqona*-drinking because, being by definition open to anyone who brings an *i sevusevu*, it takes in the widest possible social group. By making it appear that balanced reciprocity in exchange relations gives way to 'tribute to chiefs', *yaqona*-drinking seems to contain the challenge that balanced reciprocity poses to hierarchy. The apparent transformation in exchange relations is paralleled by a transformation in space: the orientation of houses in terms of *veiqaravi*, 'facing each other', implies balanced reciprocity across groups; but in *yaqona*-drinking *veiqaravi* denotes hierarchy in attendance upon chiefs. The chiefs and the people 'face each other' but now the chiefs are *i cake*, above the *tanoa*, and the people are *i ra*, below it – the relation between them being transformed by the medium of *yaqona* through which chiefs access the ancestral *mana* from which they partly derive their authority. The *sevusevu* and *yaqona*-drinking form the paradigm for all presentations to chiefs and for their redistribution. Thus *yaqona* ritual transforms a fundamentally balanced exchange into one that is hierarchical. The image of stratified relations exemplified in people's positions relative to one another around the *tanoa* is one encountered virtually every day in the village of Sawaieke.

I have argued that the centrality and significance of *yaqona* ritual are such that people's disposition in space when they gather to drink *yaqona* provides an image of social relations as properly hierarchical. In the gathering the ambiguities inherent in the nature of hierarchical relations beyond the household are made to disappear –

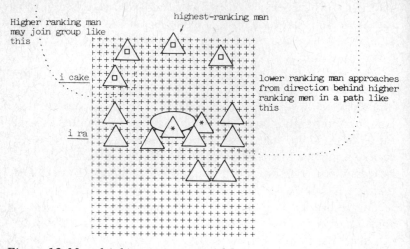

Figure 12 Men drinking yaqona *out of doors*

at least with respect to the relative status of chiefs and commoners in interaction with relative age; gender, however, remains a problem. That is to say, the presence of women at the *soqo* inevitably raises the issue of how rank, seniority and gender interact in constituting hierarchy, and whether any one principle of ordering may be given analytical priority over the others. This matter will be discussed at length in Chapters 9 and 10, so I do not go into it here; however, the reader should bear in mind that the nature of Fijian hierarchy is not rendered less complex by the apparently clear image that may be derived from either the gathering or the meal at home.

6 Hierarchy and space in the church

I argued above that hierarchical kin relations are manifest and in part constituted by the way the above/below axis enters into behaviour in house and village hall. I showed too how chiefly authority is associated with transcendent power. This association is also manifest in church. The church has been assimilated to 'the way according to the land', but even so the new ideas it has introduced pose something of a challenge to hierarchical kinship. The church is both literally and figuratively central to the lives of Sawaieke villagers. Like the village hall it is built to one side of the village green [*rara*] and is a focus for community activity.

Formal organization of the Wesleyan Church in Gau

Virtually all Fijians are practising Christians. In Gau, most people are members of the Wesleyan Church and every village church is Wesleyan in denomination. There is too a scattering of Catholics, Jehovah's Witnesses, Seventh-Day Adventists, and so on. The Wesleyan Church in Fiji has its offices and training college in Suva; here ministers are educated and ordained and sent out to the districts. Usually there are only one or two ministers for a large area; they serve a five-year term in each posting. In Gau lives a 'senior minister' [*i talatala qase*] who oversees the islands of Gau, Batiki and Nairai. Under him are the ministers [*i talatala*] for Batiki and Nairai. Ministers rank above lay preachers [*na i vakatawa*]; there is one trained and certified lay preacher per church district – eight for Gau's sixteen villages. If there is no lay preacher in a village, there is a catechist [*na i vakatavuvuli*], who ranks below lay preacher in the church hierarchy. These offices are always filled by men.

The minister has a salary from head office in Suva; lay preacher and catechist are paid a fixed sum monthly out of villagers' weekly church contributions. Catechists are selected by ministers; lay preachers take a stiff written examination prepared in Suva and marked there. A man who passes such an examination has been nominated to sit for it by the Church Council, which meets once a quarter [*Bose Vula Tolu*], its members coming from all three islands. The successful applicant is offered a post as lay preacher only when one becomes vacant and this may be in another village, not his own, within the area of the local Church Council.

To attain the influential position of lay preacher a man must work his way up through the ranks; *curu siga*, one who does menial tasks such as opening the church doors for services; *qase ni siga*, church elder; *dau vunau*, occasional preacher; *i vakatavuvuli*, catechist, and then *na i vakatawa*, lay preacher. There is also in every village a man who is *Tui Rara* (literally 'king of the village green'); he acts as a bridge between congregation and church and seems to be viewed as a spokesman for the people in church matters. He heads the village church committee that helps the lay preacher or catechist to run church affairs, administers money, etc. Church elders also figure quite largely in church affairs and are very 'visible' in everyday life in respect of the number of things forbidden [*tabu*] to them; for example, they are not allowed to dance or to drink alcohol and must be seen to abstain from these activities in order to set a good example to others. Finally there is the Methodist Youth Fellowship [*Na Mataveitokani*], to which all young people in Sawaieke village routinely belong.

The senior minister answers to head office in Suva; ministers are responsible to the senior minister, lay preachers to the minister, and so on. Lay preachers are ranked, and I believe paid, according to their experience and seniority in office. Salaries are not high. Sawaieke's village preacher (the most senior on Gau during the period of my fieldwork) received F$40 per month out of church funds; he was a Sawaieke man and had his land, animals, etc., nearby. Had he not been so, gardening land would have been provided for his use. A piece of land went with the house occupied by the minister (the largest and, people said, 'the best' house in the village) during his five-year term. *I talatala* – as the minister is called – is expected to keep any mats given him at the christening of a first child, a wedding or a funeral. When there is a big feast the minister and the lay preacher receive a generous share of the *dalo* (taro) and the cow or pigs that are killed. During my stay in Sawaieke, the senior minister and his wife were 'looked after' [*qaravi*, literally 'faced'] by the wife of the lay preacher whose house was nearby. It is customary on Sundays to send a plate of something special (i.e. cooked food, *na tale ni vunau*) to whomever has preached the sermon that day; this means that both minister and lay preacher often receive such contributions.

Church funds are raised from collections made during services and every family is expected to give a minimum of 50c. per week. Anything from F$15 to F$20 is collected every Sunday; on special occasions – for instance, a hymn-singing competition – several hundred dollars may be taken depending on the number of village choirs involved. This *soli* (literally 'giving') is competitive and one is honoured to be a member of the village that gives most money. (People always ask who won the *soli* and how much it was, before they ask who won the singing competition.) The *soli* by house – that is, the obligatory minimum of 50c. a week – is also competitive: at the end of the year a prize is awarded to the family who has given the most money over the year. This *soli* is obligatory not in the sense that it is enforced, but rather in the sense that one can hardly avoid giving when one's contribution is announced every Sunday in church and a record is kept and read out at the end of the year.

The church calendar is highly organized, certain weeks being devoted, for example, to 'the family' or 'the work of the church'. These may involve gatherings in the village hall, etc., that are additional to ordinary church services. I understand that church organization, the style of church services, the tenets of the religion, the way it strives for community involvement, etc., are all very much what they would be in Wesleyan churches in England or Australia, but this similarity stops with formal structure; the 'flavour' of Fijian Wesleyanism is undoubtedly different from that found elsewhere (cf. Peck, 1982: 229–34, whose account of church organization in Gau largely accords with my own).

The significance of Christianity in everyday life

Religion figures largely in everyday life. No meal can be eaten, even morning or afternoon tea, and no meeting undertaken, without being sanctioned by prayer. One says grace even if a meal is taken informally outside; prayer begins every meeting of every village committee; and the name of God figures in every ceremony, for example in the *sevusevu* (presentation of *yaqona*). If people are elsewhere drinking *yaqona* when a church service begins on a weekday evening, there is a pause in the proceedings while someone gives out a long prayer and all present bow their heads; people do not actually desert the *yaqona*-drinking, but it is unthinkable that the church service be ignored in the circumstances of a public gathering. Villagers hold to the notion that 'God is with us' at all times and so they constantly acknowledge Him. Moreover, as a member of the community one is willy-nilly involved in religion; to avoid being so would be to ostracize oneself from village life.

In Gau there are three services on Sunday plus Sunday school for children and at least three other evening services during the week: *lotu ni marama* (women's service), *lotu ni mataveitokani* (service for the Methodist Youth Fellowship – all young unmarried people), *lotu ni matavuvale* (household service) and often another one, referred to as *lotu ga*, 'just church'. There may be prayers at dawn every morning [*lotu masumasu*], for example for Christmas, Easter, or 'church work' week. Not everyone attends all these services all the time, but there was only one person in the village who was not reasonably regular in attendance. Young people seem to require little urging to attend services, and women and children are especially regular. The children's pews are always full; babies in arms are held by their mothers or some elderly female relative, but by the time they are two or three years old children are likely to be seated with older children in their own part of the church, under the eye of an elder who carries a long stick for poking those who fall asleep or giggle too much.

Other church-related activities are *vulisere*, learning hymns (for choir members), intervillage hymn-singing and *soli* competitions, intervillage *mataveitokani* meetings for unmarried young men and women, and church services for the first Sunday of the month – the two villages involved alternating as hosts. Services, competitions, gatherings, are all entertaining and do much to break the monotony of village life; people enjoy a good sermon and complain if the preacher, and thus the service, is 'lazy' [*vucesa*]. Intervillage affairs are said to be more fun than others: one can get dressed up to some purpose and after the service one can catch up on gossip, drink *yaqona*, possibly meet one's current boy- or girlfriend and generally relieve any tedium arising from daily life. This is not to say that villagers take their religion lightly, but they do enjoy any socializing that church membership entails. They do not attend services merely as a matter of duty, or out of fear of sinning, or because they have been told to do so by those in authority.

Villagers take God, prayer, and the church absolutely for granted – the associated beliefs and behaviours are woven into the fabric of daily life. In virtually every house hangs a cardboard plaque that reads: 'The head of this household is Christ, he eats with us and listens to us' [*na ulu ni vale oqo ko Karisito, sa kana vata kei keitou ka vakarogoci keitou*]. If there is no plaque there will at least be a holy picture: Leonardo's 'Last Supper'; a heavenly angel guarding a European sailor as he stands at the wheel of his storm-tossed boat; the prodigal son, head bowed over his staff, standing amidst a herd of frolicking pigs; the sacred heart of Jesus, and so on. These are Roman Catholic rather than Methodist productions, but villagers like them and it seems the Wesleyan authorities tolerate them. The plaque and the pictures hang on the beam dividing the living from the sleeping area in any house.

Religion is so much a part of people's lives that they cannot imagine how one can live at all properly without it. One is routinely asked what church one belongs to and all Christian sects are tolerated (Judaism is popularly supposed to be one of them because Jews are people of the Bible). One has to give an account of oneself as a member of some congregation. In my early days in Sawaieke I found it impossible to deny that I was a church member. People were so dismayed – 'So you live just like that – just anyhow?' one woman said – that I had to follow my denial by the statement that as a child I was a Catholic, and this would bring sighs of relief and a general relaxation in the tension that had resulted from my earlier denial.

The church *is* civilization, it is often referred to as 'the light':

'In the old days, before the church came here, the people of this land served devils. They made magic to injure their kin – our ancestors did not know it was a sin. It was just because they didn't know the light. Just at that time, when the church came here, a man was living at village X who knew magic very well. He had a book about it in which was written everything concerning magic, and that magic was very powerful [*mana*]. When he died the book about it was found in his house and then everyone knew the source of that man's knowledge. But the book of making magic was so terrifying that the chiefs said that it should be burnt. Then the book was burnt and thus all the knowledge of magic was lost. Today there isn't anyone in this island who knows the kind of magic that our ancestors knew.'

These are the words of a man of sixty, but this story was told me several times, always with a mixture of relief and regret: relief that such power was no longer available to one who might wish to do evil, and regret that the wonders contained in the book were lost. Villagers are commonly ambivalent about the lives lived by their ancestors; they both respect their ancestors for their knowledge and power and fear them on account of the practices they associate with them. Also, when people talk about their ancestors they more often than not refer to the coming of the church and the change this wrought in behaviour that had once been usual. In this connection I was told, for instance, that 'In the old days, men would steal women and carry them off to their own village, and because of this there was also a great deal of murder. The church was not here then and it was because of this perhaps that they sinned.'

In their malign aspect the ancestors are *tevoro* – devils; people take their existence for granted. They may visit the living (as may the ghosts of the dead, especially in the first days after their death while the first funeral ceremonies are being performed) and there are places where the ancestors used to live, in the 'time of the devils' [*gauna vakatevoro*], where an evil influence remains. One is afraid to walk past these places at night, and in the daytime too if one is alone. The original ancestral owner of the land where the local secondary school stands was ritually placated before building began; even so there have been attacks on boys and girls who board at the school. They are said to have woken at night with this 'devil' sitting on their chests trying to choke the life out of them. Then there is Daucina, famous throughout Fiji, who haunts coastlines and takes women who bathe alone at night; he makes them his 'wives' and this is revealed when the woman goes into a fit and Daucina speaks out of her mouth. There are also female devils who try to possess men; they have been seen dancing in a Suva nightclub, one frequented by villagers on holiday in the capital. These beautiful female devils are easily recognized as such because their feet do not touch the floor when they dance.

In short, people are very afraid of devils and one has the impression that they feel that only the church saves them from being subject to such terrible evil influences. The church saves them from fear and evil because the one God is more than a match for the many small gods and devils that held Fiji in their sway in the past (cf. Henderson, 1931: 261). And it saves them too from the strong and evil magic that some unscrupulous people used against others. All in all it is said to be a good thing that this magic is gone and one does not have to be so afraid of it any more.

This is not to say that people have ceased to believe that there are others who perform magic to the detriment of their neighbours. People often discuss magical knowledge as they sit drinking *yaqona*; they are especially interested in tales of people who can exert such a fatal and magically inspired charm on the opposite sex that they can cause to follow them any person whom they desire. Sometimes the power is attributed to a certain medicine [*vakadraunikau*, i.e. leaf charms or magic] but often it is said to be an attribute acquired through attending on a devil [*qaravi tevoro*]. These persons are supposed to live in other parts of Fiji, not in Gau. However, one death and a severe case of illness were attributed to witchcraft during my stay.

The illness was that of a Sawaieke man in his thirties; it was said to be witchcraft only when the European medicines from the clinic in Qarani (a village some three kilometres away) had failed to help him. He was said to have been 'struck by a Fijian illness' [*mate vakaViti*]. This was made clear in that every day he dreamed or had visions of two devil women who were ancestral gods of the Nadawa clan; they appeared to him in the guise of living women whom he knew (either born or married into Nadawa clan) and he would hear them talking about him. Once he heard one of these women call out to the other: 'Come, let us two go and throw X outside, that he may be killed', and he knew then that his illness was caused by witchcraft. Speaking of this man's illness, a Nadawa clanswoman said to me: 'It is because of our ancestor gods; it's been a long time since those two devil women, our ancestor gods, appeared. They were seen before Y married and again before Z married [this being at least sixteen years before]. Perhaps someone is attending on them. Someone wants X to die.'

I asked her if she knew anyone who would want to do such a thing; she said no, but it was clear that his illness was caused by witchcraft 'because of the visions' [*rai votu*]. She said: 'A Fijian doctor could help him, one of those who "causes to drink"' – a reference to the use of *yaqona* in curing ritual. Why then did the sick man not visit such a doctor? 'Because he doesn't believe in traditional things; he thinks himself wise – a wise person he is,' this in an ironic tone. Who then could it be who was attending on Nadawa's ancestor gods – did it have to be a Nadawa person? No, she said. It could be anyone, *kaisi se turaga*, 'one who is low-born or one of chiefly birth', anyone could do it; even someone as far away as Vanua Levu could have 'made *yaqona* to call those two [the female ancestor gods of Nadawa clan] and then told them what was desired.'

The woman with whom I discussed all this was a devout churchgoer, a married woman in her early thirties, usually undeviating with respect to Christian doctrine; neither was she especially easily convinced of witchcraft; here it was the visions that decided her. These constituted sound evidence because dreams, hallucinations, etc., are believed to be actual 'out-of-the-body' experiences (cf. Herr, 1981). However, in telling me of a couple in the village who were several times supposed to have 'attended on devils' – people, moreover, on whom she could be severe in other respects – she said: 'I don't believe it because I haven't seen it. No one has seen them doing anything so no one is able to relate anything properly about this thing.'

The point is that the ancestors [*kalou vu*], the ghosts of the dead, and the gods of old Fiji such as Daucina have still to be reckoned with. But their power is said to have waned considerably, specifically because it is only the rare person who is believed to 'attend on a devil' and it is this very attendance or service that is said to increase incrementally their strength. On the other hand, it is because one has to reckon with the ancestors that the installation of a high chief may be delayed or not performed at all. I was told, for instance, by a young man of twenty-five that: 'After Takalaigau has drunk [the installation *yaqona*] all the ancestor spirits in the whole of Gau island will then stand behind him. The meaning of this is that if he calls us to work at Tautu, to cut coconuts or something like that, it won't be possible to refuse. If a person refuses the work it is possible that he might die.'

I never heard any 'hell fire and damnation' preaching in the village church. Preachers dwell rather on the loving and forgiving nature of the Christian God, who seeks to help His erring children and is bound to do so. So the ordinary church member takes the view that even if one is not married in church, even if one did steal cassava last week from a neighbour's garden, even if one does gossip and vie with one's kin and resent giving to them, one *does* go to church, pray, give money for missionary efforts and church support and above all one believes, has utter faith in the existence of God, and so one is not afraid of Him. But perhaps I exaggerate the preachers' emphasis on the Christian God's loving nature, or perhaps times have changed or Sawaieke preachers are especially benign, for a Fijian woman friend has since told me that when she was a child in the 1960s she heard a lot about being *kama e na buka waqa*, 'burnt in the fire', both at Sunday school and in church.

It seemed that people often turned their thoughts to God; many times I was told spontaneously how one had prayed for divine guidance and received it, or prayed for success in some enterprise; one young man told me that he began each day in his garden with a short prayer that God would look after him during the day, prevent any accident to him and ensure the fertility of his garden. A middle-aged woman told me how, after years of suffering from rheumatic pain and years of praying to God to release her from it, she was cured by being shown in a dream a form of massage that relieved her pain. I was told of this experience shortly after it occurred; the woman was euphoric with relief and gave thanks to God many times in telling me her story.

People often speak of having prayed for something and received it, but this personal relation with God does not necessarily give rise to specially pious behaviour or self-righteousness; rather the most prevalent attitude seems to be that provided God is acknowledged, He will look after one and one is bound to be a basically good person, bound to be redeemed, provided one observes all the outward forms of religious practice and attends on God in prayer.

The church and Fijian custom

The church and customary behaviour support each other. Religion, or rather prayer, enters into virtually every ritual performance: marriages, deaths, the welcoming of special guests, the installation of chiefs, everyday *i sevusevu*, and so on. All ceremonies are carried out in the sight of God, and this is always stated to be so. The paramount chief, all the clan chiefs and many older men and women are church elders – the hierarchy of the church being partially accommodated to hierarchy in the secular domain.

On special days – the first Sunday of the month, at Easter, New Year, Christmas, Father's Day, and so on – the high chief speaks from the pulpit as do, in proper order, other clan chiefs and high-status men. Honorific titles are used in addressing the congregation; so the opening words of every speech acknowledge the ranking of clans: 'You the chiefs [or gentlemen] of Takalaigau and you the ladies, you the gentlemen of Raitena . . .' and so on down through the clans whose members are present. Honorific titles are also used in secular rituals such as *sevusevu*, and while each title is inclusive, the primary reference of the order of their announcement is to the status of each *chief*. This is so in church where any given speaker (except the minister and lay preacher, who are usually exhorting the congregation to righteousness) turns so that he addresses the clan chiefs directly. Chiefs are the leaders [*i liuliu*] in church – as they are elsewhere – but when the time comes for the collection, the order in which households are named suggests that rank alone orders differential status. This is the only situation I know of where it seems that *all* members of the chiefly clan, Nadawa, would rank above *all* members of Koviko clan, Sawaieke clan, Navure clan and Voda clan in descending order. As we shall see later, this particular status order is at odds with seating in church.

The church, in the person of the minister and the lay preacher, apparently upholds all that is 'in the manner of the land'. It blesses chiefs on their installation; it prefers marriages arranged by the young people's parents to elopements; it supports all the claims that kinship makes on those within its compass. *Na i tovo vakavanua*, Fijian custom, is not only *vakavanua*, 'in the manner of the land', but also *vakamatanitu*, 'in the manner of the government' and *vakalotu*, 'in the manner of the church' – and this is explicitly stated to be so. The church *and* the chiefs [*turaga ni vanua*] disapprove of any encroachment of European manners that may threaten the status quo: licence in dress and behaviour of young people, dancing, beer-drinking, young people leaving the village for the more heady delights of Suva or Lautoka, young people making their own decisions as to work, marriage, etc. However, the church does not always gain its ends. Early in the present century the Fiji Methodist Synod tried hard to persuade its congregation to pledge abstinence from *yaqona*-drinking. They were unsuccessful and 'gradually retreated to the point where they asked only that ministers limit themselves to strictly ceremonial drinking, whereas ordinary church members could do as they please' (Forman, 1982: 114).

The close ties embedded in kinship hierarchy are the very basis of church power, for it is primarily within the household that the tenets of Methodism are inculcated. I noted above that the domain of tradition may be equated with that of kinship in an analogy between the household and the village or the country, in such a way that the political community is represented as the household writ large. This analogy is made in contexts like that of *yaqona*-drinking or village meeting where the political community is the primary reference. In church the primary reference is to the household, to the congregation as the children of God. So, in sermons, the analogy tends to take the opposite direction with the household being seen as a microcosm of the village or country: it too has its chief, who orders the conduct of the household for its well-being and prosperity and whom the others must respect and obey; its members should do their duty according to their position relative to the 'leader of the household' [*i liuliu ni matavuvale*]. Above all is God. He is *Turaga* (literally Chief with a capital 'T' – no qualifying words are necessary.

The household is characterized by the same sexual division of labour as is the village or the country, and its members are subject to rules of avoidance and permitted familiarity. God approves proper 'respect' between family members and the fulfilling of kinship duties; many times I heard St Paul referred to as justifying the subjugation of women and a man's position as head of the household. Similarly, Nayacakalou (1975: 113) notes the emphasis on parental authority in church teaching. God is *Turaga*, and Father of us all, head of the household, head of Sawaieke country and ultimately head of state; He is acknowledged as such by the prayer that precedes nearly all activities from family breakfast to birthday party, traditional ceremony, village meeting and Provincial Council Meeting.

Church hierarchy is associated with chiefly hierarchy in that Sawaieke village is always the home of the senior minister for the three islands of Gau, Batiki and Nairai. Sawaieke, I was told, is the seat of 'the high chief of the whole of Gau', so 'it is right that the minister makes his home here'. Chiefs of the other two countries on Gau are unlikely to admit themselves to be of lower status than the high chief of Sawaieke country, but certainly he had a larger number of villages under his – sometimes nominal – sway, and it would seem that either the Wesleyan Church was aware of this when they made Sawaieke the official residence of the minister, or that Sawaieke chiefs manoeuvred so as to obtain this distinction.

Be that as it may, one who ranks high in the religious hierarchy has to be closely associated with those who are chiefs in the secular hierarchy. When the Roman Catholic Bishop of Fiji and the South Pacific visited Gau in 1982 he was received and lodged in Sawaieke village, where he was paid all traditional honours – though not a single Catholic lived there. Catholics from villages all over Gau (perhaps twenty to thirty people) made their way to Sawaieke too and remained there as guests for the duration. I believe the matter of the Bishop's lodging was decided in the *Bose Vakavanua*, the bi-monthly meeting of chiefs, officials and representatives from all the villages in Gau. Nobody seemed to find it incongruous that most Catholics lived in a village on the far side of the island. The Bishop's religion was irrelevant beside his status as a high officer of his church. He could properly be received only in Sawaieke, for this is where the chiefs are 'for the whole of Gau'.

The Wesleyan minister's behaviour at the time aroused adverse comment. A deputation of chiefs was said to have asked if the Bishop might use the village church. They were told it was their church and they must do as they saw fit. This was taken to mean opposition from the minister – who was not Fijian. The problem was solved by the chiefs asking the Bishop if he would *like* to use the church, and he – a Fijian accustomed to the nuances of polite behaviour – properly declined the offer. The Mass, confessions, marriages and baptisms were performed in the house of one of the chiefs. Talking of this matter, various people expressed opinions similar to that of a much-respected man in his fifties: 'Although the organization and beliefs of the Catholic Church are different, we are all Christians, we are all Fijians.' The Bishop was 'leader of the Catholic Church' and 'it is right that we should look after him here'. He could properly be associated only with the leaders of the community, the chiefs; on this count alone he should be shown all proper attentions.

The church's association with the chiefs is recognized in 'the customs of the land' [*i tovo vakavanua*]; so when *yaqona* is presented in *sevusevu* God's blessing is called down upon the chiefs and the people and the speech may end with: 'Let the following of the chiefs and the minister become ever greater' [*sosoraki cake tu yani vua na kena turaga kei na i talatala*]. A minister present when people are drinking *yaqona* is served what is called 'the second bowl' – the actual second bowl is discounted; it goes to the chief's herald, who is *not* second to him in status.

Thus the chiefs, and indeed all people in authority in the community, actively support the church and are seen to do so. The church bolsters chiefly authority and in so doing exacts support from chiefs who, in their turn, urge the claims of religion, give generously in money contributions and are apparently assiduous in fulfilling their religious duties (cf. Nation, 1978: 26). But men of chiefly birth who are in line for some high traditional office are unlikely to become ministers or lay preachers. For commoners, the church is one way of gaining a high-status position; this is not to suggest that those who do so are all self seeking men, but I did hear certain men in the higher church posts described as 'arrogant' or 'ambitious' [*viuvia levu*].

Use of church space

In the seating arrangements of the village church the semantic load carried by above/below is ratified by association with the divine. I attended services in five of eight churches in Sawaieke country and four of eight churches in other districts of Gau. The description and analysis of church space given here applies in general to any of these churches, though details differ from one to another. Figure 13 shows Sawaieke's church – because it is the one I know best and because the seating arrangements there were at their most highly different-iated and refined. This accords with Sawaieke's pre-eminence as the chiefly village and the residence of the senior minister.

Reference to Figure 13 reveals the plan of the church to be at least roughly analogous to that of a house in that it has an area above and an area below, the area above being highly exclusive, like the sleeping area of the house that is used only by *na i taukei*, 'the owners'. I have labelled the 'end door' as the chiefs' entrance, not because it is so

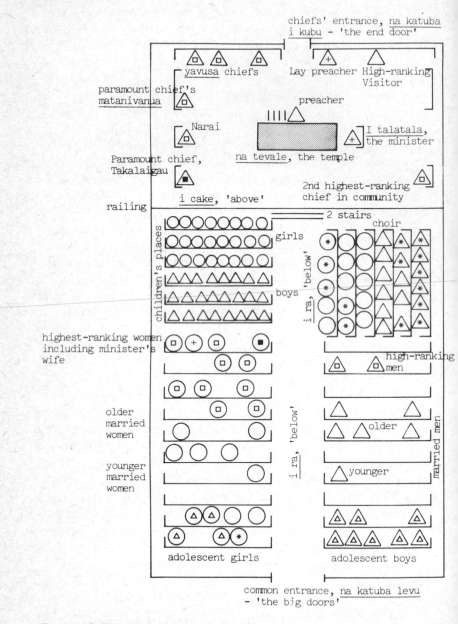

Figure 13 Floorplan of Sawaieke church

called but because it is so used. Only the highest-status men sit in this area: the paramount chief, the chief who ranks next to him, the clan chiefs, the minister, the lay preacher and any male visitors who are of high status or whom the Sawaieke chiefs wish to honour. This part of the church is raised some eight inches above the rest of the space that is below, and is marked off by a railing. The *tevale* (temple) is very high; the preacher stands on a platform behind it and looks down the church. He or she (women may be *dau vunau*, occasional preacher) also, literally, looks down on the chiefs. In Sawaieke village church, which is older and larger than most, the seating arrangements for chiefs are such that the paramount chief and the man who ranks after him – another lineage chief in the chiefly Nadawa clan – both have their own armchairs. So do the minister and the chief of Sawaieke clan (entitled to install a high chief of Sawaieke country). Other clan chiefs sit on church pews. The people, in their various sections, sit on a literally lower level than the chiefs in the space below. The people face up the church towards the preacher and the chiefs; the preacher and the chiefs face down towards the people. All in all the arrangements are such that the chiefs can be seen to be chiefs in the eyes of God, while the people occupy their own places in the eyes of the chiefs.

For the rest, Figure 13 reveals that seating does not strictly follow the arrangement that might be expected given the use of house space and the way people seat themselves when drinking *yaqona*. Both children and the choir seem to be seated relatively above, nearest the chiefs; this is said to be because children are inclined to be noisy and restive and must be placed in sight of their elders so that they can be seen and quietened if necessary; the choir is seated as it is so that the chiefs and the people may get the full benefit of their singing and the pleasure of being able to see them well. (Any secular entertainment is also performed so that the chiefs have the best view of it.) Seating arrangements for men and women are segregated, but they are also apparently near equals across gender and according to relative rank/ seniority. So women of the highest status (the wife of the paramount chief, the elder sister of the man who ranks after him, the wife of the minister and other elderly ladies of chiefly birth) sit at the top of the women's section of the church, and on a level with male elders of chiefly birth who do not have a place in the exclusive section above. Married women and men sit below them and adolescent girls and boys take the most humble positions nearest the lower doors (see Tippett, 1968: 170; Geddes, 1945: 384).

This departure from what is normal in the secular domain – where in general women sit below men of all ages – is visible evidence for an argument to the effect that the church has raised the status of women relative to their status both historically and in the traditional domain. A number of older women had reached the status of occasional preacher in the church hierarchy, though they could not become lay preachers in charge of a church. However, I was told that the *Konfiredi* (the annual conference for the Wesleyan Church in the Pacific) in 1982 had decided that women must be allowed to take up such posts. Women with whom I discussed this matter were on the whole pleased with the decision, though they themselves denied any wish to become lay preachers. Men, however, found it unacceptable, saying that according to Fijian custom, 'it is not right than women should be leaders'. Italatala, the minister, took the same view, but he often stressed the importance of women in the home and in his sermons advised men to consult their wives and to help them with the rearing of children, with housework, and so on – advice that most men seemed to find difficult to take. Thus the official church view is that women are almost, but perhaps not quite, the equals of their menfolk, particularly in respect of the partnership of husband and wife and as parents, and this is reflected in the seating arrangements in the body of church buildings. Not all Christian sects in Fiji are so minded; Sekaia Loaniceva's radical Christian 'Congregation of the Poor' excludes women from the ranks of seniority in the movement and segregates seating at services (Rokotuiviwa, 1975: captions for photographic centrepiece).

Being rather puzzled by some details of the church's seating arrangements, I asked a number of people about them: could the high chief and the second in rank be described as seated above the other clan chiefs when the latter were seated at the topmost end of the space? (see Figure 13). I used a diagram of the church in questioning people, and the exchange would go something like this:

Q: This is the church and its arrangement. Please look at the arrangement of the chairs. Takalaigau [the paramount chief] sits here, and here Tunimata [his herald] and here Tui Voda [a clan chief]. Is Takalaigau seated above Tui Voda?

A: No, Tui Voda is not seated below, he is seated above.
Q: What about Takalaigau?
A: He is also seated above.

After several exchanges of this kind I decided the answers might be an artifact of the way I was asking the question in Fijian, or rather, of the way one compares in Fijian. A literal rendering of 'Is Takalaigau seated above Tui Voda?' runs 'Is Takalaigau seated above and Tui Voda seated below?'. It seemed that people were reluctant to describe *any* chief as seated below, because the problem was finally solved by someone saying: 'Tui Voda is seated above but Takalaigau always sits *right up* above [*i cake sara*].'

Subsequently several other people agreed with this way of putting the thing though others, apparently as confused by the rights of the matter as I was, would only go as far as to say that all the chiefs were sitting above and would not commit themselves to any statement that implied that one was sitting above the other. Indeed, one person said that the clan chief and not the paramount chief was *dabe i cake sara* – 'sitting very high' – and added that it was having one's own chair that was important; this distinguished the position of the paramount chief.

My own view of the chiefs' section as a space in its own right is that the two highest-ranking chiefs sat above the others because they were farthest away from the door by which all chiefs entered church. Moreover, the orientation of their chairs, and the way clan chiefs' pews stood behind the *tevale*, meant that effectively the clan chiefs faced the highest-ranking chiefs (a situation reminiscent of that time when the chiefs inverted the space of the village hall; see Chapter 5). The position of the preacher in the pulpit behind the *tevale* is ambiguous: he 'faces the chiefs' from a literally higher position. Perhaps it may be said that as God's representative he is above the chiefs but as a man, below them; God is unquestionably above the chiefs, but His representative may attend on them. One could also liken the *tevale* to the *tanoa* used in *yaqona* ritual, but this may be to stretch resemblances too far. The ambiguity of the preacher's position together with the chiefs' being to either side emphasizes that here it is God, not the chiefs, who is focal to the proceedings. The chiefs are clearly acknowledged, but here they are themselves 'facing God'.

I received differing accounts of church seating. People were by no means unanimous and very few agreed that the general arrangement was like that for a house. It was the church, it was where one prayed; how could it be anything like an ordinary house? One religious and educated man objected strongly to the notion that there was any discrimination at all evident in the seating arrangements of the church, telling me that the church was built for all the people and we are all equal in the sight of God. He did admit that no one other than the paramount chief would sit in the paramount chief's chair, but maintained that the chair was placed where it was only to enable him to see well. He claimed that respected guests could sit in any of the other places in the chiefs' section – except, of course, in the minister's chair – and that people may sit where they will in the body of the church: 'There is no law about it'. No one of the chiefs could be said to be seated lower than any other, he said. I asked him then to describe the arrangement to me as he would had I never attended a church service in Sawaieke; he said: 'the chiefs sit above' [*e ra dabe i cake na malo*], thus discriminating between the upper and lower parts of the church. He also made much of the way the minister from Rotuma (i.e. not Fiji) usually sat in the body of the church, and told me in approving tones that this was because the minister wished to see well the face of the person who was preaching.

For most of my stay in Sawaieke, *I talatala* sat halfway down the men's section in the body of the church, but in a village meeting shortly before I left he agreed to return to the chair allotted him beside the *tevale*. He was formally requested to do so by a high-ranking married man in his early thirties, on the grounds that it was not right for him to sit in the body of the church. The man appeared to be speaking for others when he said: 'We people in the congregation don't like the look of it.'

Observations like this, and actual behaviour, do, I believe, confirm the importance of 'correct' seating arrangements in church. People often denied that these arrangements corresponded in any way to those in the house or the village hall, but it is surely significant that chiefs were allowed a large amount of space in the area above; also, in facing up the church, the congregation faced not only God's representative in the person of the minister or preacher, but also the chiefs arrayed at his side. No one ever denied that chiefs 'sit above' in church, even when they were reluctant to admit that the people 'sit below' or that some chiefs sit 'lower' than other chiefs. Geddes noted, as I have done, that church seating is indicative of a Christian challenge to the traditional status quo. However, where I see the crucial change as concerning the status of women, he argued that it is 'rank' that is challenged by Christian beliefs; that the prestige of the chief is undermined by that of the minister who, 'unlike the heathen priest ... is in no way subordinate to the chief' (1945: 385–7). Certainly the minister is not *subordinate* to the chief in the religious domain, but neither is he superior to him. Moreover, the religious domain is accommodated to the domain of tradition where the chief is paramount. The power conferred on a chief in his installation brings him closer to transcendent power than the minister can be; the latter stands to God as a herald does to his chief, while an installed paramount chief, in respect of his relation to both God and ancestor gods, himself manifests divine power (see Hocart, 1952: 13–21; Toren, 1988).

I have dealt in this chapter with the church and its partial assimilation to the traditional status quo within the domain of religion. In the next chapter I extend this discussion to show how the church penetrates the secular domain of political relations in the traditional hierarchy. I show too how the latter is articulated to the formal structures of democratic authority, and how this is manifest in the space of the village hall.

7 Government and traditional hierarchy

Formal political structures

Fiji has four Divisions, each headed by a Commissioner and further sub-divided into Provinces, each headed by a Roko (a title of honour); the Province is sub-divided into islands and/or districts and further, into villages. Sawaieke is the chiefly village of Sawaieke country – eight villages in all – on the island of Gau, which is part of Lomaiviti Province in the Eastern Division. During the period of my fieldwork traditional and democratic methods of government were closely articulated at the level of civil administration and local government. Traditional values were recognized at the highest level in that the Council of Chiefs advised central government on matters to do with the Fijian population and also appointed eight members to the upper house, the Senate.

Administrative matters that are solely the concern of a given village are in the hands of its chiefs and the village committee, an elected group headed by *turaganikoro*, 'the village chief', who is also an elected administrator (not a *turaga ni vanua*, 'traditional chief', literally 'chief of the land'). Village policy is decided, in accordance with decisions handed down from higher levels, in the Village Council [*Bose Vakoro*], which all adult villagers are welcome to attend. Proposals requiring support and co-operation from other villages – such as those affecting the single secondary school on the island – are carried to, discussed, and decided in the Country Council [*Bose Vakavanua*]. Here men are elected as Gau's representatives to the Provincial Council [*Bose ni Yasana*; see Nation, 1978: 108–24].

The Provincial Council decides matters such as the allocation and use of development aid allotted to a province by central government. Its members are advised by civil servants in the Public Works Department, Medical Service, Department of Agriculture and Fisheries, Education, etc. Only elected representatives have voting rights in this council, which is chaired by one of their number.

Elected Provincial Councils were instituted in part because it was thought that traditional leadership was holding back development (Spate, 1959: 102) and that new leadership was required (Watters, 1969: 206–11). However, Nation argues that 'the leadership of the new bodies bears strong resemblances to the old leadership even though the personnel has changed' (1978: 18). Gau also has a permanent island council [*Bose ni Yanuyanu*], largely appointed by the Minister for Health; it is concerned with public health and administration of medical and other services.

All persons over twenty-one could vote in general elections as long as they were registered on two electoral rolls; at that time the electoral system provided for an ethnic balance in the legislature between ethnic Fijians, Fiji-Indians and others (i.e. ethnic Europeans, Chinese, etc.). The Alliance Party was re-elected during the course of my stay; it is 'the Fijian party', with strong European and some Indian support. Most Fijians with whom I discussed politics professed themselves Alliance supporters. Only a handful of Indians were resident in Gau, so the political process described below refers exclusively to Fijians.

Traditional authority

Gau is divided into two *qali* – a division of villages subject to another land or country (cf. Nation, 1978: 20). The eight villages of Sawaieke country are traditionally '*qali* to Batiki' but Sawaieke villagers say they never warred with the nearby island of Batiki and were never subject to it; they say they are '*qali* to Sawaieke'. The other eight villages are subject to Bau [*qalivakaBau*], whose chiefs gained ascendancy before and during the early days of colonization; the high chief of Bau is still said by some to be *the* paramount chief of Fiji. Each of the Sawaieke villages 'listens to' [*vakarorogo*] a certain clan chief in Sawaieke village. Early in my fieldwork I was told there were four clans in Sawaieke and that their chiefs and the villages owing allegiance to them were as follows:

Name of village	Sawaieke chief	Clan
Lovu	Takalaigau	Nadawa
Vadravadra	Takalaigau	Nadawa
Yadua	Takalaigau	Nadawa
Nukuloa	Narai	Sawaieke
Levuka	Narai	Sawaieke
Nawaikama	Tui Navure	Navure
Somosomo	Tui Voda	Voda
		(Naividamu)

Narai, Tui Navure and Tui Voda all 'listen to Takalaigau', so Nadawa clan ranks highest in Sawaieke country. Across villages this ranking has relatively little effect on a day-to-day basis; the villages are largely independent of the Sawaieke chiefs with respect to internal administration (including that of profitable co-operative businesses). However, the rank order of chiefs and the inferior status of the chiefs of subject villages is obvious at gatherings and in council meetings; I show below how Sawaieke chiefs are both seen and heard to dominate these proceedings.

Sawaieke village may be unusual in having many clans; the model of Fijian social organization taught to children in primary school makes the clan [*yavusa*] coterminous with the village. Abandoned house foundations [*yavu*] are found close to the present village, as well as in the hills above it. These old village sites are small, their *yavu* crowded together. The present village of Sawaieke is said to be the same age as its large stone and mortar church, and a woman of eighty-three, the oldest person in the village during my stay, to be the first child born there. Most people agreed as to the origin of the village; a typical story ran as follows:

Before, the people of this village did not live together in the manner of kinship. No. Each of the little villages stood alone and there was much quarrelling and fighting between them. ... During the old time, in the time of the devils, the church came here; civilization came here. It brought the light to us. Before, all of the old villages on this piece of coastline had stood alone; then they wanted to be nearer each other because if all the villages moved here it would make easier their attendance upon one another [*veiqaravi*, their fulfilment of mutual traditional obligations]. The owners of this village, of this land, were Sawaieke clan. ... They called to the people of the little villages that they should come here: 'Takalaigau, come here' – and they came; 'Tui Navure, come here' – and they came. And the Voda people also came here. The Buli [district head under the colonial administration] decided that house-building should begin. Then they built the church, and this was the beginning of true kinship.

The Buli was probably also a chief, as were the last two men to hold this now defunct post in Gau (cf. Sahlins, 1962: 304; Belshaw, 1964: 236; Roth, 1953: 146; McNaught, 1974: 17). Other accounts did not mention the Buli but agreed that the church brought forth the village as it is today, most implying that the church actually pre-existed other buildings. In the Lands Commission records of 1916 the village, with all its clans, seems well established and the pattern of allegiance largely conforms to the present one.

Four Sawaieke clans are listed above. Another clan, Koviko, was reconstituted during my fieldwork. Takalaigau, the paramount chief, told me that Koviko clan ranked second after Nadawa. He gave the rank of clans, in descending order, as: Nadawa, Koviko, Sawaieke, Voda and Navure. But this conflicted with what other people said and with the order in which clan chiefs drank *yaqona*: Nadawa, Sawaieke, Koviko, Navure, Voda. Most people said of Koviko that it was 'just a lineage, counted along with Nadawa clan' and seemed unaware that it was listed as a clan by the Lands Commission. During my time in Sawaieke, those not directly involved either refused on conservative grounds to accept it or said that Takalaigau had illegitimately created it. But so far as I know, no one directly challenged the high chief about the matter; the Koviko chief was accorded the respect due to a clan chief and sat above in hall and church. During my first months in Sawaieke he had not done so, his usual place being beside or just below one of the upper side doors of the hall, while in church he sat below the most senior male elders in the body of the church below.

These observations reveal something of a high chief's influence and the salience of space in particular persons' perceptions of their own status. A man gains prominence in the community according to an interaction between his personal qualities and achievements, his rank/seniority within his own clan, and the position of that clan in the traditional hierarchy (cf. Walter, 1974: 320). This status is manifest in the man's seating position when he gathers with others to drink *yaqona*, to discuss in council the community's welfare, or to worship.

A chief is always accorded all the outward signs of respect, presumably because the principle of chiefship is itself highly valued; thus he is always *seen* to be a chief in any community gathering. However, if in fact he is not highly thought of – accused perhaps of greed, lack of true chiefly bearing, and so on – people have recourse to passive resistance (cf. Nation, 1978: 21–2). They fail to turn up for a work party he has called or neglect other duties, such as letting him know when an important visitor arrives. But a chief is always able to maintain his public position in *sight* of the people, so he is unlikely to lose his influence completely; his position in space at any gathering gives him an edge over any opposition.

Articulation of church and traditional authority

Earlier I showed how the significance of above/below is ratified by association with the divine. The importance of the church, its overarching authority, and its articulation to secular hierarchy are encapsulated in a statement made to me by a young man of perhaps twenty-five to whom I had said that in London I did not go to church:

> 'In the Fijian way, if a person is not a member of a congregation, not a churchgoer, then that person is also not a member of a household, not a member of a lineage, not a member of a clan nor a member of a village. The meaning of this is that s/he is not counted as one of the people of this land.'

This is an extreme statement, but certainly anyone outside the congregation would be in a difficult position – because the church is not only equated with civilization, but credited with the beginning of community life and 'true kinship'. The church encourages development [*veivakatoroicaketaki*, literally 'moving upwards together'], itself 'a secularized version of the theology of Christianity' (Peck, 1982: 260).

Church membership is taken for granted, so one should be seen, at least on some occasions, to go to church. One must close one's eyes and bow one's head for prayers at gatherings, and meetings of councils and committees (cf. Nation, 1978: 28). Prayers are given out extempore by any preacher or church elder called on by the presiding chief. Quoted below is a small part of the prayer that began a Country Council. In typical fashion it makes clear that our tasks on earth, and thus all traditional chiefly tasks, are divinely appointed; that the divine accords authority to men in so far as they follow the path of God (cf. Nayacakalou, 1975: 113). God is called *Saka* – 'Sir', here translated as 'Lord', this term being used by commoners to chiefs, and referred to as *Turaga* – 'Chief', here 'Lord' or 'God'. The opening sentences recall those for a *sevusevu* where the honorific titles of chiefs refer to the sacred *yavu*[*yavu tabu*], the dwelling place of their ancestors.

> Let us pray. To Heaven, to the holy dwelling place [*i tikotiko tabu*] You the true God, you the God who alone is served. ... You made the heavens and the earth too that we people might inhabit it. We people know that we are the most excellent of the creation in your hands. ... There are also the various tasks to which we have each been appointed; we know that these tasks were chosen by you and that you have trusted us in this matter, God. This morning we are very thankful that life has been given us that we may meet together in this village on this wonderful day. Our Lord [*Turaga*], that is what we thank you for. But before we begin the meeting, Lord [*Saka*], we bow our heads and serve you, God. ... Before the council begins, we bow down, Lord [*Saka*], at this time and pray in your name, which is the name of rest, the name also that gives us life. We are thankful for the life of the gentlemen [*turaga*, literally 'chiefs'], the young men, the members of this council, the leader of this council, that they live at this time. In getting ready to begin the council concerning our island, we leave up to you, God, the laying down of the law, the thinking and opinions of the members of this council, [we ask], God, that you alone should lead them. We trust, God, that you will give ideas too to the rest of the gentlemen who are representatives in this meeting ...

The presence of a church representative is said to be essential at the installation of chiefs and at community meetings. At an installation it should be a minister or senior minister who prays for God's guidance for the chief. When a minister attends a gathering he is made to sit above and is served 'the second bowl' of *yaqona*. So in the secular sphere the minister is seen to rank after the high chief, while in church he is seen to be above and central in so far as he mediates between God and others. These data seem to support Tippett's view that 'the functional role of the herald and priest have been taken over by the Fijian church' (1980: 57). However, it seems to me that the 'herald' is more correctly made analogous to the Roko and assistant Rokos employed as administrative officials of a province and, to a lesser degree, to the representatives [*mata*] on the various village and island councils who are at once advisers and executives for the traditional chiefs.

Transforming authority 'in the manner of the land'

Traditional chiefs dominated village and country meetings [*bose vakoro* and *bose vakavanua*]. Committees to organize certain sectors (for example the church or the school) were proposed and elected by those present at any given meeting; the committee members were often 'commoners', but it was traditional chiefs who presided and were seen to be dominant. A high-status traditional chief always chaired such meetings and it was always he who had the final word on a matter (cf. Nayacakalou, 1978: 15; 1975: 53–82, 83–92). Opposition was rare and when it *did* occur it was usually not made explicitly to a chief's face; a man would not normally presume to oppose another of higher status, though disagreement between lower-status men who were peers was routinely allowed an airing. However, chiefly authority requires the consent of the people, and if a chief loses this consent his effectiveness is very much undermined.

During my fieldwork an important chief was, in his absence, voted out of office as head of the secondary school committee. But he retained his prominent position in the Country Council [*Bose Vakavanua*] and only resigned some months later, apparently of his own accord. The lesser post of school committee leader passed to a commoner, but the more important office went to another, similarly high-ranking, chief. The most important office in the Country Council is that of chairman or 'leader of the meeting'. People I spoke to about it said that this post should always go to a traditional chief: 'In the Fijian way it is not right that the people should lay down the law; authority is the prerogative of traditional chiefs.' This remark, made by a man of about thirty-six who was a commoner, represented the consensus of opinion in Sawaieke village.

Villagers from other parts of Sawaieke country may have been less inclined to consensus over this matter, since it appeared to me (on the basis of limited observation) that traditional authority was probably less emphasized in other villages than it was in Sawaieke. Nevertheless, it was unthinkable to virtually all villagers with whom I ever discussed the matter that heads of government should not also be high-ranking chiefs in their own right, or at least members of important chiefly families – especially with reference to the post of Prime Minister. It was thought proper too that ministerial posts and Fijian parliamentary seats be occupied by those of chiefly birth.

From the villagers' point of view traditional authority was articulated to democratically constituted authority at the highest levels of government, just as it was at village level, where the authority of chiefs is visible on a day-to-day basis (cf. Scarr, 1970; Nayacakalou, 1975. 86). This is not to say that only those of chiefly birth attain high positions in the government and civil service. During my fieldwork, many parliamentary seats and prestigious posts in the civil service (for example that of Roko Tui, chief official of a Province, or District Commissioner) were held by commoners. Indeed, villagers thought it inappropriate for a man who had chiefly responsibilities to give much time to duties outside the traditional sphere and, more specifically, to politics.

This notion appears to contradict the one which makes it desirable for Members of Parliament, as well as the Prime Minister and Governor General, to be of chiefly birth. The problem is resolved by making local high chiefs of men who have retired as MPs, policemen, schoolteachers, etc., and returned to their natal villages. There was a conceptual separation between the spheres of traditional and of democratically constituted authority. For example, the Council of Chiefs was said not to be 'political'; people often talked as if the Prime Minister himself had nothing to do with politics because he was 'the head of the government'.

The two spheres of traditional and democratically constituted authority were articulated to one another more or less closely at the village, intervillage, provincial and central governmental level; but traditional authority seemed to become attenuated at council meetings at the higher levels of inclusiveness. As one moved from the context of the village to that of the province, high rank/seniority by birth was no longer sufficient to ensure that one's voice would be heard in council and one's opinions attended to. Of course, this could be said to be true too at village level; to be truly influential a man has to be seen not only as of high rank and seniority, but also as having the virtues that should go with these attributes – wisdom, knowledge of the ways of the world, chiefly bearing, influence with civil administration, and so on. However, men who loom large in the village or island meeting are not likely to do so in the Provincial Council, even though they may be present there in positions of honour above. This was partly because the qualifications required of administrators and people in central government were different from those required of traditional chiefs, and partly because the context in which decisions were made had shifted from traditional to democratically constituted authority – those with voting power in the Provincial Council were elected representatives. Ranking was by no means absent in the Provincial Council, but the shift from traditional to democratically constituted authority was apparent there in the way the arrangement of space (and the burden of traditional authority it carries) was partially subverted.

To demonstrate this I describe below the course of several council meetings at village, island and provincial level. Provincial Council meetings occur twice a year and I was able to attend only one of these; island meetings occur roughly six times a year and village meetings once a week or so. The appended diagrams show seating arrangements in the appropriate village hall.

VILLAGE MEETING 1

This meeting in Sawaieke followed directly on the first of a series of meetings called by the minister and church officers to celebrate Pentecost week and to discuss 'behaviour appropriate to our family life'. The church meeting was poorly attended and this perhaps explains the low attendance at the Village Council meeting that followed it, as well as the prominence of the Rotuman Methodist minister, who did not make a regular appearance at Village Council meetings; it was Naivakatawa (the lay preacher) who routinely represented the church in this context. The following is an edited extract from my field notes:

> The meeting is chaired by Takalaigau and discusses registration of voters for the coming general election, village work in connection with building at Gau Secondary School, the election of a new village chief, the response made by another village to Sawaieke's contribution to a large funeral exchange, the debt owing on the village truck, the failure of some men to carry out labour obligations to the village.
>
> The meeting ends with a speech from the minister – the gist of which is support for 'our leaders'. They help and encourage us, he says, and we must follow them, do the work they ask; we must do what is required by the demands of our lives 'in the manner of the land' [*vakavanua*]. Our chiefly village Sawaieke is the leading village of the island, he himself was brought up in just such a village; and 'it is right that we should shoulder our traditional tasks'. Our leaders are wise, they help and advise us properly.
>
> During this speech the minister, an accomplished and rousing preacher, manages to invest 'our leaders' with a holy significance so that the atmosphere in the hall becomes redolent of *vakarokoroko*, 'respect'. He refers throughout to 'our leaders' [*noda i liuliu*], rather than to 'our traditional chiefs' [*noda turaga ni vanua* or *ko ira na malo*]. I assume this is meant to allow for church leaders as well as for traditional chiefs. What strongly impresses me, however, is that, given that we are in the presence of the high chief he, as our manifest leader, willy-nilly takes on the qualities of chiefliness and leadership that the minister extols.
>
> Throughout the meeting, it is primarily Takalaigau who speaks; with the exception of the minister, only five other people do so: the village chief [*turaganikoro*], Takalaigau's talking chief or herald [*matanivanua*], the chair of the primary school committee, the chair of the Women's Association, and the lady who looks after the money to fuel the electricity generator for church services and village meetings in the hall.

Turaganikoro reports on matters looked after by the village committee, work in progress, etc.; representatives of other committees

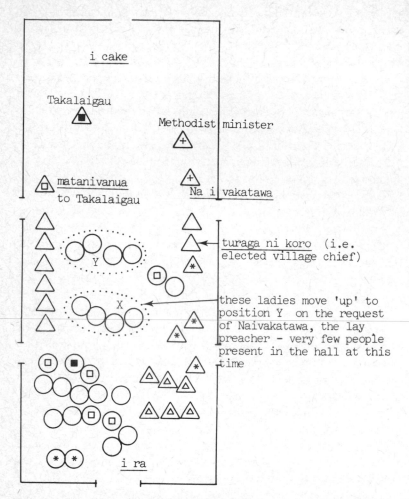

Note: For the reader who may be wondering about my own seating position –
for meetings I asked permission of the presiding chiefs to sit above, so that I
might easily hear and/or record what was going on. At other times – for example,
yaqona-drinking – I sat below along with other married women or with girls.

Figure 14 Village meeting 1

speak only when called upon. Married men occasionally speak out on
a matter of personal concern – as when cows have trampled gardens
– but on the whole they too remain quiet; women and young men
rarely speak at all and even when asked for their opinions (an

infrequent occurrence) are likely to remain silent, though they may be vociferous on the subject elsewhere. Primarily it is the high chief, clan chiefs, other holders of traditional titles, *turaganikoro*, and older married men who speak up in meetings. When I asked others why they did not do so they would either shrug or, in the case of women, say they were afraid [*rere*] or too shy or ashamed [*rui madua*]. One man, married and in his mid-thirties, who in other contexts was not slow to give an opinion, proud of his reading and broad general knowledge, his interest in politics, and so on, said to me: 'It's not my duty to lay down the law; it's right that the *malo* [traditional chiefs] should meet in council, that they should discuss everything to do with the village – discuss it, explain it, make a decision about it. My duty is just to listen.'

The Methodist minister was allowed to be the focus of attention for the earlier meeting; thus for Village meeting 1 Takalaigau, the high chief, left free for the minister the top central position (see Figure 14). The minister, equally polite, declined to take it. Their positions express rather neatly the relative status of high chief and church minister in the context of the village hall. This is the high chief's domain, so he sits above the minister; normally he would take the top central place whether the minister was present or not, but the initial meeting was a church affair, so he took an off-centre position, thereby making an accommodation to this legitimate intrusion of the church into the chiefly domain.

The four women who moved from X to Y were seated unusually high; they were told by the lay preacher to 'move up' during the earlier meeting when few people were present and no men were seated in the vicinity of Y. The women shown at the bottom left entered the hall much later and did not presume to seat themselves so far 'up' the space where men were already seated, even though they included the high chief's wife and two other high-ranking women.

VILLAGE MEETING 2

This meeting took place in the absence of the high chief, who was on a visit to Suva; it was chaired by *turaganikoro* and preceded by a long prayer from the lay preacher, who left soon afterwards. The four men seated above and *turaganikoro* did most of the talking; two contributions were made by middle-aged married men. Below is an edited extract from field notes and tapes:

> The meeting discusses fund-raising for the secondary school, the division of men's labour for the village; the young men are reprimanded for their use of bad language and a man complains about an insulting piece of graffiti referring to his teenage daughter; the young men are castigated for this by each of the traditional chiefs in turn and later lectured about football practice, their game not being up to scratch. This is by way of taking attention away from an argument between two clan chiefs that preceded it.

> The chiefs' argument concerns which people of a neighbouring village are 'theirs'. Chief A claims people whom Chief B says are his. Chief B feels that Chief A has those in power on his side, that he is about to be deprived of his rightful due. It is Chief B who brings up the matter and demands that the other tell him what is going on. The argument lasts a good twenty minutes. At first the speakers use the allusive and indirect style characteristic of accusation in meetings. Later they become more explicit. Throughout their argument Chief A constantly insists that they should not discuss the matter at all, that they should wait for Takalaigau. I quote here a small part of their exchanges, those that occurred right at the end of the argument.

Chief A: Yes, it's enough. Takalaigau will come here and it will be clear. Nothing bothers me. If you want Village X as yours, let it be so.

Chief B: It is not that I am bothered by anything, I want to know the truth, the correct thing. Before one talks about anything one should see that one stands in a correct moral position.

Chief A: Fine. The mistake will then be proved when one of us is suddenly lost to this world, that is ... [i.e. God will strike dead the one who has asserted what is not the case, for the domains of traditional chiefs are given in the divine order of things.]

Chief B [interrupting]: What mistake? I know that my path is the right one and there is no mistake. This is what I'm talking about here. However, I shall fight on behalf of my establishment. But if it's going to cause continued ill-feeling, no.

Chief A: It's not correct to denigrate Takalaigau like this. [Implies that Chief B denigrates Takalaigau by attempting to oppose him.]

Chief B: I don't denigrate anyone. I speak the truth.

Chief A: This is the first time I've heard anyone denigrate Takalaigau. It's not possible for us to denigrate Takalaigau. He is our death. [The ancestral power vested in a properly installed paramount chief means that it is death to disobey or to act against him, whether with or without his knowledge.]

Chief B: It's not possible in what way? No matter. Let us speak correctly.

Chief A: Tell Takalaigau that there's no point, that we two [the speaker and Takalaigau] stand apart. Thank you very much.

Chief B: I am just very sorry that you advise him in a contrary way.

Chief A: I don't give him contrary advice. No. I still follow my rank. [Do not presume to give advice.]

Chief B: No. You lie. I know very well.

Chief A: I shall just do my duty to the chief of Naboginibola [Takalaigau]. That's what I do, I do my duty throughout every year. We two [the speaker and Takalaigau] are accused of this: that we are in error.

Chief B: Yes. Just so that the right thing be known.

Elder [soothing]: No, this is a good discussion. The day will come when we'll make it all good and correct.

Chief A: What I have to say to him, then, is that we two should be silent about it and wait for Takalaigau.

Turaganikoro: Yes, I thank you all very much, gentlemen, for being here and for giving ear to this matter.

This argument could not be resolved by those present, who sat in embarrassed silence throughout. Clan chief C (see Figure 15), who entered during the argument, apparently took a low place so as to stay out of it; he may have been an indirect cause of the quarrel, for

Figure 15 Village meeting 2

the fact that Chief A's clan had suffered a loss of members to Chief C's clan may have made Chief A anxious to secure those in Village X.

With respect to seating, no one present has sufficient status to take the top central position. The four men above are of very similar status. Had only one of them been present, he might have taken a more central place. *Turaganikoro*'s position reflects his much lesser status. He was 'in the chair', but he did not attempt to interrupt or to curtail the clan chiefs' argument – his junior status relative to these men would not allow him to do so.

The disposition of people in Village meeting 2 is unusual – a number of married men are clustered in the bottom right-hand corner; they may have been inhibited from taking higher places by the chiefs' argument. Also, if he was present when they entered, the position of the lay preacher below the midpoint of the right-hand wall would have inhibited married men from taking vacant places above him. The young man who sits above a married man on the left-hand side of the diagram is only technically a 'young man' (because he is unmarried); at that time he was village treasurer and also took the minutes; this explains his relatively high position.

VILLAGE MEETING 3 – EDITED EXTRACT FROM NOTES AND TAPES

The meeting is half over when Takalaigau enters; after the routine business is done Chief A raises the matter of whose people live in Village X. He and Chief B have a brief, heated argument. Chief B says they are his people and Chief A says yes, this is so, but not all of them. There are, says Chief A, *some* B-people in Village X and they are the descendants of some who were driven away from their original place. He says that he and his opponent should 'be silent' and allow Takalaigau to examine the rights of the matter.

Takalaigau: It's right that an explanation of it should be brought to me. This matter is important, it's not right to quarrel about it. . . . The answer which was quite correct was reported by Chief A: B-people live in Village X – one division of them. . . . They went to stay there because of a quarrel that happened here. This was confirmed at once in Suva. Just this thing is clear in this story: it was like this because I was away. The correct thing to do in case of a problem of the land is this: a clan leader who is worried about something concerning him should come to me. The most important thing is not to wave it about. The mistaken report of it will then move on to others.

I am revealing a matter of continuing importance: when I go to a village and explain this thing no one from here goes along with me. The meaning of this is that what is yours is in fact my own –

because the history of it belongs to me. I will reveal it here.

I was much concerned in the beginning of this thing. In a discussion of the chiefs of this land you, Chief B, were absent. This was the reason we faced an important decision. I revealed it to the chiefs. ... We discussed it, and they confirmed I should set out at once to the place where the facts are to be found.

I went to do it; saw, took the book about it, read and discussed it with those in the information department [Native Lands Commission of the Department of Fijian Affairs]. It was approved that I might have a copy of the book about Sawaieke country for myself. ... If one of you goes to see this book, unfortunately you will not be able to do so. That's the law. But it was a blessing that it was given to me – it is given to the person who is the leader of a country only ...

I just came back here and I heard about Chief A's and Chief B's stories; they could not resolve the issue because there was no truth in the stories. What is being talked about is important because if it should be taken in the legal sense, the proof of it is there in the book. If someone lies he is likely to have another problem because of it. That book is legally ratified and the chiefs in the lands investigation [1916] swore to it at the time it was made law.

I shall not wave about *all* the actual facts ... that is not the right way of going about it. I just reveal the answer to it that was always said by Chief A: there are B-people in Village X ... they went there because of a quarrel. They went to stay there and they established a clan of their own and they listen to Chief X. I am explaining this according to the way in the manner of the land; they were established legally in Village X. There a clan was given to them, and a piece of land that they might stay there.

Chief A: Therefore, Chief B, it's enough. I am very thankful that it's been resolved [*ni sa mai seavu*]. Look, please

	don't hold a grudge about it. I shall not hold a grudge about it.
Chief B:	No one is bad-tempered. Bad temper avails nothing.
Chief A:	You are revealing that you are a B-person. [a compliment] However, let us two listen here to what Takalaigau has explained. Just that eh, Father of ... [appealing to another senior man]. You younger ones, listen: this thing is clean once and for all, finished. Concerning it you will now say as follows: there are no B-people in Village X. They are a clan and they are established, they wrote their names and they wrote the names of their living descendants [as members of that clan]. It is over. That is the whole of it, ladies and gentlemen.

It may seem to the puzzled reader that I have muddled my As and Bs, but the crucial point in Takalaigau's speech occurs when he says that B-people in Village X 'listen to' Chief X and that he is explaining the matter 'in the manner of the land'. This means that if once there were B-people in Village X, there are no longer. They are a clan subject to Chief X, who is subject to Chief A in Sawaieke, so the disputed people ultimately 'belong' to Chief A.

The disposition in space of the persons concerned is shown in Figure 16. Takalaigau, who entered the meeting late, took his place – which had been left free for him – in the top central position of decisive authority. The two disputing chiefs faced each other at more or less the same level on opposite sides of the room, Chief B being a little below Chief A – each of them being seated at the side of the hall nearest to their own section of the village.

Ordered speech is here analogous to above/below: status differences are at once expressed and constituted in who 'listens to' whom. Chief A makes much of this in his continued insistence that he and Chief B must wait for Takalaigau, that they should not even discuss the matter in Takalaigau's absence. Takalaigau makes the same point in saying that the quarrel would not have occurred had the matter been brought to him in the first place, and that only he has sufficient authority to talk about it because the history of it 'belongs' to him. Speech in a public context is a prerogative of persons of high status; so no one tried to interrupt the chiefs' argument in Village meeting 2.

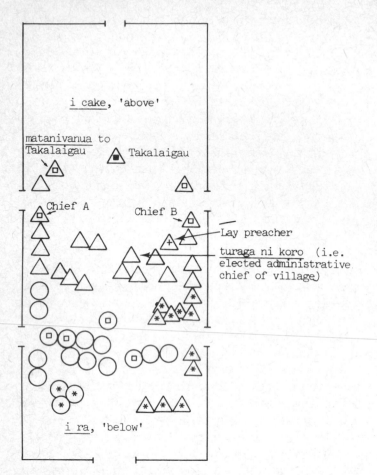

Figure 16 Village meeting 3

Reference to Figures 14 and 16 reveals that women seem less concerned with their relative status as manifest in space: several senior women are below much younger married women. It is also clear that young men may sit above, on the same level as, or below women (considered as an undifferentiated group). On the whole young men do not sit above married men in village meetings. This situation may be compared with that of *yaqona*-drinking where, because they look after the *yaqona*, young men may appear to be above married men; but this appearance is undercut by the description of them as 'right in the middle' [*e loma donu*] between the chiefs who are above and the women below. The disposition of people in Village meeting 3 is closest to people's conceptual model as derived from their descriptions of seating arrangements.

COUNTRY COUNCIL 1

This meeting for all Gau villages took place in Sawaieke village hall after the traditional welcome to a visiting government minister of chiefly rank and another government Member of Parliament. Owing to the guest of honour's high chiefly rank, the welcoming ceremonies were carried out with the utmost formality. A welcome is extended to all state and church officials, but distinctions are made between these men. For this occasion, the preparations were elaborate and the ceremonies strictly rehearsed. The chiefly *yaqona* [*yaqona vakaturaga*] was performed by men wearing traditional leaf skirts and other decorations befitting their status. The *yaqona* was prepared and served using prescribed gestures, orchestrated by the men's chant.

The full series of welcoming ceremonies entail many ritual presentations of whale's teeth, mats, *yaqona* and *magiti* (feast food); only when these were over and the company had drunk tea and rested did the Country Council itself begin. The following is an edited extract from notes taken at the time and refers only to the actual council meeting.

The government minister, the *vulagi dokai* [honoured guest], is above, central and seated in a chair. He has lots of free space around him. The council chairman directs the order of questions to the government minister, who is relaxed, at his ease, affable. A man who asks a question rises to his knees so that he may be seen and heard amongst all those others who are seated on the floor; each question is prefaced by a lengthy formal acknowledgement of government minister, chairman, high chief and *malo* [traditional chiefs], with full honorific titles being used. Humility is nearly always apparent in the demeanour of the questioner, who rarely challenges whatever answer is given and says *vinaka, vinaka* ['thank you'] at intervals during the answer. There are questions about education priorities, copra prices, the air service to Gau, the duties of the Public Works Department, lack of dental services, etc.

There is only one confrontation, and this embarrasses most people. The questioner is a non-Sawaieke man, not of chiefly rank. He complains. He says this is the first time the government minister has been to Gau in five years and only now, in election year, has he come. He [the speaker] is fed up with the Alliance [the party of government]; if they do not shape up – and judging by their present performance they are unlikely to do so – he is going to found a new party, etc., etc.

Takalaigau is angry and I hear him ask the chairman, 'Is it right to talk like that in this traditional council? It's not fitting, it's disgusting.' The chairman is angry and embarrassed. He curtails the man's speech, not without difficulty, by saying 'Thank you, X, thank you, thank you, X' over the man's own words. When the man first complains the government minister answers him, but the answer is not to his satisfaction; he goes on objecting. Then the minister relaxes back in his chair and leaves it to the council chairman to squelch the speaker.

Later I discuss the incident with a few men, commoners aged thirty to forty, including a teacher from N, two Sawaieke men and others from two of the villages of Sawaieke country. The Sawaieke man says: 'We Sawaieke people vote Alliance; all Fijians vote Alliance. At the coming election, this year, we shall vote for them again. But lots of things concerning us are not done. They are not concerned with us people who live in small villages. X [the complainant] spoke the truth when he said that no one [from the government] had come here during the last five years. What this means is that they don't understand the life of villages like this one; they only know about life in the capital. So what about the lives of us who live in this village? I shall not vote for a different party, I am on the same side as the Alliance, but they do not care about us. What can we do to change their way of doing things? What do you think, Mother of Manuel?' [cf. Nation, 1978: 128–31, 134.]

I say I think X was right to speak up; if one is dissatisfied one should complain. Someone says it is not their way to complain and argue. We discuss how, in any case, it is difficult to do so in a meeting like the one just held. The Sawaieke man and the

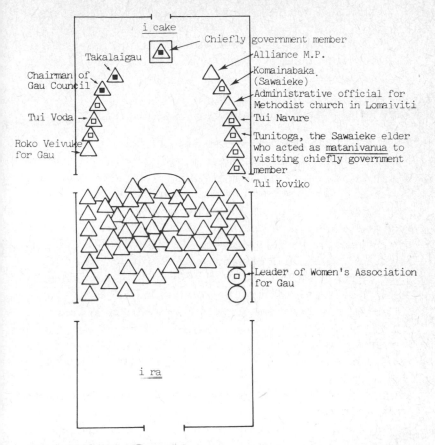

i cake

Chiefly government member

Takalaigau   Alliance M.P.

Chairman of   Komainabaka
Gau Council   (Sawaieke)

Administrative official for
Methodist church in Lomaiviti

Tui Voda   Tui Navure

Roko Veivuke   Tunitoga, the Sawaieke elder
for Gau   who acted as matanivanua to
visiting chiefly government
member

Tui Koviko

Leader of Women's Association
for Gau

i ra

Figure 17 Country Council 1

schoolteacher from N are quite clear about what constrains them.
The Sawaieke man says: 'It's difficult to speak up in a big meeting.
X is a bold-tempered man, strong. The chiefs are sitting above
and he is below, but still his voice is heard there. He is not afraid.'

The teacher from N chuckles and says: 'The guest of honour
and the *malo* – all the chiefs – are present and the ceremony of the
chiefly *yaqona* is performed, but X is not shy [or ashamed], he
speaks and reveals his knowledge.' Someone else objects to this,
saying: 'He only reveals his own ambition [or arrogance]', but on
the whole these men seem to support X's action.

We also talk about the Council of Chiefs, how it gives advice to the government. People have previously told me that it is 'not a political council', but the schoolteacher from N disputes this, saying: 'The Council of Chiefs is also political, it is political in its very organization.'

COUNTRY COUNCIL 2

This second island-wide meeting was routine; it took place in Nawaikama and many representatives from other villages were not able to attend. The meeting began with a *sevusevu*, the *yaqona* being presented by a member of the host village to the visiting chiefs who were named in order of status, using honorific titles: 'To Nadawa gentlemen, to the chief Takalaigau; to Naiviqeleqele, to the chief Ratu; gentlemen, the chief Tui Vanuaso. All of you who are *malo* [chiefs] gentlemen, in our chiefly island, Gau.'

The *i sevusevu* was accepted by a Nawaikama man acting as herald. Then there was '*yaqona* in the manner of the land' [*yaqona vakavanua*] – prepared and served using prescribed gestures; the 'three bowls' went to Komainabaka, the chairman – a much-respected Sawaieke chief – to Takalaigau and to a Navukailagi man who, not himself of chiefly rank, was honoured as the representative of the highest-ranking village owing allegiance to Bau. After a number of speeches the chairman called for prayer. Then a short break until the council meeting proper began, it having taken an hour or so to get through the preliminaries.

I include Country Council 2 here for comparison with Country Council 1. There the disposition of men in space showed careful acknowledgement of differential status in the presence of the guest of honour (see Figure 17), with the attendant chiefs sitting in an ordered semicircle below him but above the *tanoa*. On that occasion it was married men who looked after the *yaqona*, and the man who prepared the *yaqona* and the one who served it were themselves of chiefly birth. No young men were present; the two women, who sat in the humblest positions, represented the Gau Women's Association, the chairwoman being a senior lady of Takalaigau's own family. The ceremonies preceding both meetings, as well as the prayer that opened them, made it abundantly clear that the chiefs were men in authority.

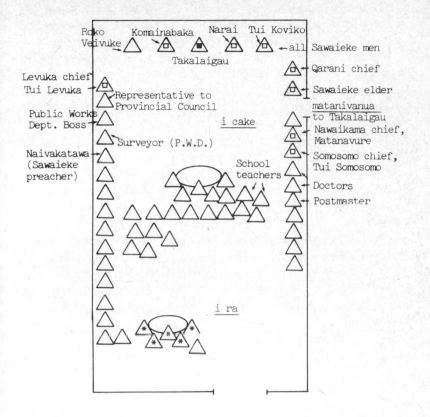

Figure 18 Country Council 2

At Country Council 2 (see Figure 18) *all* men in the top positions were Sawaieke men and all of them, with the exception of Roko Veivuke (assistant Roko, a provincial administrator), were chiefs. The prominence of Takalaigau in the top central position was somewhat undermined by the first of 'the three bowls' of *yaqona* being served to Komainabaka, who was acting chairman. This did not prevent Takalaigau from having his say whenever he wanted to do so; nevertheless it was clear that Komainabaka was in charge, and he ran the meeting with quiet efficiency.

The chiefs of inferior villages of Sawaieke country (present were chiefs from Levuka, Nawaikama and Somosomo) sat in rather humble positions below the Sawaieke chiefs but above the *tanoa*, which was so placed that all the higher-status men were seen to be above it. At Country Council 1 these men were unambiguously below the *tanoa* – they hardly appeared to be chiefs at all by comparison with the very high-status guest of honour.

The tributary offering of *yaqona* root – the *i sevusevu* – is always made to the highest-status men present, even if they are not householders in the village concerned. In the past powerful chiefs were able to dispose of all and any property and while this is illegal now, the notion survives in observances like the *i sevusevu* (Sawaieke chiefs give permission for the council members to be in Nawaikama, a village that owes allegiance to them). Also a chief sometimes helps himself to goods, etc., that are not his own, and this despite the resentment aroused by the action; however, he cannot dispose of land in this way.

PROVINCIAL COUNCIL

The Provincial Council [*Bose ni Yasana*] meeting, held in Natokalau, Ovalau, largely concerned development on the various islands of Lomaiviti Province and financial aid for development projects. It took place in the presence of the then Deputy Prime Minister, Ratu Sir Penaia Ganilau, who, as chiefly guest of honour, was accorded welcoming ceremonies of formal magnificence. These preceded the Provincial Council proper and took perhaps two hours or so.

The ceremonies were performed outside the village hall on the village green [*rara*] adjacent to it, with the Deputy Prime Minister and some very few other guests being seated on chairs on the verandah of the hall. The DPM's armchair was in the central position, set apart from the other, straight-backed chairs. The DPM's herald sat at his feet, below the verandah, while those involved in the presentations and the chiefly *yaqona* [*yaqona vakaturaga*] sat on mats on the grass, directly opposite and facing the DPM. Council members and villagers who were watching sat far away and some people who were standing up for a better view were told to sit down by one of the chiefs, even though they must have been a good thirty yards from the DPM's chair. So the Deputy Prime Minister was accorded the full traditional authority of a very high-ranking chief of Fiji.

This status shifted somewhat once the meeting began inside the hall. The DPM was seated in an armchair beside the island chiefs, who were seated above on mats, but their collective traditional authority was here less relevant because this meeting came within the domain of central government and the democratic process. This was manifest in the seating arrangements; despite the presence of the *tanoa* and of the chiefs above, attention was perforce focused on those who sat on the floor at the low tables in the centre of the room. The DPM did not sit in the top central place, which had become irrelevant here, but at the top right-hand side of the room, where he was at once prominent and had a good vantage point on the proceedings (see Figure 19).

The elected island representatives who had voting power sat at the central tables, the top table being presided over by the chairman of the Council (an elected island representative) and two civil administrators, who could not vote. These men, significantly, *had their backs to the chiefs* who were seated above. This was the only time I saw a seating arrangement of this kind.

The root *qara*, 'to face', forms the basis of all the terms used for attendance on God in worship, or on chiefs. In the prayer quoted earlier, God is addressed as 'You the God who alone is served' [*qaravi*, literally 'faced']. This service or attendance is the actual source of power; so the old gods are said to have lost their power because 'no one attends on them'. Their power was derived from offerings made in human sacrifice and the pouring of libations of *yaqona*, and would be made manifest again if that attendance were reinstated (as it is in witchcraft). Similarly, a chief's power is derived from people's attendance upon him, from their offerings of first fruits, their obedience to his wishes, their installation of him as chief and their *yaqona*-drinking. Thus a Kabara man could report to his fellow villagers of an important ceremonial exchange that 'the Kabara delegation had ... "shouldered the carrying pole of empowering the chief" ... they had not only physically supported the chief by participating, but in doing so had ... empowered him' (Hooper, 1982: 228).

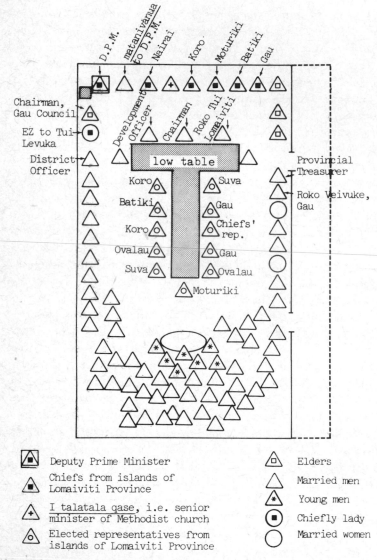

Figure 19 Provincial Council

A chief's authority derives from people's attendance on him and is manifest on a daily basis in the orientation in space of people to chiefs, especially in the widest public contexts of *yaqona*-drinking and meetings of the village and country councils. The collective term for welcoming ceremonies is *veiqaravi,* literally 'facing each other'; and if one attends on a chief, serves or ministers to him, one literally 'faces the chief'. Similarly those who look after the *yaqona* 'face the *yaqona*' (see Chapters 3 and 6). It follows that the seating arrangements for the Provincial Council to some extent undermined the authority of chiefs even while the formal properties of above/ below continued to be observed. That is to say, attention was focused on the elected representatives around the table, whose chairman sat with his back to the chiefs, but the island chiefs were still accorded the position above. With the exception of the DPM, who was literally and figuratively the highest person present, they were on the same level and so did not acknowledge the superiority of any one of them over the others. This recalls Erskine's observations of over a century ago: 'chiefs were generally most careful . . . to avoid being placed in a position of the slightest inferiority. They avoided one another as much as possible, preferring any business to be conducted by intermediaries' (Erskine, 1853: 202). In the contemporary context chiefs of different areas have to meet together; however, their concern to avoid any appearance of inferiority relative to one another is still in evidence.

In Figure 19 it can be seen that the people sat below the chiefs; civil service advisers were at the side walls with the humblest of them seated below the *tanoa,* along with the men of Natokalau, who were looking after the meeting [*qarava na bose,* literally 'facing the meeting']. These advisers were called upon at will by the chairman and the island representatives. Questions from the latter to the DPM acknowledged him as a member of government, as an elected representative of the people, rather than as a man of high chiefly status. Thus questions were *not* couched in humble terms, few men using the chiefly honorific form of address, and some rep- resentatives even tried to improve the occasion by seeking the DPM's support for their own ends.

Conclusion

Comparing all levels of council meetings, it is clear that the coercive power inscribed in space in traditional contexts can be made at once to contain and to signify democratically constituted authority.

Village meetings are formally democratic, with the chairman and other committee members being elected representatives; nevertheless traditional chiefs are able to dominate the proceedings, and their domination is inscribed in the prominent positions they occupy in space and in the fact that it is they who speak and others who at once 'face' and 'listen to' them (see Nayacakalou, 1975: 90; Spate, 1959: 35). However, in the more inclusive context of the Provincial Council, where the conduct of the meeting is governed by law, democratically constituted authority comes into effect. Thus a shift became apparent as one moved from the highest level of inclusiveness in the traditional context – the Country Council, where the chiefs dominate – to the context of the Provincial Council, where elected members seemed to dominate. Nevertheless, continuity was maintained in that the island chiefs were accorded the position of honour in the gathering, and the meeting was preceded by the traditional ceremonies of welcome to the presiding chief, Ratu Sir Penaia Ganilau. This, taken together with the fact that the DPM is both of very high rank in his own right *and* was then the holder of high office in the democratically constituted government, effectively allowed traditional authority to emerge unscathed from the encounter. Indeed, it could be argued that Ratu Sir Penaia's position in the space of the meeting conveyed the notion that democratic procedures took place by virtue of chiefly dispensation.

8 Learning about seniority and gender

A change of focus

The preceding chapters provide data and analysis on spatial constructs. The hierarchy that is constituted within the household and made concrete in the design and use of house space pivots on a transformation of balanced exchange relations between men and women into one where a man's contribution is valued above his wife's. This hierarchical exchange relation is in part constituted and expressed in the seating for family meals. Across groups and across persons the apparent transformation of balanced exchange between groups into tribute to chiefs has its paradigm in the *yaqona* ceremony. This transformation is also constituted in space: the essential equality of *veiqaravi*, 'facing each other', in the layout of the village becomes clear-cut hierarchy *inside* buildings on the above/below axis. Here the relations between men as equals and affines (i.e. as cross-cousins) are contained by and subordinated to hierarchical relations between kin.

Further, the use of space in church ratifies chiefly authority by association with Christian divine power, which becomes analogous to – or partially identical with – the ancestral *mana* derived from *yaqona*-drinking. Chiefly authority is articulated to democratically constituted authority in such a way that at the level of the village and the country [*vanua*] chiefly authority seems to be coextensive with that of central government. In council meeting (as in church) authority is given at once by a prominent position above, and by the prerogative of speech. Those who sit below are those who listen; they are of inferior status.

The salience of above/below allows Fijian villagers to merge the different hierarchies of household, church, chiefly and governmental authority; so ambiguities and possible conflicts of interest tend to be ignored in favour of an apparently unitary and overarching construct that governs all. Seniority, gender and rank are all implicated here, but as yet each of these notions remains problematic

– most obviously in respect of how they are articulated to one another in any given person's understanding. This chapter looks at children's early experience of seniority and gender distinctions; rank, by which one is either 'chief' or 'commoner', seems to be articulated to seniority, and I discuss this later. The next chapter deals with how children construct over time the meaning of above/below.

Children and adults

A village child grows up in a context that stresses close kin ties, adult expectations, relative seniority and gender distinctions. Most examples of child–adult and child–child interaction described below are in respect of food exchange, orders and discipline. The giving of food, in any context, is an act that constitutes kinship; within the hierarchical household it connotes authority in its benign and nurturing aspect. Affection, orders and discipline are also defining markers of hierarchical kin relations and encompassed by the term for love between kin, *veilomani* ('to love, care for, pity or have mercy on one another'). In any interaction the senior party is in control, the junior party has only to listen and accept. In the political context, 'to listen' is to owe allegiance; for a child, 'listening' is inherent to the constitution of hierarchical kin relations. Frequent adult injunctions to behave in certain ways enter into children's constitution of the meaning of relative seniority. By contrast, the constitution of gender distinctions seem to depend more on observation and imitation of elders and peers.

Heredity is taken to be a factor in a person's good and bad qualities, abilities and sensibilities, but my knowledge of villagers' notions of conception is sketchy. People whom I asked denied any specifically biological form of transmission of inherited qualities, but would sometimes explain them in a general way as 'just because of the blood of kinship'. Certain inherited qualities or abilities – like the power to cure a certain illness – are bestowed on one by the *mana* of the ancestors (or the power of God).

It is generally held that children have to learn to become adults, and to do so they must be taught. The knowledge, rights and responsibilities appropriate to the child at different ages, and impressed upon him or her by peer group and elders, are an amalgam of *i tovo vakavanua* – custom (literally 'behaviour in the manner of the land'), *na vuli* – school education (literally 'learning') and Methodist precepts and principles. In adult notions of teaching the accent is upon discipline – rebuke, ridicule, or punishment – when the child errs. Questioning of adults is usually actively discouraged and obedience is stressed. So a child's most active and participatory learning takes place in the company of peers and slightly older children. According to my observations, the peer group is narrowly defined in behavioural terms – twelve to eighteen months differentiate one group from another; there are no formal age sets.

The childhood stages most often acknowledged are baby [*gone dramidrami,* literally 'sucking child'], little children [*gone lalai*] to age five or so, and schoolchildren [*gone vuli*] – those at primary school and in the early years of secondary school. *Gone tubutubu* (literally 'grown-up child') is sometimes used in reference to early adolescence. From their mid-teens on people are reliably differentiated as to sex, with young women being referred to and addressed (i.e. as a group) as *gone yalewa* (literally 'girls') and young men between fifteen and seventeen as *cauravou lalai* (literally 'little young men') to distinguish them from older unmarried men, who are *cauravou* ('young men'). Marriage makes one an adult; but young men are allowed a good measure of autonomy, young women rather less. The data in this chapter and the next refer primarily to children up to age fourteen.

Birth, naming and baptism

The birth of the first child of a legitimate marriage is properly surrounded by ceremony, irrespective of the child's sex. Mother and child are sequestered within the house for four nights and attended by older women who come to drink *yaqona* there. On the fourth night the child is shown to the father and there is a feast called *lutu na nona i vicovico,* (literally 'falling off of the umbilical cord'). *Tabua* (whale's teeth) are exchanged and relatives come to make presentations of goods, etc. Little or no such attention is paid to later births, and it seems that the ceremonies for the first-born have also fallen off because nowadays most women have their first baby in hospital in Suva. The umbilical cord should not be discarded; a boy's should be buried and a young tree planted on top of it, so that he might become a skilful gardener; a girl's should be secreted under a rock in a stream or on the reef so that she will be able to supply her family with fish (cf. Brewster, 1922: 170).

The naming of the child [*vakatokayaca*] takes place soon after birth; senior male kin in the father's line have the right to name the first child. However, any person in the senior generation can do so, providing that the *tabua* (whale's tooth) they present to the child's paternal kin is accepted. The child is usually named after someone; often the name has been in the family for generations, but it may refer to some significant occurrence in the parents' or grandparents' lives – for example Lesumailepanoni, 'Returned from Lebanon', because the father was a member of Fiji's peacekeeping force in that country. Where the name of a living person is given, that person and the child are *veiyacani*, namesakes. They are usually close kin – for example, the child is named after his Father's Elder Brother (FEB); there is often a special fondness between *veiyacani*, who address each other as 'Name' [*Yaca*] and refer to each other as 'my namesake' [*noqu yaca*].

Children are usually christened within their first year but again, it is only for the first child that much fuss is made. A couple of mats are presented to the minister and there is a festive drinking of *yaqona* in the father's parents' house. Godparents [*tubutubu vakalotu*] are close senior kin, often the child's maternal grandparents. Once it is a few weeks old, the child is taken to church every Sunday – at first by one of its grandmothers; later, at age two or so, by an older sibling (real or classificatory).

Children born outside marriage are not accorded the seniority of children of recognized marriages. The first child of the marriage is *na ulu matua*, the eldest (literally 'the mature head'). He will become head of the household – *nodatou i liuliu*, 'our leader' – though he may as a matter of courtesy defer to an illegitimate elder brother in the latter's presence. Here I use 'he' because even if a girl is 'the eldest' she will not become 'our leader'; she has no formal land rights and is *ulu matua* in name but rarely in terms of authority – she is almost always displaced by a younger brother, though she should still be consulted on important matters. The father's rank decides that of the child; a child born outside marriage to a chiefly woman does not inherit her rank and is unlikely ever to be given a high position *vakavanua*, 'in the manner of the land'.

Childcare and the child's early experience

The mother is principal caretaker of the child for the first year or two. In Gau women find most of their duties in or close to the home, so babies are left to sleep under a mosquito net while awake or held by some close female relative if in need of comforting. A baby is breastfed for up to a year and sometimes longer; a child may be weaned on to the bottle, but it is not used for early feeding unless the mother's milk is inadequate. Weaning – with or without the use of the bottle – is a fairly rapid process, other foods having been introduced to the child over the preceding months (cf. Quain, 1948: 299; Levy, 1973: 445).

Babies receive a lot of cuddling and fondling from all female relatives and usually too from fathers, grandfathers and elder brothers, but they are not 'talked to' or very often played with by adults. They are picked up and soothed if crying or diverted with something to suck, and otherwise left to find their own stimulation. Until a child can sit up [*gone duriduri*] and crawl [*gone qasiqasi*], s/he spends most time lying on the mat in the same room as the mother. Village children may begin to walk as young as nine months and *should* be doing so by twelve months. A healthy and robust child who fails to walk by the age of fourteen months or so is 'lazy' and treatment may be sought from one of its grandmothers, who inserts into the child's anus a small piece of cloth soaked with the juice of chilli peppers. This painful treatment, I was told, invariably induces a child to walk. It is also obtained for children – usually between one and five years old – who cry too much or are dilatory in one way or another. Once I saw this treatment given to a child of nearly five whose mother said to me in explanation: 'He is always crying, acting like a baby. When this is over then his childishness will be over too.'

Children are expected to say a couple of words: *Na* or *Nana* (Mummy) and *'Atu* [*Ratu*] or *Tata* (Daddy) around one year of age. I recorded a variability of between eleven and fifteen months from maternal reports of the age at which the first words are spoken. But it is rare for mothers to converse with children even once they have begun to talk; rather, they are encouraged to sit quietly and not to run about inside the house or draw attention to themselves in the company of adults. A crawling child who ventures too far from Mother in someone else's home, or the village hall, or who goes near the kitchen hearth or some other object of interest like a cupboard or cooking utensils, is scooped up and set down again near her mother, usually without any comment. A toddler who understands a few words is reached for, set down beside the mother or other adult, and told: 'Don't. It's forbidden, forbidden. Sit down.' Or, if the child tries to examine something – a jar of tobacco, a box of matches, a woman's handbag – it will be told: 'Don't! Inquisitive child! Bad child!' The reminder that something is forbidden, the command to sit down and the rebuke for inquisitiveness are the remarks most often made to toddlers by adults. So, by the age of thirty months most village children are remarkable for their quiet passivity in adult company, able to sit for long periods beside their female elders, mostly silent and only rarely addressing their elders or demanding something of them.

Babies and toddlers are often kissed and cuddled on the laps of women and, less often, by men. Physical interaction also includes slaps, punches and knocks; these gestures are graduated from a gentle blow as an expression of fondness or friendliness to one that is meant to cause pain. Kisses, in which one presses one's nose to the cheek of the other and sniffs, also range from the gentle to those rough enough to make a toddler cry. Many times I saw two mothers, each encouraging the baby in her arms (aged about eight months or more) to punch out at the other, both children grinning and crowing with glee until one took too hard a blow and began to cry; then he or she was kissed and laughed over by the mother. Children up to age five hold hands and walk with their arms around each other; once the child is in school this behaviour is confined within sex and is common for all ages up to late teens and early twenties.

A child over four is no longer kissed and cuddled by mother or younger women, though grandmothers and older women may still do so. One who shows too much affection for her children aged four or so may be criticized by other women: 'She dotes too much on her children.' The word for 'dote', *vakamenemenea*, implies that one treats children like babies by showing a foolish fondness for them (cf. Quain, 1948: 300); *menemene* also describes the behaviour of a child who, beyond the normal age, still shelters behind Mother. Children brought up by their grandmothers (usually Mother's mother) are often said to be *either* presumptuous and 'too inquisitive' *or* 'childish' and unable to take on the tasks proper to their age. Both forms of behaviour are attributed to the grandmother being unable to refrain from doting on the child and allowing it have its own way.

Parental expectations of children

What is desired of village children is that they should grow up; this is apparent in a variety of stock comments that adults make on a child's behaviour.

A baby, a toddler who does not yet speak much, or one who is behind the behavioural norms for his or her age, has a 'mind like water' [*yalo wai*, literally 'spirit (like) water']. Once when I was with some women who were mat-making and some children, a toddler of sixteen months stumbled against my back and righted himself by grabbing my hair. His mother snatched him up, slapped his hand, and sat him down on the mat beside her, saying: 'Don't. It's forbidden. It's forbidden to touch her hair. Sit down.' To me she said: 'Forgive him, Mother of Manuel. His mind is like water and he does not yet know what is forbidden.' Here the child was being taught to observe that aspect of the above/below axis that requires one to 'respect' the head of another person.

The term *yalo wai* is opposed to *yalo matua* – applied to a child who is polite in speech, who sits quietly busy in some useful task, who protects and cares for younger children by correctly guiding them or giving them a large share of some food, and so on. *Matua* is also used of root crops like taro which, when ready to eat, are still hard (compare *dreu*, meaning 'ripe', of fruits). To be *yalo matua* is to have maturity, firmness, a mind in which injunctions to behave well are firmly fixed; unlike those who are *yalo wai*, whose thoughts run like water (despite its similarity, *matua* is not derived from 'mature'; for loan words in Fijian, see Schutz, 1978: 1–50). An adult may compliment a child by saying that s/he is *yalo matua* – for example of a five-year-old who wished to go to a special church service, of a nine-year-old who, unasked, had prepared and cooked cassava while her mother was out fishing, of a seven-year-old who took it upon himself to wash his school uniform, of a three-year-old who could recite a prayer. The injunction to be *yalo matua* is a favourite one for preachers and often figures in the Methodist instruction that begins every child's school day.

Matai! – 'clever!' is the compliment more commonly paid to children under school age; for example, in admiration of a three-year-old who carries a glass of water without spilling it or shows mastery of some other physical or intellectual skill like being able to sing a song or recite. *Yalo matua* is reserved for more exceptional occasions. But children do not look to their elders for notice of their achievements, probably because when adults *do* notice childish activities they do so mostly to forbid them, spontaneous praise of children being comparatively rare. In observing children under five I only once saw a child call for notice; he was a precocious two-year-old who will be mentioned again below. He was climbing a small tree and called in triumph to his mother: 'Mummy, Mummy, I am climbing, I am climbing!' However, children are normally warmly thanked for performing some small task, for example fetching something.

Parents want children to grow up, take on appropriate tasks in house or garden, be quiet with adults, polite, respectful, obedient and well-behaved (cf. Levy, 1973: 439, 461). To shirk responsibility or to behave behind the norm for one's age is to be wilfully childish; in a child over three or so this behaviour may be punished. So a child of twenty-four months was rebuked when he pestered his mother to carry him: 'You're being babyish. It's forbidden, it's forbidden to be babyish.' And a five-year-old who was taken out of church feigning sleepiness and later discovered playing out of doors was beaten by his mother and scolded: 'You don't want to go to church? You have behaved childishly [younger than expected]. Bad child! Crazy child!'

Parents want their children to grow up, but will not tolerate what appears to be presumption or any assertion of will that goes against their wishes. So a girl of four years ten months was beaten because she avoided the task of watching her younger brother (three years six months) and sister (one year three months) to amuse herself in the company of her old grandfather. The angry mother, rebuking her, said: 'Impudent child, not willing to do what you're told! Arrogant child, bad child! It's forbidden to act as if you were grown-up, understand?' The term *viavia levu*, used twice in this admonishment, means to have pretensions to being 'big'; it also means 'ambitious' as a derogatory term. It is used to criticize any type of presumptuous or arrogant behaviour, including that of a man who pretends to high status.

Learning contexts: peer group, home and school

I remarked above that children's questions are actively discouraged, as is any form of self-assertion; adult speech with children tends to consist of commands to do or not do certain things. The cumulative effect of this interactional style is to make the children very quiet and passive in the company of adults. This does not hold true for the same children in the company of their peers or somewhat older and/ or younger children. At first I was surprised to come upon a child, previously encountered only in adult company, and find him or her gaily loquacious, self-assertive, full of liveliness and curiosity. But this behaviour is reserved for one's peers – this being as true for five-to-thirteen-year-olds, teenagers and young men and women as it is for the under-fives. The point is that an active *exchange* takes place in the company of one's peers and slightly older children.

Young children often talk to and play with babies and toddlers, attempt to interest them in some object, and so on – the older child being perhaps between two and a half and three and the younger one, say three months to one and a half. A child of four or so may already shepherd younger ones around and direct their play. The example below records a typical instance of the running commentary children often make on their own actions – one that allows a toddler to add to his or her own knowledge. I heard only one instance of a woman talking in a similar way in the presence of her child (aged one and a half); she was preparing *tavioka* (cassava) for cooking. The following behaviour is common in children up to the age of seven or eight. The oldest child in this example is four years ten months; note how she adopts the attitude of a nurturing parent towards the youngsters.

She is in the company of her YB (three years two months) and her YZ (one year three months). They are collecting fallen mangoes, the eldest child putting them into the lap of her skirt, which she holds up in front of her. She talks aloud to herself: 'Good one, bad one, bad one, bad one, good one. This is a good one, just ripe, this one's mine to eat. This is a bad one, it's overripe.' To the youngsters beside her she says: 'You two pick up mangoes. Go on.' Having found a few good mangoes, she examines the three her YB is clutching to his chest and discards two of them: 'Bad ones. Look, this is a bad one, it's too soft.' She discards the mango her YZ is trying to eat: 'Don't eat it, don't. It tastes bad. It's too ripe. Look, do you want to eat mango?' The little one looks at her, says nothing. Her EZ continues: 'Yes, you want to eat mango. Let us three eat mango.' She selects one from her hoard, peels it, takes a big bite and then offers it to her YZ: 'Do you want to eat mango?' The little one looks back at her, says something that might be 'yes' and is given the mango, her EZ repeating: 'Yes, you want to eat mango. Mango tastes good. Nice.' Then she gives a mango to her YB, who has said 'I do' every time she asked her YZ if she wanted to eat. He cannot peel it and she takes it back, peels off some of the skin and returns it to him. He bites and eats. His EZ asks: 'Does yours taste good?' He answers: 'Yes. It tastes good. Another one for me!' in clear tones, attempting to take one from her lap; she slaps his hand and then, when he has drawn back, gives him another one, saying: 'Yes, let us three eat more mango.'

Older children may stand *in loco parentis* to younger ones, and by the age of nine children of both sexes – but especially girls – are efficient childminders. An age gap of eighteen months, particularly once a child has started school, is sufficient to allow an older child to assert authority over younger ones. One often hears a six-year-old rebuking someone under five with: 'Inquisitive child! Bad child!', but they are not so inclined to ridicule efforts at speech as adults are. I often heard school-age children engage in deliberate teaching, for example a seven-year-old saying earnestly to one of two: '*Yaloka. Oqo sa yaloka. Sega ni 'loka. Yaloka.*' ['Egg. This is an egg. Not 'gg. Egg.']

The habit of talking pretty much only to one's peers continues throughout the school years and into adulthood. Younger people do not usually question or address remarks to older people; they wait until they are spoken to, or respond to orders and requests. Among children between five and thirteen, exchange of gossip and information escalates. I heard children relate to others garbled versions of adult scandals, tales of ghosts and devils, stories read to them in school; they discuss other children, the residence of God, where London is situated, and so on. *Veitalanoa*, telling stories, is a favourite activity for all. Stories are not confined to myth or legend; for example, anyone who has returned from a journey should relate the experience. Below is a seven-year-old boy's highly articulate account of his first trip to Suva:

'I awoke in the early morning, got up, had breakfast. Then we went to wait for the truck. The truck came, then we went to the airfield. Then the plane came into land. Weeee! We got on. I was not afraid. The sky looked lovely. My little mother [MYZ] was waiting for us. We got on a bus, went to Suva. I saw the capital city, I went to the cinema, I saw the wharf, I went shopping – they are *huge*, those shops. Grandma bought my watch and then I sang a song at a gathering in a big park in Suva.'

Though unadorned, this comes close to the adult style of storytelling; the child did not use the verbal particles that signfy tense, but the delivery and general style was fluent and much appreciated by an audience of six children between five and ten and two women (including myself), and the child was encouraged to go on by questions and urgings for more from the assembled children. In the company of adults outside his immediate family – adults he knew well – this child was tongue-tied and embarrassed, barely able to get out a few words in reply to questions about his trip.

To be *siosio*, inquisitive, is a childish trait worthy only of admonition. But one village mother let her children be inquisitive without much hindrance; they engaged her in conversation and she answered their questions, but even so she laughed over their behaviour and described it as 'too inquisitive'. These children were considered precocious, the youngest being described as a 'wise child' [*gone vuku*] by village women. His exploits were often discussed and adults engaged him in talk, apparently for the pleasure they took in his performance, and he responded to them in a way that seemed to me to be unique for the village.

This child engaged in the kind of imaginative play with his mother that is common amongst middle-class English children; once I saw him climb on her back, pull her hair, then stand in front of her, take hold of her nose and say: 'Bring me the medicine for Mummy to drink', this being his mother's practice when *he* had to take medicine. At this point he was two years four months old, articulate, active, happy to wander about on his own between the houses of his close relatives (his grandparents, his MZ, his FB); his MZ's house was a good 100 yards from his own and out of sight of it. His articulate self-confidence and independence were unusual in so young a village child. Up to the age of three and a half or so children usually stay within sight of their houses unless they are with an older sibling aged four or above.

Most children's games up to the age of five imitate adult behaviour. Children over two of both sexes like to have a bit of cassava and a sharp knife to play at chopping up food while women prepare a meal, or a few strips of dried pandanus so that they too may 'weave mats' alongside women engaged in this task. They play in water while someone washes clothes or dishes at a water outlet, make mud pies, squat in groups on the sea wall for fishing with a pretend line. They pretend to smoke, play the guitar by strumming on a piece of wood and singing, put flowers behind their own and each other's ears, follow older children about to gaze large-eyed at their antics and listen to their talk. They also spend many hours just sitting and quietly watching men or women engaged in some task.

Primary school children [*gone vuli*] play more organized games with conkers (when they are in season), jacks or knucklebones using small stones, cards (when they can get hold of a pack from their elders), chasing games like 'tag' and many others similar to those played in Europe. However, these children have a number of tasks to do in and about the house and in the gardens – collecting firewood or coconuts, preparing cassava for cooking, washing dishes or their own school uniforms, and so on. Any collecting task finds five- to thirteen-year-olds going off in groups of three to five, chatting or singing, often with a couple of under-fives in tow. They do not hurry over their task but spend time collecting and eating fruit or, if one of them has a bush-knife, opening and drinking green coconuts; they may stop to swim in a stream or play or just sit down somewhere to rest and talk. Such expeditions with children two to four years older allow four-to-seven-year-olds to acquire a knowledge of the terrain outside the village, of swimming, of food-plants both cultivated and wild, and of fruit-bearing trees; along the sea front they learn which of many varieties of shellfish are fit for eating, how to catch crabs, collect bait for their mothers, and so on. Once they are over about nine, children may go with Father to the gardens or with mother to fish and then, I assume, their knowledge is extended and refined. But these occasions are comparatively rare and I think it is fair to say that the base of a child's learning about the resources to be got from land and sea and their uses, as well as general techniques, are laid down in the company of other, slightly older children. This style of learning continues from babyhood to adulthood; general knowledge seems to be 'filtered down' from adults to children through an overlap in association between members of different peer groups.

Fijian children start school at six, but Sawaieke parents were encouraged to send their children at five, so that they might become accustomed to the tenor and organization of school life. They entered Class 1 and joined in any of its activities that interested them. I spent three months towards the end of my fieldwork working in the village school; its roll of 67 was divided into six classes, the pupils coming from the villages of Sawaieke and Somosomo. I taught in all classes, the headmaster and other teachers kindly allowing me to accustom the children to my presence before I began working with them on their notions of above/below, described in the next chapter.

Fijian primary school teachers must have graduated from high school and received a two-year training in teachers' college. In Sawaieke school, all children were literate and could read and write fluent Fijian by the time they reached class 5; most had attained basic skills in arithmetic, but were not so strong on geometrical concepts. Maths is taught in a mixture of Fijian and English – all the textbooks are in English – so the maths lag is not surprising. For English the teachers use manuals that gradually introduce a wide range of grammatical forms and vocabulary by an oral method that combines rote-learning with individual participation. None of the primary school children could be said to *speak* English, but would almost certainly do so fluently if they completed secondary school.

Fijian teachers often express disappointment with children's school performance, comparing them unfavourably with Indian children who, I was told, are more likely to finish secondary school and obtain white-collar jobs. Also Fijians lament that they 'do not understand business' and do not very often become doctors, lawyers, dentists, etc. Teachers and educationalists often attribute this to a conflict between expectations at home and at school; but it may be as much a product of inequities in rural, as compared with urban, education as of anything else (Lomaloma, 1985). Whatever the case, there *is* a conflict.

Briefly, Fijian teachers are trained to encourage children to show initiative, ask questions, assert their individual needs for teaching, and Sawaieke teachers made every effort to put their training into practice. At the same time they tended to quench personal ambition by stressing inter-reliance within the peer group and submission to traditional authority, which precludes any self-assertion in a child in the presence of those who are older. This conflict in expectations may be better dealt with by girls, who may spend longer in school than do boys – a view based on the fact that Christmas saw the return to the village of ten to fifteen teenage girls who were at school on the mainland, but while at the same time there was a great influx of young men, only four or so came from school. My observations led me to suppose that traditional expectations dominated, this being attributable to the ambiguity in teaching methods and to the half-hour of Methodist teaching that began the school day; this was often devoted to impressing children with the obedience and deference they owed to senior kin.

Politeness and the correct use of kin terms

Positive parental teaching prompts children to observe various formalities and politenesses and to use proper kin terms. So, when people are eating and someone passes their house, a mother may prompt a child *sotto voce*: 'See Little Mother [MYZ]. Call her: Little Mother, come and eat.' The child calls as instructed and the reply is made: 'Thank you, thank you, my child. I've already eaten.' The mother may prompt the child again to say: 'Come and eat again here' or, as a joke compliment to the hearer: 'Come here and just touch it', and the child calls out as prompted and the reply comes again: 'No thanks, no thanks'.

This prompting begins when the child is about two and a half, when s/he can understand and call out with some clarity. S/he is especially prompted to call to peers and as s/he goes about the village, the child over three is in turn greeted, or invited to eat: 'Cama, where are you going?' or 'Mere, good morning!' or 'Mika, come and have breakfast!' When the greeting comes from someone very familiar, the child under five may respond as s/he has heard others do; but where the person who calls is not one of the child's immediate neighbours or close kin, s/he is likely to ignore the call. Where the child under five responds brightly and audibly, any adults present laugh and comment: 'S/he is not afraid'. But it is rare not to be afraid [*rere*], for shyness or shame [*madua*] has already been fostered in the child by a variety of mock-serious behavioural threats from seniors, and by many injunctions to 'sit down' [*dabe i ra*] and 'be quiet' [*tiko lo*] in the company of adults, especially when they go with Mother to other people's houses.

A child's habitual method of locomotion inside a house that is not his or her own is on hands and knees. This is in imitation of older children from the age of six to sixteen (women also sometimes go on their knees in the company of other adults in the house or village hall), reinforced by constant adult injunctions to 'sit down'. Children up to age four are as likely to walk about inside a house that is not their own as they are to go on hands and knees; a toddler is more likely to do so. But by the age of four and a half a child is imitating older peers and so sits down immediately inside the house entrance, and crawls or goes about on the knees inside. Children may even adopt a humble, squatting posture *outside* a house entrance and maintain it inside in the presence of their elders, but when on their own, children up to age thirteen walk and run about the house – their body postures being markedly different in the company of their peers or children who have not yet reached puberty.

When children are about four adults begin to prompt them to use the polite apology *tulou, tulou* ('Excuse me') when they have to stand to walk among seated adults, and also to ask permission to stand, to walk past someone, etc. Below is an extract from notes describing a community gathering:

> The woman beside me calls to a girl (aged four years three months). She rises and walks *lolou*, her body bent over in a near caricature of the proper respect posture. But the girl says nothing and as she approaches us, weaving her way between the seated women, the woman who has called her says *tulou, tulou* on the child's behalf, her voice loud enough for the child to hear. The woman gives the child some Fijian tobacco: 'Give this tobacco to "Big Mother" [*nana levu*], to Grandmother Di Ma [*bubu Di Ma*].' The child takes the tobacco, and as she gets up to pass me on her way to another part of the room, the woman prompts her: 'Excuse me, excuse me [*tulou*], Mother of Manuel', and the girl whispers a barely audible *tulou*.

In telling the child to give the tobacco to 'Big Mother' (a term normally used to address MEZ), the woman made use of the term the child herself should use in addressing her grandmother and then extended it to show that 'Big Mother' and 'Grandmother Di Ma' are the same person. The term *Nana levu* ('Big Mother', normally used in address to MEZ) was not used by other children in addressing their grandmothers, nor was it used by *this* child to all her grandmothers (i.e. her classificatory grandmothers). Rather this was a special case where the term was used to a woman of high rank, where *Bubu* ('Grandmother') was used to commoner grandmothers and to less high-ranking chiefly women; so *Ratu levu*, 'Big Father', is used to address FEB, but also by some children to address or refer to a grandfather of high rank. This unusual use of the terms may be derived from a literal translation of the English 'grandmother' or 'grandfather'.

Adults actively teach children to use kin terms and forms of politeness. There are stock ways of initiating verbal exchanges with children. One may greet the child, for example 'Where are you going?' If the child replies, more questions follow about what the child ate at the last meal and where its mother is at present; or one may incite the child to sit on one's lap or beside one and then ask a series of questions about how to address the people sitting nearby. For example: 'Who is this?' and the answer comes: Father's Sister [*Nei*] or Little Father [*Tata lailai*, FYB] or Mother's Brother Maika [*momo Maika*] or Grandmother [*Bubu*]. If the child's replies are audible and correct, the adult may say: 'Oh my, thank you, my child. You *are* clever!' This type of conversation tends to occur with children between the ages of two and three and a half who are talking fairly distinctly. Sometimes, with a child under two and a half, there are also exchanges that teach the names of body parts, for example 'Where are your feet? Your nose? Your eyes?' And the child will grab his or her own foot or nose, or blink eyes in response. This interchange is a common one between children under two and a half and older children over six.

Seniority and discipline, fear and shame

Children rely on their peers for play and conversation; they are lively and forthcoming 'authorities' with younger children and humble audience with older children. This pattern appears to be set in

infancy and goes along with a timid and self-effacing deportment in
the company of those senior in age; this is commonly ascribed to
'shyness' or 'shame' [*madua*] or to 'fear' [*rere*; cf. Quain, 1948: 301;
Levy, 1973: 447–50). These sentiments are inculcated in the child
by ridicule, mockery, laughter or plain disapproval on virtually all
occasions that the child draws adult notice. By the age of four or so,
most children give the impression that they positively do not *want* to
be noticed by adults or, rather, by most people who are senior to
them. This behaviour is carried through in adult life: deportment
that combines humility with a quiet dignity is 'chiefly', while the
quintessence of bad manners is to presume beyond one's station (cf.
Quain, 1948: 302).

What is being impressed upon a growing child in *all* interactions
with people are the distinctions to be made among them with respect
to seniority and, ultimately, to rank. By the age of five the general
pattern for social interaction is set: one may assert oneself only in the
company of one's peers and one's juniors. All those who are older –
even by only a couple of years – have the right to tell one what to do
and to enforce compliance or punish disobedience by means of
physical discipline or the threat of it. One has no champions among
older people who may be *relied* upon to stand up for one, to save one
from a slap or a knock, or to rebuke the one who has administered it.

It must be stressed that the rights of seniority accrue to *all* those
who are older than oneself. A young child who disciplines one even
younger with a slap or a sharpish knock with the knuckles on the side
of the head is rarely rebuked – at least, I never saw any disapproval
other than an enquiring look from an adult to which the older child
would respond with an explanation. It seems to be a feature of the
importance given to seniority to take for granted the right of those
who are older to discipline younger ones. A child under five who
complains to Mother of another, perhaps only slightly older child, may
be sympathized with, but the other's behaviour often goes unques-
tioned. Indeed, sometimes the mother or other adult will side with the
older child and threaten a beating. Even if the mother is sympathetic,
others present may laugh and ridicule the child's tears, saying:
'Serve you right! Nice' [*Vinaka sara ga! Maleka*] This response to
childish distress becomes even more common as the child approaches
five, and once they are at school children are rarely seen to approach
their parents for support in any dispute with another child.

Seniority distinctions are strengthened by parental attitudes that *encourage* children to assert authority over younger siblings; a child of eleven stands virtually *in loco parentis* to a one of six and even to one of eight (cf. Quain, 1948: 308; Levy, 1973: 456). I often heard children aged nine to eleven told by Mother or other adult female kin to take the whisk broom or a stick to aid them in forcing compliance from a younger child who had ignored commands to come in or made some other show of defiance – the stick usually being used as a threat rather than in fact. If a child complains of bullying, no effort is usually made to redress the situation. The bully may be described as 'a bad child' and the other told to stay out of his or her way, but the situation is one that is accepted: older children are bound to assert themselves with those who are younger; a child has to sort out the matter for him- or herself.

While older children can, and do, discipline those younger than themselves, they are more often loving and indulgent and tend to patronize; an age gap of two or three years is sufficient for the older child to act as loving, as well as disciplining, parent. The loving 'parental' response is seen in spontaneous gifts of food to younger children. It is very common for an older child to give up some desirable snack food – fruit, a scone left over from breakfast, a piece of taro – to a younger child and to go without himself. My son, who accompanied me in the field, often told me that at mid-morning break at school he and the youngest child of our hosts' household were given scones or home-made doughnuts or a piece of taro by the older children of the house. My son was at this time aged eight; the youngest child of the household where we lived was six and the older children were both eleven.

Older children dry tears, break up quarrels, soothe unhappiness and dispense cuddles with as much readiness as they command and discipline. But they are unpredictable: they may pounce on one for some childish misdemeanour only to follow up with a series of squeezes and kisses that are well intentioned but may be rough enough to induce tears. I do not want to overemphasize the following conclusions, which are based very much on the general demeanour of village children under the age of five, on behaviour that I often saw repeated and led me to assume an attitude towards their elders that could not be elicited in speech. However, I think it is fair to say that children under five view their elders with a 'respect' that is compounded of fear and a desire to be like them, and to gain whatever their elders may have to give. Where those elders are co-siblings, parents and other close kin, 'fear' (perhaps too strong a word) is mixed, no doubt in greater measure, with love; this is evident in the concern which, in later life, is apparent in relations between close kin. Where the child's elders are less well known than are very close kin, the child under five is likely to treat them with a degree of circumspection and restraint that is remarkable given that by this age the child knows and is known by everyone in the village. The child's demeanour with all his or her elders other than those within the household is, I think, best described as apprehensive, a conclusion derived from observations like the following:

A boy aged three years four months is walking at breakfast time past the house of some close kin. The adults of the house are his FFZ's children; they and the boy's father are immediate cross-cousins. The relationship being a close one, he is called many times: 'Timoci, come here and drink tea. Come and have breakfast.' He gives a quick look round, but without altering his steady progress – somewhat faster than a child's usual dawdling pace. The woman (the boy's classificatory mother) holds up some food and calls again: 'Timoci, look. This doughnut is yours. Come here. This is yours to eat.' A home-made doughnut being a highly desirable item, the child pauses, turns, and begins walking slowly up to the house while the cries of the woman continue: 'Yes, that's right. Come here. This is for you.'

He comes to the common entrance near which the woman is sitting. But he does not come up the stairs and enter the house, nor does he put his head round the door. He stands to one side of the steps outside, in the woman's (and my own) line of vision but outside the line of vision of the others who are present. He looks at her with large eyes but says nothing and she takes two doughnuts and holds them out to him, saying '*kemu*' (yours to eat) in the flat tone that signifies the intention to give (the interrogative *kemu?* is a polite offering, meant to be refused.) She says: 'Are you afraid? Yes, you are afraid. Here, take it.' The child puts out his hand, takes the doughnuts and, without actually running, hurries away as fast as may be consistent with dignity. Meanwhile many remarks have been addressed to him by his *momo* (FFZS, classificatory mother's brother) to the effect that he must enter the house and drink tea, as well as questions about where he is going and what he had at home for breakfast. He answers none of these questions, all of which are asked in a jocular, bantering tone, and as he hurries off the woman laughs and remarks, loud enough for him to hear: 'He is afraid. He is always shy.' And all the others present laugh too.

On other occasions I saw variations on the same behaviour – for example once he took the offered food, and as soon as he had regained the flat ground at the foot of the *yavu* (foundation), he ran off towards his own house and was pursued by loud laughter and mocking cries of 'Run! Run!' [*Cici!*] Another time he came inside and sat down at the cloth to eat rice, only to be surprised by his *momo* (a man of twenty-five) who stealthily pressed the hot spoon taken from his tea against the boy's upper arm, causing him to shrink away and begin to sulk, though he did not cry out or burst into tears.

The children of the house who were his classificatory siblings (FFZD's children, a girl aged eleven and two boys aged five and eleven) treated his behaviour with indulgent or mocking amusement; they always gave him food when they could, but were likely to accompany this generosity with a gentle knock with the knuckles on the side of the head – a gesture with painful implications – or to aim a mock punch at his jaw. In their company the child entered audibly into conversation, but the adults could not elicit any speech from him that went beyond a whispered 'thank you' [*vinaka*] prompted by an adult who gave him food. This child was the youngest of four siblings, the one nearest him in age being a sister four years his senior.

Timidity in the face of those who are older is also fostered in young children by older boys and young men who will tease them by shouting or pretending to come after them with a stick, or make as if to punch them and laugh when the children scuttle away or shrink from the approaching fist. Many times I saw a young man take the spoon from his hot tea and suddenly place it against the arm or leg of a child seated nearby – on one of these occasions the child was aged one year and three months. This behaviour in young men and the mock-threatening behaviour of older boys of twelve or so is rarely objected to. Sometimes the mother or other female relative will prompt the child, saying: 'He is bad. Punch him.' A very young child may then punch out at the offender (as did the child of fifteen months mentioned above), but older children simply shrink away. Tears give rise to laughter and ridicule, as does any childish display of anger or sulking. The extent to which an inability to 'answer back' is internalized by Fijian children is apparent in Profile 31 in Stewart (1980: 111–13). Here a young man recounts his adolescent experience in a family where distressing arguments between his parents were common. He describes how his alienation from his family culminated in early manhood in a rebellion against parental authority: he drank alcohol and went dancing and 'didn't listen often to what they said'. However, in all this time, he only 'once exchanged arguments, which shocked them'.

This does not mean that older boys and young men are invariably harsh in their interaction with children. Indeed, those up to five or so may be hugged, kissed and sat down in the older boy's or young man's lap; but their behaviour is not predictable and by the age of three and a half or four most children seem to have learned to avoid them. Older girls and young women are more gentle and nurturing, much more likely to kiss or cuddle a child, to dispense food, engage the child in conversation and in general tolerate the presence of children in their near vicinity. However, they too are fairly strict disciplinarians and expect obedience and retiring behaviour from children.

Person and gender

Tamata, meaning 'person', also means a 'commoner' as distinct from a 'chief'. So while the term is sometimes generally used, it is impolite to use it in direct reference to another person. People tend rather to use specific terms – 'child', 'lady', 'gentleman', 'girl', 'boy' – in both reference and address. Note that with the exception of 'child' [*gone*] all these terms are gendered.

As the eldest legitimate child, a girl receives the same ritual attention at birth as does a boy. However, this is not true for her subsequent life. A boy's circumcision is attended by four days and nights of feasting, *yaqona*-drinking and ceremonial exchange and is a proud occasion for the child. Boys in Sawaieke are usually circumcised at around the age of eight or nine (cf. Quain, 1948: 134; Williams, 1858: 166; Erskine, 1853: 254). In Gau there is no ritual for a girl at puberty and her first menstruation seems to be entirely ignored, but menstrual blood does not seem to be in any way ritually defiling (cf. Thompson, 1940: 89; Quain, 1948: 315, Geddes, 1948: 317). However, Profile 27 in Stewart (1980: 99–101) recounts in the first person the memories of a young Fijian woman whose first menstruation was marked by four days of feasting, the use of a special ointment to make her skin smooth, and special teaching from her senior female kin as to the correct way to behave with male kin. We are not told where in Fiji this took place, but judging from the young woman's description of her dress, it must have been somewhere in Lau. In Moala there is a ceremony for the first time a girl goes sea-fishing (Sahlins, 1962: 187); I was told that this *should* be the case in Gau but that nowadays the occasion is not ceremonially observed. Hocart (1929: 149) speaks of a ceremonial confinement of the adolescent daughters of chiefs, but this practice no longer took place during his own time in Lau. Thomson (1908, 1968: 217), whose account owes much to Williams (1858, 1982: 160), describes the tattooing of girls' buttocks and pudenda just before puberty, a practice that was stopped by missionaries, presumably in the last century (see Milner, 1969; Gell, forthcoming).

A girl's sexuality must be 'taken care of' [*maroroi*] so that she does not shame her kin. Girls and women keep their genitals and thighs covered even while bathing only with other women; men, I am told, swim naked. A boy of six or seven may be laughed at for allowing his genitals to be seen; a little girl of the same age is soundly smacked. If a boy of two or three handles his genitals someone might remark drily, 'he takes hold of his *boci*', and others present will laugh. The reference to *boci* (uncircumcised penis) is not *tabu*. A girl of the same age who behaves similarly is smacked and scolded in outraged tones: 'Don't! It's forbidden. It's forbidden to touch it!' and no specific reference is made to her genitals (cf. Quain, 1948: 317–18). The only polite term is *ka vakamarama*, 'female thing', and it is rarely used. The common term *maga* is a term of abuse, as in *maga i tinamu*, 'your mother's cunt', said to someone in anger or to express surprise and disapprobation. 'Male' insults come a poor second in vehemence and popularity and are given by *kaisi na tamamu*, 'your father is low-class' (literally one taken prisoner in war) or, as a joking reprimand to a young man who speaks out of turn, *tiko lo o iko boci*, 'keep quiet, you're one of the uncircumcised'.

The division of labour within the subsistence economy means that men's and women's work tasks rarely overlap. Children's tasks do not so clearly differentiate boys and girls, but the distinction is 'set' by the time children reach puberty and their elders' example means that they are likely to be aware at a much earlier age of what constitutes appropriate work for each sex (cf. Quain, 1948: 311). Here I must remind the reader that men also govern. Women take part in local government via their leaders' attendance at council meetings. But their part in discussion and decision-making is minimal and tends to be confined to women's work, as when the village has to donate mats for an intervillage ceremonial occasion or to act as hosts to some central government delegation. Both men and women may become church officials, but all high offices are held by men. Similarly, though women teachers outnumber men, the post of head teacher in Gau's primary schools always fell to a man.

There is little differentiation in the tasks allotted to boys and girls. Children above age eight or so contribute significantly towards the everyday work of the household. They sweep, wash dishes, prepare and cook root vegetables, gather firewood, coconuts and fruit, grate coconut for *lolo* (coconut cream), watch younger children, lay the cloth for meals, carry water from pipe outlet to house or kitchen, shop and run messages, pick up rubbish and tidy up outside the house, and carry out innumerable other small tasks. The only gender-defined tasks for primary school children are, for girls: washing clothes and gathering shellfish and bait and, for boys: chopping firewood, weeding and helping in the gardens, feeding pigs and tending animals.

Children who attend Gau's secondary school are always weekly boarders, at home only on weekends, so children between thirteen and seventeen are not so noticeable in the divison of labour. But by the time children are twelve or thirteen there is a reliable division of labour such that girls carry out tasks traditionally allotted to women (with the exception of mat-making, which they have not yet learned) and boys confine themselves to work traditionally allotted to men. Boys of fourteen may even be cultivating their own garden as distinct from simply helping their fathers or older brothers.

Children have many opportunities to observe *yaqona*-drinking, village meetings and the rituals attendant upon church services, weddings, funerals, and so on, so a child's experience allows for learning the significance of gender distinctions. For example, a boy sees that even though his elder sister can order him about, the situation with adults is different: once a male attains the status of 'young man' [*cauravou*], his EZ ceases to give him orders. Avoidance relations come into full effect when people are in their late teens, but while an EZ may, on occasion, *ask* her YB to do something – for example to bring certain vegetables back from his garden – an EB's communication with his YZ, like a husband's to his wife, consists almost solely of orders. Elder sisters may formally expect both respect and obedience from younger siblings, but their influence is less powerful than that of elder brothers (see Stewart, 1980: 113 fn.).

Children's own conceptions of gender distinctions for adults were culled from an essay I set for the children in Classes 5 and 6 in the local primary school. There were twenty-three essays in all, of varying length; the children who wrote them ranged in age from ten years eleven months to fourteen years two months. The average age of Class 5 children was eleven and three-quarters; of Class 6 children twelve and three-quarters.

The essays were analysed to reveal their main themes and children's attitudes. One of the most interesting and striking points was the way children interpreted the theme set for them. They were asked to imagine the time in the future when they would be *turaga levu* or *marama levu*, words that may be taken to mean either adult man or woman on the one hand, or chief/high chief or chiefly lady on the other. An unambiguous reference to high rank in a man or woman requires the use of the terms *turaga bale* or *marama bale* (real chief or real chiefly lady) rather than *levu*, which may be taken simply to mean 'big'. *Turaga* means 'chief' and *marama* 'chiefly lady', but the words are always used politely to refer to men and women, irrespective of their rank by birth. The words *tagane* (male) and *yalewa* (female) are used for adults only when the speaker is being mildly rude – usually out of the referent's hearing. In their essays, nine out of twelve boys chose to interpret *turaga levu* to mean 'chief' or 'high chief' and nine out of eleven girls took *marama levu* to mean 'chiefly lady'.

These children emphasized how they would direct, oversee, teach and advise others, or simply tell them what to do; how they would call council meetings and how others would 'listen' to them (thus implying that others would owe them allegiance). They described how they would be admired and how they would 'lead'. One might assume from this that boys and girls saw themselves in similarly exalted positions in adult life, in command of themselves and of others; however, there was one highly important difference between boys and girls in this respect. While boys spoke of directing, advising, overseeing, leading and ordering 'people', girls spoke of doing all these things only in relation to women and children (cf. Amratlal *et al.*, 1975: 44–60). The extracts below are intended to give some idea of this marked difference between boys and girls.

> *Boy, 13 years 3 months*: I lead the district council meetings. I make a speech at the outset of a big gathering. When I have finished my speech I tell Komainabaka that he should also speak.

Note that district council meetings are those where representatives from every village meet to discuss matters of concern to the whole island, and that Komainabaka is the title of the man who was second in status to the paramount chief and would therefore speak after him.

> *Boy, 12 years 10 months*: When there is a big gathering I always go there and I just sit there above. I also do the village meetings [and they] also always listen properly to me. ... I want to show the people of the village that they should work hard at their duties.

Note that village meetings involve the entire community – men and women, young men and girls – and that to sit above is a sign of high status.

> *Boy, 11 years 10 months*: On other days I go to council meetings. I always sit 'above'. I always speak to the people. I give advice to the [male] elders, young men, women and girls.

> *Boy, 12 years 7 months*: Accordingly I lead [or am in charge of] us all in this land. When I am tired of business, such as

> when work is to be done, I just say once and for all that the [other, lower-status] people should do it.

Boy, 11 years 10 months: If I am a High Chief in Gau I shall help my people every day. I shall always care for them all ... Let me speak softly [i.e. gently] to my people. ... Let me lay down the law to my people.

Boy, 11 years 5 months: I shall see to it that the people work. I shall help the people in working every day ... I shall teach the people in the land every single day.

Boy, 11 years 3 months: I shall always teach my people that they should be good-tempered [i.e. kind-hearted]. ... My orders are good ones since the people always follow them. ... My people will grow so as to always follow my chiefly example.

Girl, 12 years 10 months: Every day I advise the ladies about their everyday life. I also advise the children about their going to school. I teach the ladies ... I order them to do their duty [or tasks] well. I lead them. ... I see to it that they eat good food. ... It is also seen to that the men do their duty well.

This girl speaks specifically of advising and teaching women and uses the active voice throughout in speaking of what she will do. However, when she talks of overseeing men she uses the passive voice, so that the matter of who is in fact doing the overseeing becomes equivocal.

Girl, 12 years 8 months: I always call my ladies that we may go to council. One day I call the men, women, young men and girls. When they are all there inside the hall, Takalaigau then makes a speech. When Takalaigau's speech is over, then Tui Koviko speaks.

This girl sees herself in a position to call all the people together, but she does not, when they are gathered, take a leading part in the proceedings and allots the speech-making to the paramount chief and one of the clan chiefs. Later on in her essay she speaks of a communal meal, but does not say that she initiates it; she describes herself as thanking those who cooked it, but the thanking is of the informal rather than the speech-making variety.

> *Girl, 12 years 6 months*: I advise the ladies that they should clean up their sides of the houses and their kitchens. ... Each time it is I who sound the whistle that we may gather [i.e. for a meeting] in the village hall.

This girl refers exclusively to women throughout her essay. She makes no reference to 'people' or to men; the whistle is sounded only for Women's Association meetings. It is the conch that calls people to a village meeting.

> *Girl, 10 years 11 months*: I lead all the ladies in Gau. I always call all the ladies here that we may have a council meeting.

> *Girl, 13 years 2 months*: I inspect [or oversee] the ladies. I lead our women's meetings.

> *Girl, 11 years 8 months*: It is my work to lead the ladies in Gau. It is for me to oversee the ladies in the whole of Gau. So that they may do the things they should do.

> *Girl, 11 years 6 months*: If I shall say that they should each bring here a mat and a bottle of oil, they will approve [this proposition]. It is my duty to oversee the women in Gau. Accordingly I initiate [literally 'make happen'] the meetings of the Women's Association in Gau.

The bringing of mats and coconut oil for a ceremonial exchange is always a woman's duty in the case if mats, and usually so in the case of oil, though bottles of oil are sometimes prepared and brought by men. It is unlikely that the first 'they' above includes males, because in the rest of her essay the girl refers exclusively to women.

> *Girl, 10 years 8 months*: I shall help my people. I shall always care for them. I shall always help weak [or ill] people. I shall not be arrogant. I shall be present at all the gatherings. I shall lead them in [doing] the right thing.

This girl is the only one who refers unequivocally to 'people' and envisions herself as one who will be in a position respected by the entire community. However, she does not speak of advising, ordering, teaching or leading – except that she 'leads' in setting a good example. She emphasizes throughout how she will care for the people and does not make any mention of commanding them.

Only one of the girls (aged thirteen) saw herself in adult life as in a position where she would be able to tell other people, specifically including village chiefs, what to do. However, she envisions herself as *outside* the traditional system, as an employee of the government whose work it is to inspect villages. Part of her essay reads:

> I always go to each of the village chiefs to tell them that I come from a government department. I want to put down here the things that I am going to show [or reveal to] the village chiefs: one, that the grass in the village should be cut; two, that [all] parts of the village should be cleaned; three, that the [empty] tins should be picked up ...

This girl does not talk of telling traditional chiefs [*turaga ni vanua*] what to do; she refers only to village chiefs [*turaga ni koro*]. This post is held by a man elected to it; it is entirely administrative and one that, by comparison with the position of traditional chief, has very little kudos attached to it.

These children's essays reflect values predominant in the village, the value accorded to high rank and to seniority in general. All the children, with the exception of two of the girls, emphasized the power they envisioned would be theirs in adult life. Of the three boys who took *turaga levu* to mean simply adult man, or 'big man', one saw himself as a doctor, one as a policeman, and the other as *turaga ni koro* (elected chief of a village). They tended to focus on the powerful or bossy aspect of these positions, on the ability they would have to oversee others and direct their behaviour. With the possible exception of the boy who saw himself as *turaga ni koro* they too, like the boys who wrote of being a traditional chief, assumed that they would be in positions of power over 'people' – i.e. including women.

It is readily apparent from these essays that gender is bound to be a factor in the ascription of status, and that it is therefore also going to be a factor in the way hierarchy is constructed in terms of above/below.

Conclusion

I have tried in this chapter to give some general ideas of the way children's understanding of their rights and responsibilities, of gender and of relative seniority, is learned in interaction with their peers and seniors. It is no accident that a number of the examples of interaction described in this chapter are concerned with the dispensing of food, affection and discipline. All these behaviours are defining attributes of kinship, especially of the close and always hierarchical relations *within* the household, and are encompassed by *veilomani* – love between kin. It is perhaps unnecessary to point out that disciplinary procedures such as ridicule, mockery or beating are not precluded by this love; proper parental concern requires that a child be surely taught that presumptuous behaviour in relation to one's seniors is virtually always rude and even entirely antisocial. It should also be stressed that the general adult style of interaction with children is such that the adult speaks and the child has only to listen and obey. On the other hand, open, outgoing and lively behaviour is expected amongst one's peers and it is in this context that one can – and should – assert oneself, joke, play and even fight. Note, however, that one's peers, by definition, *cannot* be members of one's own household.

9 Understanding above/below

This chapter concerns a series of tasks I set for primary school children. These tasks were intended to discover what children of different ages understood about people's relation to one another on the above/below axis. In social intercourse inside the house, church or hall and especially in ritual contexts, this is the dominant spatial construct; moreover, the behavioural constraints it imposes are striking, so it seemed important to look at the process by which children come to constitute its 'meaning'.

Within the house, above is the place of senior men; in most public buildings, it is the place of chiefs; below is the place of females. Church space is used somewhat differently. There above is the place of chiefs, but the space below is occupied by the congregation in such a way that high-status women are on a level with male elders, above married women and men, who are seated above girls and young men – the sexes being segregated with men seated on the right as one faces the pulpit, and women on the left. Here, for rank/seniority statuses below chief, males and females are on the same level for a given rank/seniority category, an observation that underlines the ambiguity of women's position in the contemporary hierarchy.

These data suggest that in Fiji hierarchy is merged with the representation of space – but is this indeed the case? What does above/below mean to those whose behaviour it appears to govern; do they take it to be an attribute of certain spaces or an attribute of persons in relation to one another? If it is an attribute of persons, do notions of gender interact with notions of rank/seniority to constitute hierarchy? Further, it seems that ritual – meals, *yaqona*-drinking, church services, meetings – is crucial to the constitution of the above/below axis. But *do* the ritualized aspects of people's behaviour work to constitute social hierarchy at the ideological level? Does the image in ritual of ordered, stratified social relations merely reflect an ideological order apparent in notions of the relations between ranked lineages, chief and commoner, husband and wife, and elder brother and younger brother? Or is the image that may be derived from people's ritual behaviour *itself* the primary source from which contemporary hierarchy is derived?

By looking at what children understand about above/below, one can perhaps begin to answer these questions.

Children's drawings of 'a gathering'

Children are not admitted to *yaqona*-drinking, though a toddler or two may be present on informal occasions, especially at home. But children do have ample opportunity for observation. Those as young as four or five have the habit of 'peeping' [*iro*]; so any lively gathering in house or village hall attracts small groups of children, who range themselves outside the building and peer in at the proceedings through chinks and crevices in the bamboo slats or other material that form the walls. School-age children may have to penetrate a *yaqona*-drinking group to deliver a message or suchlike. So, despite their formal exclusion from *yaqona*-drinking and other adult activities, children are in a position to form their own ideas about their nature. 'Little young men' [*cauravou lulai*, boys aged about fifteen and over] are admitted to *yaqona*-drinking at around age seventeen primarily as mixers and servers of the drink; young women [*gone yalewa*, literally 'girls'] begin to attend village-wide gatherings at around age seventeen or so.

The data below come from my analysis of drawings and commentary on them provided by sixty-seven children who, in 1982, made up the entire roll of the Sawaieke District Primary School. These children ranged in age from five years ten months, the youngest child in Class 1, to fourteen years two months, the oldest in Class 6. The drawings, commentary on them and the essays written by older children were the first tasks I set. They were freely devised so as to elicit relatively unstructured information on children's notions of status distinctions on the above/below axis and to find out the extent to which they themselves made use of this dimension to differentiate status.

For their drawings children were given the following instructions in Fijian:

but what kind of big gathering? Perhaps relations are diff acc to gathering

198   *Making sense of hierarchy*

Just imagine that there is a big gathering going on in the village hall in Sawaieke. All the people are sitting in the village hall: the women, the young men, the girls and the men. They are drinking *yaqona* and having a good time. Please draw nicely everything that you can. Show all the people who are there drinking *yaqona*.

The children did the drawings in class, each child being separated from the next to prevent systematic copying. Later they gave me their drawings, and in individual conversation with each child I labelled the drawings in accordance with the answers to the following questions:

Who are these people? Are there any women here? Where are they sitting? Please point them out. What about the men – are there any men? Please point to them – where are they sitting? Is the high chief here? What is his name? Where is he sitting? And are there some young men? Show me the young men – where are they sitting? Is there a chiefly lady here? Where is she? What is her name? Where is she sitting? And what about the girls – are there any girls? Where are they sitting?

Often I had no need to go through all the questions; once they were started off, many children volunteered the desired information. Or one of the early answers might forstall further enquiry – for example, one boy aged nine told me that there were three chiefs sitting above and all the other figures represented were young men. Were there no women or girls? No, there were none. Where I had to ask the full series of questions, I tried to alternate their order so as to minimize bias due to order effects across children. Note that my questions distinguished only three levels of rank/seniority with respect to each sex: I asked about a high chief and a chiefly lady, men and women, and young men and girls. However, the children spontaneously distinguished up to five different levels of rank/seniority as being possible for men and four for women.

In the examples shown here, I have substituted symbols to differentiate status, but otherwise the arrangement and density of the figures, their relative size, and so on, are exactly in accordance with the drawings themselves (see Appendix 1.).

Owing to the difficulty I should have in analysing the above/below problem in tandem with variation in respect of the way children approached perspective, I have entirely ignored perspective to concentrate on what children *told* me was the case. In other words, I might be told that a figure pointed out to me as 'the high chief', *na turaga levu*, was seated 'right up high', *i cake sara*, and that others were seated 'below', *i ra*, even when the layout on the page would not perhaps have led me to this conclusion. Ignoring perspective, then, the drawings were analysed to discover:

(a) the pattern of opposition given for the positions above [*i cake*] and below [*i ra*]
(b) the number and kind of rank distinctions made for each sex
(c) marks of distinction that set one person off against the others.

PATTERNS OF OPPOSITION (SEE TABLE 6).

When the poles above and below are taken together, a total of 37 oppositions may be distinguished from one another across all 67 drawings. However, considered alone, the position above has only 6 possible variations, the position below 17 possible variations. Looking at the two poles of the opposition as they varied together, the 37 different types were further broken down into 10 distinct types of drawing. The results across all 67 children are shown in Figure 20, together with a description of the various opposition types.

In reference to Figure 20, the reader will see that I have numbered each drawing type. The progression from Type 1 to Type 10 accords with the median age of children whose drawings display a given pattern of opposition; this is shown in symbol form with a key at the bottom of the page. Children are grouped according to age and sex: a small circle represents a single girl and a small triange a single boy, their respective ages being apparent by reference to their position on the horizontal axis. So, for example, the youngest child to produce a Type 5 drawing may be seen to be a boy aged six years three months, while the eldest are two boys aged nine years seven months.

WHO SITS ABOVE?

The first problem to be answered concerns who sits above. Looking just at the pattern of opposition shown for Drawing Types 2-10 and

Drawing Type	Pattern of Opposition		Number of children
1	?	?	1
2	▲	?	2
	△	?	1
3	▲	△▲	2
	▲	▲	1
4	▲	▲○/▲○⊙	8
	▲	▲⊙	1
	△	▲▲○⊙	1
5	▲	○/○⊙	12
	▲	⊙	3
	△	○	1
6	▲	△	3
	▲	▲▲○	1
	▲	▲▲○/▲○⊙	2
	△	△	1
	▲	▲⊙	1
	△	○	1
	△	▲⊙	2
7	▲⊙	▲⊙	1
	▲⊚	△△⊚○	1
	▲◉	△△▲○⊙	1
	△	▲⊙	1
	▲⊚	○	1
	▲⊚	▲⊙	1
	▲⊚	△▲⊚○⊙	1
8	△	○/○⊙	5
	△	▲⊚○⊙	1
9	△	▲○/▲○⊙/▲▲○	5
	△	▲⊙	1
10	△	▲▲○	3
	△	▲○⊙	1

Total no. of different oppositions: 37

Possibilities i cake:

?	Drawing Type 1	1
▲	Drawing Types 2, 3, 4, 5, 6	35
△	Drawing Types 2, 4, 5	3
△	Drawing Types 6, 7, 8, 9, 10	22
▲⊙	Drawing Type 7	1
▲⊚	Drawing Type 7	4
▲◉	Drawing Type 7	1
	Total:	67

Possibilities i ra:

△▲	Drawing Type 3	2
△	Drawing Types 3, 6	4
▲○	Drawing Types 4, 9	4
▲○⊙	Drawing Types 4, 6, 9	9
▲⊙	Drawing Types 4, 6, 7, 9	8
▲▲○⊙	Drawing Type 4	1
○	Drawing Types 5, 6, 7, 8	15
○⊙	Drawing Type 5	5
⊙	Drawing Type 5	3
▲△○	Drawing Types 6, 9, 10	6
△	Drawing Type 6	1
△▲⊚○	Drawing Type 7	1
△▲▲○⊙	Drawing Type 7	1
△▲⊚○⊙	Drawing Type 7	1
▲⊚○⊙	Drawing Type 8	1
▲○⊙	Drawing Type 10	1
?	Drawing Types 1, 2	4
	Total:	67

Table 6 Patterns of opposition for cake/ra *in drawings*

excluding Type 7 (which I discuss later), it is clear that the matter of who sits above is a relatively unambiguous one for the children. Thirty-five out of 67 children showed the high chief above alone, while 22 showed a small group of chiefs, *including* the high chief, as 'sitting above' [*dabe i cake*]. So 57 out of 67 children said that figures in their drawings whom they designated chiefs (i.e. *turaga ni vanua* or *o ira na malo*) were 'sitting above'.

In other words, high rank is seen to pertain to a very few individuals; other people are classified into groups that are very

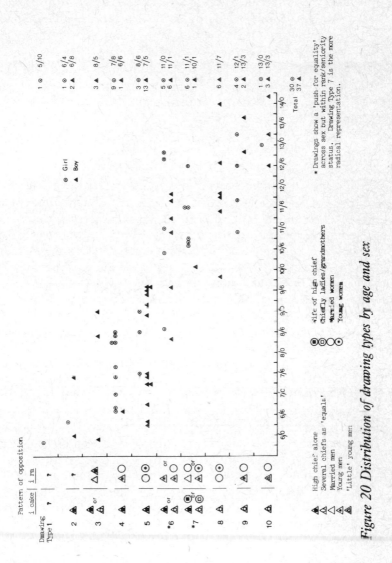

Figure 20 Distribution of drawing types by age and sex

much more inclusive and less highly differentiated with respect to internal variations in seniority which, for example, might make one married man superior to another married man by virtue of higher rank or age seniority. This finding holds for all children, and is indifferent to variation in the number of rank/seniority distinctions children make. There is a noticeable change with age so that children eight and a half and over tend to show two to four chiefs together above, with only 15 out of 43 children showing the high chief above on his own. In accordance with these data, above may be defined as the place of chiefs.

WHO SITS BELOW?

The question of who sits below is a more difficult one. Drawing Types 4 and 9 show females, considered as an undifferentiated group, intermingled with and so on the same level as young men. The entire group is said to be below. However, Drawing Types 5 and 8 show females only seated below, differentiated from and definitely below young men. Type 10 may be read as similar to Types 5 and 8 in that here females are shown intermingled with 'little young men' and, as a group, are said to be 'below' young men.

However, there is a strong interaction here between the task and the sex of the child who is carrying it out. For Types 4 and 9 it is girls (13 out of 16 children) who say that young men too are seated below along with women. For Types 5, 8, and 10 it is boys (22 out of 26 children) who say that women only are below or, in the case of boys doing Type 10 drawings, below alongside 'little young men' [*cauravou lalai*], this being the humblest of the rank/seniority statuses for men. In other words, girls prefer to say that young men are below along with women and girls, while boys prefer to say that only women and girls are below. This preference holds for older children (twelve to fourteen) with 4 out of 6 girls continuing to place young men along with women below, and 5 out of 7 boys either giving women the low position or seating them alongside 'little young men' and below young men.

A 'PUSH FOR EQUALITY' ACROSS GENDER

Drawing Types 6 and 7 show a 'push for equality' across gender and within rank/seniority levels, with Type 7 being the more radical representation. The disposition of figures shown in these drawings of *yaqona*-drinking is virtually never seen in real life. This is especially true for Type 7 Drawings, which may show the high chief seated beside his wife above, with other chiefs seated beside their wives, and so on 'down' through the rank/seniority levels, with young men and girls seated together below. Husbands and wives practise avoidance in public gatherings; they do not sit side by side. The typical disposition of people in a mixed gathering is that shown earlier in Figure 8: men and women do not mingle together but rather form discrete groups according to their gender and rank/ seniority status. Only two or three times in eighteen months did I attend a gathering where the situation came anywhere near being like that shown in Drawing Types 6 and 7.

One of these times occurred during the New Year holiday season in 1982, when the ladies of Sawaieke (some twenty or so) visited the neighbouring village of Nawaikama (about 3.5 kilometres from Sawaieke) in response to an invitation from Nawaikama men. No Sawaieke men accompanied the ladies on their visit. Sawaieke women, considered as a group, rank above or on the same level as Nawaikama men, whose village is one of eight owing allegiance to Sawaieke. So, on this occasion, several high-status women from Sawaieke sat above the *tanoa* side by side with Nawaikama chiefs; the Sawaieke women as a group sat towards the top of the room and along one side, on a level, and sometimes intermingled, with Nawaikama men; all Nawaikama young men [*cauravou*] were definitely below Sawaieke women.

This unusual situation arose largely because no Sawaieke men were present and because it was a holiday occasion from which lots of fun was expected – dancing, flirtatious joking, and other daring behaviour. It is true that when Sawaieke women visit villages that owe allegiance to their own, a few chiefly ladies from Sawaieke are always invited to take their place above the *tanoa* and will do so as a matter of course; but, if their own men are present, these ladies are bound to adopt seating positions that are unambiguously below their men (husbands, elder brothers, fathers-in-law, etc.). Only when unaccompanied by their own men may chiefly ladies from Sawaieke, in another village, sit on a level above the *tanoa* and side by side with the traditional chiefs of that village.

This means that children who did Drawing Types 6 and 7 can only rarely, if ever, have actually seen anything like the situation they depicted. Type 6 Drawings are less extreme than Type 7. They show the high chief or a very few chiefs together above, and it is only for rank/seniority levels below 'chief' that one finds a 'push for equality' – that is, women may be intermingled with men, girls with young men. Type 6 Drawings vary widely in disposition of figures, but they all share a certain feature: at least some, possibly more senior, women are said to be on a level with or just below men, and unequivocally above young men.

Yaqona is drunk every day, and each week there is at least one gathering of men and women in the hall for the same purpose, so it seems unlikely that children would choose to depict a highly unusual situation when asked to draw people drinking *yaqona*. Rather it looks as if some children were asserting what would be the case according to rank and age seniority *if gender were not a factor*. So, around age eleven, some – but not all – children had abstracted from their experience a notion of status relations as ordered in terms of rank and seniority, and ignored the gender principle that makes females in general inferior to males on the above/below axis. They therefore depicted situations they can never have seen – for example a man seated beside his wife in a gathering.

It is interesting to note that of the 18 children who asserted a certain quality of gender within rank/seniority level, 11 were girls, while of the 7 who made the more radical representation in Type 7 Drawings, 6 were girls. Reference to Figure 20 shows that the preference for Type 6 and 7 Drawings is most prevalent between ten and twelve, with 12 out of 17 children in this age group making rank/seniority the main principle in ascribing social status. Type 7 is the more radical choice in that it asserts equality across gender within status for most rank/seniority statuses from high chief's on down. This radical assertion of an interaction between rank and seniority in ascribing status does not occur before Class 4 nor beyond Class 5. Two older girls in Class 6 (the final year of primary school) did Type 6 Drawings, where a less extreme version of the rank/seniority principle puts married women above young men, who are put on a level with girls. All other children in Class 6 show a high chief or a small group of chiefs above, with women and girls, or women, girls and young men at the pole below. Those seated below seem to be regarded as a group whose members are of more or less equal status.

But to put *all* females over age seventeen or eighteen on the same level with young men is, effectively, to ignore rank/seniority differences among women.

RANK/SENIORITY DISTINCTIONS

Children who produce Type 7 Drawings showing a radical 'push for equality' across gender use three, four and five rank/seniority distinctions for men and two, three or four for women; those who make Type 6 Drawings – the less radical choice– tend to make fewer distinctions within women, the majority showing only one or two categories of women (9 out of 11 children); see Table 7.

Table 7

(i) *No. of rank/seniority distinctions made for* MEN
by children doing Drawing Types 6, 7, 8, 9, & 10

	5	4	3	2	1	
Type 6	4	3	4			re.11 chn 8:4 −12:10
Type 7	2	4	1			re. 7 chn 10:1 12:6
Types 8, 9, 10	7	9				re.16 chn 9:10–14:2

(ii) *No. of rank/seniority distinctions made for* WOMEN
by children doing Drawing Types 6, 7, 8, 9 & 10

	4	3	2	1	
Type 6		2	5	4	re.11 chn 8:4 −12:10
Type 7	3	3	1		re. 7 chn 10:1 −12:6
Types 8, 9, 10	3	3	7	3	re.16 chn 9:10–14:2

Looking now at Table 7 (ii), if we compare the number of rank/seniority distinctions made for women by children doing Drawing Types 6 and 7 with those by children over nine and three-quarters who have made other choices, we can see that the latter children make as many rank/seniority distinctions for women as other children. Nevertheless they decline to *use* them. Despite their ability to distinguish female statuses they seem to prefer to class all women together, or to class all women together with young men, and effectively assert that the different categories may be equated so that all members are considered to be seated below.

Young men (or 'little young men', if both distinctions are made) may be considered the defining marker for the place below when rank differentiations are made for men. However, women may be treated as an undifferentiated group and placed as such below, even when rank distinctions have been made for them, and so it seems that the term 'below' is defined by being the place of women.

AGE VARIATIONS

With regard to overall variation by age, the drawings show that above/below figures in the youngest children's ideas: the high chief

Table 8: *No. of rank/seniority distinctions*

No. of:	Distinctions for MEN						for WOMEN				
	5	4	3	2	1	0	4	3	2	1	0
AGE											
5 yr+			1	1					1		1
6 yr+			3	4	1			1	2	5	
7 yr+		1	3	4	1			1	2	6	
8 yr+		4	4	1					5	3	1
9 yr+	1	5	2	1				1	3	4	1
10 yr+	3	2	2				2	1	3	1	
11 yr+	3	5	2				1	4	3	2	
12 yr+	3	3	1				1	1	3	2	
13 yr+	3	1					1		2	1	
14 yr+	2						1	1			
Total:	15	21	18	11	2		6	10	24	24	3

is above and females, or females and young men, are below; but they are not yet using the above/below axis to make further rank/seniority distinctions. Table 8 shows that up to age eight the majority of children are making two or three distinctions for men and one or two for women. At eight-plus they begin to distinguish further ranks of men using three and four distinctions, but still only one or two for women. Not until age ten do they begin to use with any reliability three or four distinctions for women, but over half of the children are still making only one or two.

Table 9

(i) *No. of rank/seniority distinctions made for* MEN

	5	4	3	2	1	0	Total
By boys	10	13	4	8	2	–	37
By girls	5	8	14	3	–	–	30

(ii) *No. of rank/seniority distinctions made for* WOMEN

	4	3	2	1	0	Total
By boys	2	5	8	19	3	37
By girls	4	5	16	5	–	30

There is an interaction here with a child's sex (see Table 9). Boys differentiate statuses for men more finely than do girls; girls differentiate statuses for women more finely than do boys. So the majority of boys (23 out of 37) make four or five distinctions for men, where most girls (22 out of 30) make three or four. For female statuses the reverse finding holds: the majority of girls (25 out of 30) distinguish two or more statuses for women, while the majority of boys (22 out of 37) show one or none at all.

Despite this interaction, there is a noticeable tendency around age eleven, even given the introduction (at age ten) of four possible statuses for women, for older children to continue to distinguish only one or two rank/seniority statuses for women. For children over eleven, 8 out of 13 boys and 5 out of 10 girls make only one or two distinctions among women. It seems that while they are probably able to make more than one or two distinctions for women, these children do not regard such distinctions as of any great significance and tend to ignore them.

This accords with the way drawings by children of twelve and over are fairly equally distributed over Types 8, 9, and 10 (10 out of 13 drawings): Here children seem more conscious of ambiguity in the position of 'high chief' when compared with other chiefs, but they seem to reconstitute too a definition of below as the place of young men against other ranks of men, or of women as an undifferentiated group against the ranks of men and on a level with, or below, young men.

In other words, these older children have constructed a principle of hierarchy in terms of a relative ranking on the above/below axis, a principle that incorporates gender as a complexly interacting factor that tends to make status distinctions for women of marginal importance. Children doing Drawing Types 8, 9, and 10 no longer construct a simple hierarchical relation like the majority of six-to-nine-year-olds; they do not see only its extremes: chief above and women, or women and young men, below. Nor do they attempt to make status differences solely the product of an interaction between rank and seniority, like some of the nine-to-twelve-year-olds. So they no longer depict older persons of chiefly birth as always above younger persons whose rank by birth is irrelevant. Rather, they now seem to realize that the rank/seniority principle, though it may be expressed in general terms, also implies possible exceptions, and that these are largely clustered around a gender distinction that makes females in general inferior to males.

I take Type 9 Drawings to be the most sophisticated, because they introduce some ambiguity at both poles of the above/below axis. They allow that several chiefs, including the high chief, may be considered more or less equals, and that the high chief is not – at least in Sawaieke – always unambiguously the 'highest'. In addition, young men are said to be below on a level with women, and again this gives a truer picture of day-to-day relations, for whether young men as a status category may be said to be above all women is a matter that varies according to the status of the women who are present and the sex of the person making the judgement. Given the relative sophistication of Type 9 Drawings, it is perhaps not surprising that they do not appear before age ten years eleven months and are not a popular choice – only six children making this type of representation.

MARKS OF DISTINCTION

There is little tendency up to age seven and a half to separate the high chief off from other figures, though he may be shown aligned with the *tanoa* (containing the *yaqona*) and next to it. However, at seven and a half children begin to leave more space around the figure they designate high chief or, in a few cases, show him seated in a chair, so that he is literally above others. This use of the chair to mark high rank shows that children are extrapolating information from contexts *outside yaqona*-drinking where, except in the case of a high chief of the most exalted variety (like the Prime Minister, Ratu Sir Kamisese Mara, or his former Deputy and now Governor General, Ratu Sir Penaia Ganilau),no one ever sits in a chair, and using it in their drawings to make the chief's position clear.

The four youngest to draw in a chair were aged five years eleven months, six and a half, seven years three months and eight years five months. There are two drawings by older children where a chair appears, but these are more sophisticated. So, in a Type 7 Drawing by a girl aged ten years eight months, the high chief is on the same level on the page as his wife and each of them is said to be above, the high chief has below him a couple of elders, married men, and young men, while below his wife sit grandmothers, married women and young men. This child said of her drawing: 'Both the high chief and his wife are sitting right up above, but it is different because the high chief is sitting in a chair and his wife is sitting on the mat.' In other words, both the high chief and his wife ranked above all others, but within their relationship the high chief ranked above his wife.

The oldest child to draw in a chair was a boy aged twelve years seven months, who produced a Type 8 Drawing for which he described a small group of named chiefs as 'sitting above' [*dabe i cake*]. But he seemed a bit concerned about the ambiguity of this situation and wanted to distinguish the high chief from other chiefs. He said to me: 'Look, these few chiefs are all sitting above, but the high chief is sitting in a chair and the *tanoa* is facing him.' I asked him if the high chief usually sat in a chair and he said. 'No, only here [i e in his drawing] so that he may be seen.'

From age seven years three months up to twelve years ten months rank is also marked by drawing the high chief larger than other figures and/or leaving more space around him. Older children who show a number of chiefs seated together above tend to draw them the same size, but leave plenty of space both between the chiefs themselves and between chiefs and all other people shown. This strategy is introduced at age eight and a half and still in use at age fourteen; as a rank marker it is a matter of fact: chiefs *do* sit with more space between them, and between themselves and all others (see Figure 8).

Two other rank markers are commonly used in the drawings. The first is given by the child's showing the rope that leads from the *tanoa* to the high chief. This rope is used only on important ceremonial occasions *before* the serving and drinking begin, when it is coiled back under the *tanoa*, but it is an empirical rank marker and the children use it as such. The depiction of the rope occurs between the ages of nine years ten months and twelve years seven months, but is most common for children from eleven and a half to eleven years ten months (5 out of 8 children).

A more subtle and at the same time more ambiguous marker is given by showing the *taki*, or serving of *yaqona*; 23 out of 67 children depict one or more young men in the act of serving. Most children show *yaqona* being served to the figure designated as high chief and to one or two other people (men and women). Older children may display a better understanding of the *taki* by depicting only one young man in the act of serving the high chief: 5 out of the 11 children over twelve who use this rank marker do so in this manner. In the empirical situation, no one *ever* drinks or is served at the same time as the high chief. In depicting a single young man serving the high chief, some of the older children appear to be drawing on knowledge that the order of drinking is important, and that 'the high chief drinks first' and on his own.

Children's essays on 'the gathering'

After they had completed their drawings, but *before* they were questioned about them, children in Classes 3 to 6 inclusive wrote a story about a gathering. This task was meant as a simple check on the drawings, so I do not go into much detail about it. Suffice it to say that children were asked to write a story about a big gathering in the village hall where people were drinking *yaqona* and having lots of fun.

Since the topic was so freely described, the essays were not necessarily related to the drawings; but in no case did the two forms of representation by a given child contradict one another; often the essay independently corroborated the coding type I had ascribed to a drawing. Of a total of 43 essays, 32 refer either to 'rank markers' and/or describe the social status of the participants with reference to their disposition in space.

The essays were virtually unstructured by myself and written *before* children were questioned about the drawings, so the significance of spontaneous description like the following cannot be discounted. 'The chief sits above, the young men sit round the *tanoa*, the women sit below' – this by a boy of nine years two months who did a Type 5 Drawing showing the high chief above and women below. The following two extracts are both by girls who did Type 7 Drawings showing a radical 'push for equality' across gender and within rank.

> *Age 11 years 6 months*: Takalaigau [the high chief] and the Minister and Lady Takalaigau and the Minister's wife are seated above.

> *Age 12 years 6 months*: Takalaigau sits above. The men also sit above. Some of the men sit below. A few of the women sit above and some of them sit below ... those who look after the *yaqona* sit in the middle.

And finally this, from a girl aged eight years five months who did a Type 4 Drawing showing the high chief alone above and women and young men together below:

> Takalaigau sits above and Ratu Laua [considered second in rank] comes next. The women sit below and so do the young men who look after the *yaqona*.

Children's labelling of prepared drawings

This section describes data derived from the next task I set for 47 children ranging in age from six and a half to fourteen years two months. (A minor flu epidemic, which affected many of the younger children, prevented all 67 children from participating.) The children were given 10 prepared drawings and asked to label them in response to my instructions.

The prepared drawings showed seated figures drawn in a simple and schematic style so that they could be said to be male or female, young or old, according to my own or the child's wishes. (That they are also rather odd-looking may be blamed on my lack of drawing talent and the exigencies of fieldwork.) The drawings fell into one of three categories according to whether they showed people drinking *yaqona*, eating meals, or in meetings. Specific instructions were given for each drawing, but in general children were asked to label the figures to show which were men, which were young men, which were women and which were girls. They might be asked to show the high chief or his wife or asked to decide themselves whether this person was present at all, and if so to indicate which figure represented him or her; they were also asked to indicate the position in which each of the figures was seated.

Responses to these drawings were analysed to discover the extent to which children used the plane of the page to distinguish various status categories, and how consistently they did so. Note that the disposition of figures on the page and their orientation to one another, and to salient objects like the *tanoa*, was varied in such a way that the place above might be at the top or the bottom plane of the page or to one side; similarly the place below might be at the top or the bottom plane of the page or to one side.

The prediction tested was that for drawings of meals and *yaqona*-drinking children would be more likely to make consistent use of the plane of the page to distinguish statuses than they would for drawings depicting 'meetings'. Each response was judged as 'consistent', 'inconsistent', or 'not using' the plane of the page to establish an above/below axis, on which statuses were distinguished from one another. The drawings were rated by independent judges using a measure that gave a score of 3 to a response judged 'consistent', 2 to an 'inconsistent' response and 1 to a response judged to be 'not using'. The means for boys and girls across the three categories are shown in Table 10.

A sign test was used to compare these results. The prediction was that there would be no difference in consistency for children's responses to drawings depicting *yaqona*-drinking and meals, and that

Table 10 *Summary of means*

	Meetings	Meals	*Yaqona*-drinking
BOYS	2.48	2.76	2.81
GIRLS	2.29	2.79	2.79

the consistency of their responses to either of these situations would be greater than the consistency of their response to drawings depicting meetings. Thus, for both boys and girls, their responses were compared for drawings showing (i) *yaqona*-drinking and meals, (ii) *yaqona*-drinking and meetings, and (iii) meals and meetings. See Table 11 for results (these are not independent tests; the same data were used twice).

Tables 10 and 11 show that not only was there, overall, a high level of consistency in children's responses to the drawings, but that they fulfilled the prediction that there would be greater consistency of response to drawings of meals and *yaqona*-drinking than to drawings of meetings.

Table 11 *Summary table of significance levels*

HO: H1:	*Yaqona*−Meals *Yaqona*=Meals	*Yaqona*−Meetings *Yaqona*>Meetings	Meals−Meetings Meals>Meetings
BOYS	no significant difference	*Yaqona*>Meetings significant at 0.001, one tail	Meals>Meetings significant at 0.004, one tail
GIRLS	no significant difference	*Yaqona*>Meetings significant at 0.001, one tail	Meals>Meetings significant at 0.032, one tail

Note: Tables 10 and 11 summarize data based on my own judgements. As a check on their reliability, the data relating to *yaqona*-drinking and meetings were independently assessed by four Anthropology students. Their assessments were very close to one another and to my own. They were not asked to make a similar assessment of the data on meals because of their unfamiliarity with Fijian kinship organization, and the fact that a number of the children had used given names to designate the figures shown in the drawings of meals.

Constructing hierarchy on the above/below axis

Children's responses to the various tasks described above show that the image of social relations to be found in *yaqona*-drinking and the image of the hierarchical household to be found in the conduct of meals are, for villagers and their children, powerful. To recognize this one has only to see that the disposition of figures in children's own drawings is (with the exception of the very youngest child) entirely non-random, as is their labelling of prepared drawings. Children construct their notions of differential status by reference to spatial categories; thus social hierarchy *is* merged with the spatial dimension given by above/below; to say that someone sits 'above' is the same as saying that this person is of high status. Neither can notions of gender here be axiomatically isolated from hierarchy.

The sequence of the process of constructing meaning apparent in children's own drawings is interesting. However, before going on to discuss this I must point out that I do not consider this sequence to be, in all its details, a hard-and-fast one. I do not want to suggest that the process of cognitively constructing above/below will be always and inevitably the same for all children. The above/below axis is given in the social environment and so is open to the possibility of radical change; moreover, it is not demanded by *all* social environments but is specific to particular contexts inside Fiji. Thus it cannot be said to have built into it the same 'necessity' that characterizes above/below as a relation between objects on different planes, or other notions constructed in terms of invariant properties of the physical environment.

This said, it is interesting that the process apparent in children's own drawings is such that the notion of the chief's being above is primary for the context of *yaqona*-drinking and is found in children as young as five years ten months. The pole below comes next, and is defined as being the place either of women or of women and young men, depending on a child's sex. I do not make too much of this finding, since the simultaneous manipulation of *both* poles of the axis is found in children as young as six years three months. Further refinements in differentiation of rank/seniority statuses within gender come somewhat later with a mature and highly differentiated understanding of above/below being found as young as ten years eleven months (a girl in Class 6 who did a Type 9 Drawing).

Again, I would not wish to assume, on the basis of my data, that all children will show the 'push for equality' that I described for some of them between the ages of eight years five months and twelve years ten months. For Type 6 Drawings (those showing the less radical representation, where there is equality across gender for rank/seniority statuses below that of chief) the wide age range is such that while the median ages for both boys and girls are almost exactly the same, it is not far from that for Type 8 Drawings. Thus the possibility exists that not all children are abstracting from their experience a general rank/seniority principle (i.e. older chiefs above younger persons whose rank is irrelevant), but are instead making more direct use of the imagery of *yaqona*-drinking.

Whatever the case with respect to these ambiguities in the data, it is clear that these Fijian children construct hierarchy in terms of a complex interaction between notions of rank/seniority and of gender. What we find here is an interaction between equally dominant cultural constructs about gender and rank/seniority that cannot be isolated from one another, because at one pole, being 'above' is about being a chief and an elderly male, while being 'below' is about being a young man or a female.

The merging of hierarchy with the above/below axis is found for children of both sexes as young as six years three months. Given that a partial merging is also found in children around six, one may assume that an unrefined meaning of the above/below axis is constructed just prior to school age.

There are some clues as to how this merging of hierarchy with spatial categories comes about, in that drawings of *yaqona*-drinking and meals produce the most consistent and systematic responses across all children. Children's responses to prepared drawings both confirm the merging, and produce further interesting findings. Perhaps the most illuminating, but not perhaps so very surprising, is that the position of Mother below is the anchor within the household (in drawings depicting meals), just as 'the high chief' is the anchor for community situations (in drawings depicting meetings and *yaqona*-drinking). In other words, for drawings of people seated at meals, *all* children chose the figure that was symbolically below to be Mother – and this was the case whether she was taken to be at the top or bottom plane of the page. By contrast, the figure accorded the place above was either Father, Father's Elder Brother, Father's Father, Mother's Brother or a 'guest' – presumably given this place out of courtesy. So, in these prepared drawings of meals, Mother remained the constant and the status of 'senior man' shifted between various male kinship categories.

This finding suggests that Mother is most salient within the household, and that it is her position at meals that defines the place below, while in the community it is the high chief who is most salient and it is his position that defines that place above. Had I included in the set of prepared drawings one showing *yaqona*-drinking at home and another showing a communal meal in the village hall, I should have further data on this point, but unfortunately I did not think of this possibility when I devised the task.

It may be Mother's salience below in the house that allows for the relative lack of differentiation between women in the community domain; all women [*marama*, literally 'ladies'] are by definition married and mothers of children and may thus be distinguished from girls – these being the two most reliably differentiated statuses for females in children's own drawings of *yaqona*-drinking in the village hall. On the other hand, not all men are chiefs and only one man can be 'high chief'; it is this singularity that makes him the anchor upon which children fix other rank/seniority statuses in the community domain. This 'singularity' is further confirmed by children's essays on 'the gathering', where 26 out of 43 mentioned his presence there. Of these 26 children, 20 specifically referred to his pre-eminence. In other words, they did not simply say that he was present, but also remarked that he drank the first bowl of *yaqona*, or made the first speech, or sat 'above' others, or was presented with an *i sevusevu*.

As we shall see in the next and final chapter, these suggestions are both supported by and serve to illuminate the data gained from participant observation and from historical accounts of Fijian social relations in the nineteenth and early twentieth centuries.

10   Cognition as a microhistorical process

In this final chapter I discuss how Fijian villagers construct cognitively an understanding of above/below; how this process merges with an understanding of hierarchical social relations; and what are the conditions that underlie the process and the course of its transformation over time. The discussion is at once psychological in that it addresses the cognitions of particular persons, and anthropological and historical in that it is concerned with those persons as Fijian villagers.

The modulated construction of above/below

The experimental data from children show conclusively that they do not acquire ready-made their notions of gender, space and hierarchy; nor are they explicitly taught how to articulate any conflicting aspects of these notions; rather, they *construct* their understanding out of their experience. Their perceptions have to be valid, for they must live their lives in terms of this understanding. Younger children's notions lack complexity, but the differences between them and older children are instructive, revealing the relative salience of different aspects of the notions investigated. The understanding of the oldest children is assumed to be – in its fundamentals – near that of adults.

Cognition as a constructive process is, I argue, amply demonstrated here; the processes of accommodation, assimilation, and equilibration are evident. However, in the light of my data it seems obvious that none of this cognitive activity can be unmediated; even the endogenous (self-regulated) process of equilibration cannot be immune.

The youngest children in the sample accommodate to concrete referents: to the internal spaces of a building that are called above [*i cake*] or below [*i ra*], and to the cloth at meals and the *tanoa* in *yaqona*-drinking. Their experience of the disposition of people in these situations and of the routine use of above/below to designate certain areas leads them to focus on the two poles of the spatial axis in such a way that a single high chief is always above in *yaqona*-drinking, and women, or women and young men, always below when men and women are drinking together. But for even the youngest children, experience seems to be gender-specific: boys say that only women are below, and girls say that young men too are below, along with women. Thus, these youngest children already have some awareness that to sit below is to be low in status. This awareness comes about via 'recognitory assimilation', a kind of motor recognition that Piaget reserves for babies, but that I take to have a more general application (see Piaget and Inhelder, 1969: 7; Flavell, 1963: 104–5). Thus reference to one's position in space as 'below' comes to be linked to other aspects of a child's personal experience: for example that one should 'sit down and be quiet', walk *lolou* in a stooping position or on all fours in adult company indoors, ask permission if one has to rise to leave the room, etc. These behaviours are tied to a growing awareness of the necessity for showing 'respect' by avoidance, and the entirely proper feeling of shame or shyness [*madua*] in all interactions with senior kin.

So we have to take account of children's daily experience of relative seniority, which effectively means that they may be commanded and disciplined by any older person. Childishness [*viavia gone*] being so readily rebuked, children are probably aware too of the adult desire for them to 'grow up', to be 'of mature mind'. But perhaps most important is shame or shyness, which (like obedience) is fostered in children in nearly all their relations with older people. Women and young men as well as children often describe themselves or their feelings in a public context as *madua*. Similarly, if honoured by public praise or proposed for an administrative position in council or church, men below the status of elder or *yavusa* chief would hang their heads in a show of humility and disavowal of any ambition or arrogance [*viavia levu*], and in many cases were overcome with emotion. This behaviour is a corollary of the attitude that any status one attains should be a result of public recognition of one's good qualities, not of self-seeking or ambitious behaviour. This is true even for those who, largely because of birthright and age, attain the status of clan or paramount chief. A chief should be *yalo qaqa* (of determined mind, courageous), but he should also be polite and respectful of others. So, while children tended to emphasize in their essays the powerful or 'bossy' aspects of being a chief or a lady of high rank, they also often stressed co-operative behaviour, especially with respect to gender-specific work. Anyone whose status is below that of named chief should be overtly *madua*; indeed, the behavioural expression of this quality in respect of persons senior to oneself in part constitutes their authority.

Even while they are accommodating their earliest awareness of differential status to their awareness of the above/below axis, children are also assimilating more about authority and status relations. In accommodating these bits of knowledge to one another they come to know, for example, that Father's Elder Brother has authority over Father and sits above him at a meal, or that a chief has authority over his people and sits above them in *yaqona*-drinking. But they have not yet abstracted from their experience a general hierarchical scheme that orders the disposition of people on the above/below axis according to an interaction between rank, seniority and gender. So, even though the youngest children use all three notions, they have not yet articulated them to one another. That they *are* in the process of constructing a general scheme is apparent at the point where increasingly fine discriminations are assimilated to a hierarchy-scheme where *rank and seniority alone* interact to give rise to status, and gender is largely ignored. When gender is brought back into the reckoning and assimilated both to seniority and to a more subtle idea of rank, the components of the hierarchy-scheme are in equilibrium and so 'reversible'; that is, the scheme is applicable across the variety of specific instances and so firmly attached to the idea of differential status as to be independent of the concrete referents that describe the space: a chief is above because of his 'chiefliness', not because above is the place where he sits.

People may talk of rank *or* seniority, *or* gender as a defining factor in hierarchical relations without referring to either of the other two variables. But a mature understanding of above/below as mani-festing differential status requires the simultaneous cognitive manipulation and interaction of all three constructs. Construction of a notion of this complexity requires that certain information be given priority over other, perhaps equally salient, information, and here the notion of equilibration is surely important.

For example, a girl of eleven who understands that the disposition of people in space manifests their differential status may represent them as differentiated solely in terms of rank and seniority. At this point her hierarchy-scheme is only partially equilibrated. She realises that seniority and rank together interact in status differences manifest on the above/below axis, but she has denied her previous 'simple' awareness of gender as an important factor (her knowledge that 'ladies sit below'), and this means that her existing hierarchy-scheme cannot be easily accommodated to information presented to her in situations like *yaqona*-drinking. So her hierarchy-scheme is bound at some point (around twelve or so according to my data) to be reorganized, perhaps in response to her own conscious or unconscious imitation of adult women who are especially significant to her. If their behaviour is at odds with her scheme for the relative status of such women, it may be supposed to upset the cognitive balance already achieved and so force a reorganization. One might also suppose that a 'mismatch' between her scheme for *yaqona*-drinking and her experience of how people actually group themselves round the *tanoa* forces a new accommodation of information already at her disposal.

This new accommodation can occur only when expectations generated by a scheme are falsified; its components are reorganized at the point where the child accommodates to information already at her disposal: that if people's disposition in space is about status, and, 'the ladies sit below', then gender is a factor in relative status. I do not suggest that the girl of twelve learns something entirely new about gender and relations between men and women; rather, information that was assimilated to cognitively separate schemes comes to be articulated in response to a 'push' from the child's enviroment. Thus I would argue that equilibration cannot be an entirely endogenous 'self-regulation' that takes place willy-nilly.

Whether conscious 'reflective abstraction' (Piaget 1968, 1971: 62; Flavell, 1963: 256) is inevitable at this point in the cognitive construction of the significance of above/below is, I think, a moot point. One may suppose that reorganization of an existing scheme is triggered by, for example, a subliminal awareness of the humble posture of the high chief's wife as she passes among a group of seated men. Constructing above/below entails consciousness in that its components (the terms that designate the space itself and the notions of rank, seniority and gender) are all part of a discourse in which children are included. But this is not to say that the process by which one comes to understand the interaction between components is an entirely conscious one; indeed, I show below that certain aspects of above/below militate against a conscious awareness of their own derivation and its implications.

However, I think that the notion of equilibration is necessary if we are to understand how the interaction between concepts of rank, seniority and gender is forged into a hierarchy-scheme; one that is both stable in that it has come to comprise these three components in interaction, and mobile in that it may be applied to an infinite variety of situations where the three components may be understood to interact in somewhat different ways. Consider, for example, the leader of the Women's Associations mentioned in Chapter 5. She was daughter to a Sawaieke chief and wife to the high chief of another country [*vanua*]. In 1981 it was decided that leadership of any Women's Association should be 'in the manner of the land', that the office should go to one of the highest-status members of the group. In the absence of her husband, it was respect for *his* rank and *her* office in a context that brought together in Sawaieke women visitors from several islands that made it appropriate for her to sit above for ceremonies and *yaqona*-drinking during the week of the seminar. On other visits to Sawaieke she took her place as a daughter of the village: she sat above amongst women but below her Elder Sister, and if men were present she sat below the *tanoa*. Similarly, when Sawaieke ladies, unaccompanied by their husbands, make a formal visit to a neighbouring village, those of highest status sit above, alongside chiefs of that village. It is clear from these relatively unusual instances that the adult hierarchy-scheme has the qualities of stability and mobility characteristic of a scheme that is fully equilibrated.

Despite certain important regularities, it is clear that not all children go through precisely the same process in constructing the meaning of above/below. Some children around age eleven seem to deny a previous awareness of women's position and construct a radical rank/seniority scheme to generate discriminations of relative status. Others take a less radical stance and reserve the position above for the highest-ranking man or men; that is, they make gender a factor in status, if only in this way. It is possible that yet other children – especially boys – may easily incorporate gender into the reckoning around the same time as they make the connection between differential status and above/below. Girls are more likely to discriminate statuses in terms of rank and seniority alone. It seems likely that girls' experience of their mothers, and of older women in general, generates an appreciation of female autonomy and competence (and perhaps of the high value that is, in general, placed on female labour) that is at odds with women's position below in space.

These differences across sex and across persons lend support to the notion of modulated construction – whereby cognitive activity is modulated simultaneously by the nature of the behaviour and concepts on which it bears, by age and gender, *and* by personal history; even where people have in common a sociocultural history, their personal history is always unique. The differences across sex show that the cognitive construction of gender must itself be part of the cognitive construction of differential status. In other words, the social processes that enter into gender as a cognitive construct inevitably enter into the concurrent cognitive construction of a hierarchical scheme.

The significance of gender

The significance of gender for the hierarchical scheme is evident in girls' essays on what they will do as grown-ups (Chapter 8), for they clearly hold an overtly dual notion of power and autonomy with respect to men and women. In so far as they must be able to acknowledge appropriately the relative status of different women, boys have to a certain extent to make the same distinction. But judging by girls' responses, the problem is more acute for them.

Here I remind the reader that church seating offers another image of hierarchy. In church, for all statuses below clan chief, men and women are segregated but on a level with one another in respect of rank/seniority. I have no data from children that deals directly with this situation, but it may be as salient for their understanding of hierarchical relations in space as are meals at home and *yaqona*-drinking across households.

The problem of articulating an understanding of seniority *within* the household with status relations *across* households and persons in the community at large seems to become salient for children over the age of ten or so. Most younger children are not yet trying directly to articulate the hierarchy manifest in *yaqona*-drinking or at meals with their knowledge of seniority; rather, they seem to keep their experience of authority relatively separate from images of hierarchy in terms of people's disposition in space. Older children appear to be trying to articulate to the space where *yaqona*-drinking occurs a church-derived image of hierarchy, this image being more consistent with what they take to be the significance of rank and seniority. This may be what leads girls in particular to depict a situation they can never have seen: a high chief's wife seated above beside her husband, chiefs' wives beside their husbands, married women beside men, and so on, all ordered in relation to the central *yaqona*-bowl [*tanoa*].

Girls' reasoning appears to be that even if a woman is below her husband within the household, a married couple are each other's peers according to the interaction between rank and seniority; thus for contexts across households a woman should be accorded her place only with reference to her rank and seniority, as is the case by and large in church. However, children who reason in this way are disavowing any connection between the hierarchy of meals and that of *yaqona*-drinking; indeed, they effectively deny their own experience of seating around the *tanoa*. Thus, despite the fact that their understanding of relative status is much more subtle and wide-ranging than that of younger children (as is clear from a ten-year-old's ability to make the maximum number of status distinctions), the situation they depict in their drawings is likely to be much further from the typical empirical one.

The apparent contradiction in the interaction between gender and seniority is much more salient to girls than to boys: only one boy (aged ten years one month) made exclusive use of rank/seniority to differentiate status; other boys made gender significant by according the position above only to high-status men. Moreover, by the age of eleven years ten months boys had given up any idea that adult women might rank 'above' young men, let alone be on the same level as their husbands. A few girls continued to assert the ascendancy of women over young men up to the age of twelve years ten months. However, most children over the age of eleven and a half or so represented *yaqona*-drinking in such a way that they seemed to have resolved the inconsistencies in their experience and come to accept women's status as manifest in their position below – either alone (for boys) or on a level with young men (for girls).

All children have to deal with certain discordant facts of life: as an elder sister a women has at least formal authority over her juniors within the household and both boys and girls have direct experience of this authority with respect to their own older sisters; they are, moreover, aware of their *own* authority over younger siblings. A mother has authority over her children until they are adults, but in relation to her husband she has little or no authority; children are likely to become aware of this via their observation of Father and Mother at home. By contrast, children's experience presents them with no inconsistency as regards the authority of elder brothers and that of husbands/fathers. Children have thus at some point to distinguish between women in respect of their authority over males as 'elder sisters' and their lack of authority as 'wives', and to marry this distinction to the hierarchy manifest in space when the family eats together or people gather to drink *yaqona* or to worship.

This distinction is not so easy to make. An adult elder sister is rarely resident in her brother's home; when she is, the strict avoidance rule tends to militate against any overt display of her authority. What made *me* aware of the importance of the distinction was not the fact that Elder Sister is formally senior to her brother, for this may count for little in the actual relations beween them; rather, it was the fact that it is 'Mother', i.e. Father's Wife, whom the children showed as *invariably* at the pole below within the household; in other words, it is not 'women' but 'wives' who are most salient below in the space of the house. When I then re-examined my diagrams of people at meals I found that a woman's position *within* the household varies as a function of her relation to the men who are present.

My evidence on this point is scanty; I recorded only three occasions where an adult elder sister was present at the same meal as her younger brother and his wife in the man's home. But in each case Elder Sister sat in a position that was noticeably above that of the wife and somewhat below her brother; neither did she serve the meal. However, I think it likely that when an elder sister is *accompanied by her husband* on a visit to her younger brother's home, she would sit opposite her younger brother's wife at the pole below, with her husband above in the honoured position. Certainly, when a woman and her husband's *younger* sister eat together with children in the man's absence, the wife may sit at the cloth above the sister and be served by her; however, when her husband is present she sits directly opposite the younger sister and serves the food. My ethnographic evidence, scanty as it is, confirms that a woman's position in space within the household varies as a function of her relation to the male household head, and that it is women as 'wives' rather than as 'sisters' who there define the pole below. This finding is crucial for women's position in the community at large.

I remarked in Chapter 1 that, given that humans are biologically social beings, the most salient objects in a child's environment are other people. However, with respect to gender, people of the same sex as the child have to be *rendered* salient. Forms of social relations enter into *all* cognitive activity, because the thinking self constituted in and through that activity is a locus of social relations; thus all cognitive activity is mediated by specific kinds of human interaction. This means that gender identification will enter into cognition in ways that are culturally specific. Certainly there is 'no need to choose between the primacy of the social or that of the intellect' (Piaget, 1968, 1971: 13–14) but there is a need to understand *how* social processes at the level of the group enter into cognitive developmental processes to produce culture-specific constructs of those same social processes.

The concrete foundation of an abstract scheme

The children's data show that differential status is merged with spatial categories, but how does this merging come about? Piaget has always emphasized that a child's early cognitions are tied to concrete referents, a point made also by Bourdieu (1971, 1977). This is as much the case for my own data concerning a so-called 'symbolic' construct as it is for the so-called 'logical' constructs investigated by Piaget and his co-workers.

Children acknowledge the salience of 'the high chief' above for contexts across households and of 'Mother' below at home before they are aware that the spatial axis manifests differential status. For these youngest children it appears that status is concrete. In other words, the paramount is above *because he sits or is said to be above*; a woman or a young man is below *because she or he sits or is said to be below*. Despite the immediate differences between boys and girls respecting who is below, one can argue that the youngest children are not talking about status in the adult sense of the term when they describe the seating position of figures in their drawings, but are rather expressing a simple awareness of the two poles of the above/below axis and those who generally occupy them.

This is confirmed by the way that, when children begin to accommodate what they know about above/below with what they know about differential status, they produce drawings of situations they can never have seen. The data suggest that not before age eight years five months at the earliest do children become aware that it is *relative status* that is expressed in spatial terms. An 'enlightened' merging of space with an awareness that status is derived from contexts that may be independent of it occurs for many children at about age ten, when their drawings reveal a conflict between rank/seniority and gender. They 'reorder' the image of hierarchy in *yaqona*-drinking in terms of an interaction between rank and seniority, and largely ignore gender as a variable in differential status.

The children's data show that the high salience of the spatial axis as constitutive of differential status is the foundation for complex adult notions of hierarchy with respect to kinship and political relations across clans, villages and 'countries'. Adults' notions include ideas of *mana* (effectiveness), legitimacy, personal achievement, the significance of mythical relations between the ancestors of clans, and of certain rituals such as *i sevusevu* (presenting *yaqona*), *yaqona*-drinking, and so on. Adults never say that a man's status is high *because* he sits above the *tanoa*; rather, he is accorded this place because his status makes it appropriate. As I showed in Chapter 5, adults consciously hold the notion that social status determines a person's position above or below. For adults, in direct contrast to children, where the high chief sits is above, since the quality of being above is inherent in him as high chief, and where women sit is below 'because they are women who are seated with chiefs'.

From my own observation of meetings where there was no *yaqona*, people are no more likely to violate spatial constraints in this situation than they are when *yaqona* is in evidence. But in labelling drawings of meetings children were significantly less consistent with respect to the 'necessity' for showing an elder above a married man, above a young man. Their responses revealed a heightened salience of spatial constraints at meals and *yaqona*-drinking, and one is led to ask why it should occur. It cannot be because meals and *yaqona*-drinking have a set and regular format – this is also true of meetings. Nor can it be explained by any absence of association with ideas of power: prayers precede meetings just as they precede all meals, and children's knowledge of the link between *yaqona*-drinking and *mana* is likely to be rather vague.

I argue that it is adult notions of meals and *yaqona*-drinking as rule-governed activities that produce children's heightened awareness of the spatial constraints imposed by above/below. For adults, ritual practice can be, and is, expressed in terms of explicit rules. These explicit rules mean that the cloth at meals has to be placed along the above/below axis of the house space; the cloth mediates between and emphasizes the two extremes of the above/below axis. Likewise, the *tanoa* in *yaqona*-drinking must be placed so that it 'faces the chiefs'; it marks out the chiefs' positions above it from the positions of those who are seated below. Thus the children's heightened awareness must hinge on the fact that certain concrete elements in *yaqona*-drinking and meals are *always* disposed in the same way, and it is the disposition of these concrete objects that emphasizes the above/below axis.

In meals and *yaqona*-drinking differential status is manifest both in the activities themselves and in the space where they occur. A chief drinks first when *yaqona* is served, speaks first in a meeting, and (every man being a chief in his own house) eats first at home. What distinguishes meetings from *yaqona*-drinking and meals in prepared drawings is that, aside from the figures depicted, no other concrete elements are present – no *tanoa*, no cloth – to attract attention to the necessity for a continued and *consistent* ranking in space of all those 'below' the figure chosen to represent 'the high chief'.

It seems to me that the salience of *yaqona*-drinking for an adult understanding of local hierarchy comes in time to outweigh that of any other situation where relative status is expressed. Its heightened significance for adults is undoubtedly connected with the following: *yaqona*, though non-alcoholic, is mildly intoxicating; it is drunk on *all* ceremonial occasions; the *i sevusevu* and the drinking itself are obligatory and imbued with ideas of the *mana* of the ancestors and of chiefs, whose position in life is divinely ordained. Primary school children must know something of such matters, though their knowledge is probably at best only partial, but they too apparently come to accept *yaqona*-drinking as providing the 'correct' image of the nature of local hierarchy. This conclusion is entailed by the finding that, while drawings by some children around eleven represent an image of hierarchy where rank and seniority alone govern a person's position in space and gender is irrelevant, those by the oldest children (the majority of over twelve and a half) accord with the typical empirical nature of *yaqona*-drinking.

However, it is the salience for children of material objects, such as the cloth at meals and the *tanoa* in *yaqona*-drinking, that underlies the mature conception of above/below. The continuity between a child's and an adult's conception of the hierarchy inscribed in people's disposition in space rests on the *material stability* of ritual: on the fact that certain highly salient material elements are *always* disposed in the same way. So any further meaning that accrues to adolescent or adult notions of *yaqona*-drinking is inevitably articulated to an awareness of status as being more clearly manifest, more 'concrete', in certain ritual contexts. The very fact that the adult conception of *yaqona*-drinking is richer, more complex, more 'meaningful' than the child's is itself dependent upon the initial and continued salience of the *tanoa*.

So children learn about the hierarchy manifest on the above/below axis is specific situations such as meals and *yaqona*-drinking. The cognitive process is one of gradual construction and is initially tied to certain material objects such as the *tanoa*, the cloth at meals, or the house itself, but these material objects are cultural artifacts; they refer not simply to themselves but to relations between people. So the adult conception of above/below inverts the child's concept; what was initially understood as material and concrete comes to seen as an *expression* of the explicit adult notion of hierarchy as a kind of moral imperative: the 'principle of hierarchy' as derived from an interaction between rank, seniority and gender.

A continuum of meaning

What is constitutive for children is, for adults, expressive; these data lead me to argue against a common anthropological assumption that we can demarcate a domain of 'the symbolic', that this domain is self-evident, located 'out there' – its paradigm being given by ritual. For it is clear from the children's data that the notion that above/ below is 'symbolic' – that is, stands for something other than itself – is the product of a process of cognitive construction in persons over time.

In other words, above/below for younger children is what is called a 'sign' – that is, a 'signifier' whose 'signified' is the notion that in certain spaces people are disposed in certain relations to one another; for adolescents and for adults, above/below has become what is called 'a symbol' – one that contains the sign through a process of cognitive construction so that it comes to stand for status differentiation. This finding suggests that we should drop any *a priori* distinction between sign and symbol in respect of the analysis of ritual. For where we as anthropologists – along with Fijian adults – take above/below in reference to a single plane to be symbolic of status differentiation and so implicitly metaphorical, the youngest Fijian children take it to be propositional. In the simplest possible terms this means that for children *yaqona* ritual refers to nothing other than itself; it is not symbolic in the conventional anthropological sense; it does not 'stand for' anything else (which is not to deny that for any given child it has specific significant associations, etc.).

This suggests that cognition of symbolic constructs is not, as Bloch (1985, 1986) suggests it is, very different from cognition of those apparently more straightforward constructs derived from invariant properties of the physical environment – notions of volume, number, time, space, etc. All are initially tied to concrete referents, but a mature understanding requires that 'appearances' be partially disavowed. So, for example, differential status is freed of its connection to properties of the environment that are at once material and symbolic (the house, the *tanoa*), just as the volume of a liquid is disconnected from the shape of the container that holds it.

Cognitive process as social process

I have shown above that cultural knowledge has to be cognitively constructed and that particular 'knowing subjects' – who are always 'social subjects', inevitably situated within specific social relations –

are the locus of that construction. In so doing, I have tried to show how, while children have to construct meaning anew in and through the social relations in which it is embedded, they have also inevitably to submit to the meanings that others have made before them. Thus the process of cognitive construction itself has critical implications for the nature of social processes at the level of the group.

Above/below is constructed as a cognitive scheme that manifests itself in one's behaviour and thus 'coerces' or 'regulates' the behaviour of others. So children may imitate the posture of older siblings or adults: at age three and a half or four they walk *lolou* in passing among others; at six and a half or seven they politely invite their peers to sit above themselves; by eight and a half or so they may request permission to stand, and so on. But there is no single objective meaning that defines above/below. Its meaning arises out of an interaction between notions of rank, seniority and gender – an interaction whose parts may be given different weights by the same person on different occasions, or by different persons on the same occasion. So children at different ages give different emphases to each of the three interacting components, and in discourse and behaviour adults on different occasions may favour one aspect over the others to make a particular point. Nevertheless the above/below scheme generates behaviour that is objectively ' "regular" without being the product of obedience to rules' (Bourdieu, 1977: 72); for example involuntarily shying away from any touch that approaches the head, 'peeping', seating oneself in a 'proper' position in company and so on. A person's behaviour in conforming with the demands of the above/below axis is objectively adapted to the expression of hierarchy, but there is no necessity to suppose that this same person is consciously aiming at this end or has 'an express mastery' of what might be necessary to attain it (ibid.). The notion of above/below as the product of 'modulated construction' precludes what Bourdieu calls 'the fallacies of the rule' (1977: 23).

However, to argue that people's behaviour cannot be *explained* as rule-governed is not to say that people do not themselves rationalize their behaviour in these terms. We have seen that the foundation for a notion of hierarchy as 'principle' is constructed by children via reference to the material factors given by people's disposition in space in relation to the *tanoa* in *yaqona*-drinking, the cloth at meals, the space inside houses and churches. These material factors are

reproduced by adults as necessary – i.e. rule-governed – manifesta-
tions of that principle of hierarchy. So certain adult behaviour is
rationalized in discourse by reference to this notion of principle: it
becomes traditional to arrange the space inside buildings and to
make *tanoa* to accord with the proper expression of God-given
hierarchical relations between kin. Thus adults can say that the chief
sits above the *tanoa* and is faced by his people because this 'shows our
respect for the chief' – a chief who has all their ancestors 'at his
back'.

Here Vygotsky's account of the way language mediates cognitive
development is crucial for, as he shows, 'learning to direct one's own
mental processes with the aid of words or signs is an integral part of
the process of concept formation' (1986: 108). I would argue that the
naming of the above/below axis itself forces children ultimately to
make 'aboveness' and 'belowness' attributes of persons as a mark of
differential status; that is to say, the way the terms above [*i cake*] and
below [*i ra*] are used by their seniors forces children to place a status
construction on their growing awareness that the terms cannot
merely name spaces or positions in space. The fact that adults
constitute meals, *yaqona*-drinking, etc., as rule-governed behaviour
– that is, as 'ritual' (see Lewis, 1980: 21) – is important here. It is the
interplay between rule and practice, practice and cognitive scheme
that allows above/below simultaneously in part to *constitute* hierarchy
and to *express* it. And it is in this interplay that ritual takes on its
coercive power in its claim to represent another reality – one that is
immanent rather than grossly material, accessible only through
tropes.

Roy Wagner has described what he calls 'the obviation model of
trope expansion' (1986: 96); here 'core symbols' are made –
synchronically in a ritual process or over time in a historical process –
to play against one another.

So, for example, a ritual sequence may take its meaning against
the ground provided by kinship, exchange relations, marriage; when
it is kinship that is in focus, the relation is reversed and the ritual
sequence becomes the ground and kinship the figure whose
'meaning' is posited in ritual terms. This type of 'figure-ground
reversal' is central to Wagner's 'obviation', the process by which a
core symbol comes to be at once proposition and resolution, to 'stand
for itself'. I would argue that in so far as Wagner has described the

process by which people make meaning, this process is itself likely to be predicated on one such as that described in this book.

Data from the youngest children can be understood to demonstrate a fusion between 'figure' and 'ground' with respect to the meaning of *yaqona* ritual: the material fact of *yaqona*-drinking is its own *raison d'être* and a high chief is 'above' because 'above' is where he sits. To find in *yaqona*-drinking what adults find there, children have to realize that what they see as concrete is also figurative in a specific way: they have to realize that *yaqona*-drinking is 'about' status differentiation as well as 'about' drinking. Further, if they are to arrive at an adult construct in which *yaqona*-drinking is – quite explicitly – understood as a core symbol of Fijian culture, they must come to see it as an activity in which the figurative, the 'meaning' aspect of *yaqona* ritual, is its only valid justification.

This is a type of 'figure-ground reversal' in which the adult notion of ritual as symbolic is the ground against which children are confronted with ritual as intransigent and material fact. To behave appropriately as adults children have to make the material fact of ritual merely the *symbol* of its significance, rather than its own justification.

Given that my data show that a 'core symbol' has to be constructed by persons as subjects out of their experience over time, it follows that neither cognition nor knowledge can – as in Bloch's model – be divided into the ideological and the non-ideological; nor can the meaning of what we often call 'the symbolic' be located – as in Sperber's 1979 model – in the activity of a symbolic mechanism in the mind. The process of coming to understand the 'meaning' of a complex notion such as Fijian above/below is a developmental one and is thus distinct from the 'online' process by which people derive meaning from novel metaphors. This is *not* to suggest that metaphor is irrelevant; rather that it is here a constitutive element in a developmental process. Indeed, I have suggested above that, for example, *yaqona*-drinking becomes increasingly significant for adults in so far as they assimilate to 'the meaning of *yaqona*' all the many subtle suggestions of differentiated power that it can evoke. This raises the question of how notions of the self enter into the cognitive processes of the 'knowing subject', a question I cannot pursue here, though I note in passing Ricoeur's provocative observation that 'we are assimiliated, that is, made similar, to what is seen as similar . . . self-assimilation is part of the commitment proper to the "illocutionary" force of the metaphor . . . [w]e feel *like* what we see *like*' (1978: 156).

It follows too from my data that cultural categories are not, as Sahlins (1985: 145) maintains, received 'ready-made' and then 'risked in practice'; nor are they – as Bourdieu (1977: 87–8) argues – merely reproduced as 'practice' for which consciousness and discourse are largely irrelevant. Rather, complex features of cultural practice and the discourse that provides for its reproduction are the product of a genuinely constitutive process – a process which, in terms of cognitive construction, suggests that cultural heterodoxy is inevitable and not, as Bourdieu maintains and Sahlins implies, contingent. This constitutive process has its cognitive focus in ritual. Further, it is apparent that an adequate analysis of how people make meaning requires that people be understood to be simultaneously *products and producers* of their own histories – for even contingent events can be assimilated only in terms of what one already knows, and whose meaning is made to dominate at the level of the group and how it is made to do so is a function of prevailing power relations which are thus implicated in the very processes of cognitive construction. So Scribner (1985) does not go far enough when she urges researchers to take a Vygotskian perspective on 'cultural history' and child development, for this allows only for the usual reification of one level or another of process into structure. This is a prevailing problem, and one I have tried to avoid; by analysing how 'above/below' is made apparently to dominate social relations – even while egalitarian constructs are similarly salient – and how 'ritual' comes to be the vehicle of this domination by virtue of its material stability, I have shown how persons are, indeed, simultaneously the subjects and objects of the social processes in which they are engaged.

Given that, in the specific case discussed here, a conflict between rank/seniority and gender is inherent in the mature notion of a hierarchical 'principle' that effects status differentiation, it is predictable that across sex, people will have somewhat different ideas about its nature. So it may be argued that heterodoxy is an inevitable product of the cognitive process by which that notion of 'principle' is cognitively constructed. This heterodoxy (to say nothing of more subtle personal differences) further implies firstly, that the conflict *will* emerge in discourse and secondly, that it will shape the nature of historical transformation.

Behavioural practice and cognitive scheme

I showed in my introduction that one may reject as overly inclusive Bourdieu's view that people constitute 'practical activity as an *object of observation and analysis*' (1977: 2) only in so far as this practical activity has become objectified in discourse. However, discourse is essential for some kinds of critical analysis. Villagers in Gau are at once constrained by the above/below axis and able to articulate and represent what it 'means'. What remains obscure to them – because its fundamentals are inscribed in body posture, avoidance and other respect behaviour, in the 'shame' or 'shyness' that precludes explicit ambition and in the material space of house, church and village hall – is the 'objective meaning' that above/below has for the anthropologist observer. This is because the discourse of above/below does not include discussion of the conditions of its cognitive construction, and its meaning for mature persons is that it *expresses* hierarchy rather than being itself *constitutive* of it. The notion of above/below as the product of a process of modulated cognitive construction allows for what Bourdieu has called the 'doxic' function of symbolic practice, which gives the quality of 'naturalness' to the subject's experience of the world, making its properties appear self-evident and consequently not open to challenge (1977: 164).

However, I would argue that the doxic function of symbolic practice can *never* produce complete closure, simply because differences across persons in the articulation of cognitive schemes are potentially sufficient to generate the conditions necessary for calling what is taken for granted into question. Moreover, this potential may be derived from contradictions inherent to a construct, contradictions that may be exposed by an appeal to logic (cf. Bourdieu, 1977: 164–71). Bourdieu argues (and one can only agree) that logical contradictions in a symbolic scheme may not be acknowledged by subjects and may in fact never confront them. However, he also argues that 'it is unlikely that two contradictory applications of the same schemes will be brought face to face in what we must call a *universe of practice* (rather than a universe of discourse)' (ibid.: 110).

This may be so, but it also implies that discourse becomes irrelevant in the face of practice. In discourse, contradictory applications of the same schemes *are* brought face to face – thus generating conflict whose significance is precisely that. In this respect there is a substantial problem for the interaction of gender and rank/seniority in terms of above/below.

In Chapters 3 and 4 I showed how the gender component of hierarchy is complicated both by a younger brother's obligation to acknowledge the seniority of his elder sister, and by the equal relation between cross-cousins across sex. Moreover, since 'women sit below', this gender component in above/below is bound to be at odds with its other components: that persons of chiefly birth are above commoners and older persons above younger ones. Conflicting applications of the hierarchy-scheme contained in above/below thus tend to occur across sex and can only ever be partially resolved.

One such conflict occurred where an unmarried man aged twenty-six was acting head of a chiefly household which included his older married (but separated) sister and her children. The elder brother lived in Suva, so the young man was acknowledged as 'head of household' on a day-to-day basis by village men. But his elder sister actually ran the household and when the two disagreed (for example in respect of how a certain kinship obligation should be acknowledged) the woman stood up for her own position on the grounds that she was older than he, while he asserted the right of men to 'lead' or to 'hold sway' [*lewa*] over women. Once she countered this argument by saying that only her elder brother or her husband could tell her what to do; her younger brother replied that as she was married, she and her children had no right at all to be in his household and should return at once to her husband; he threatened to use his fists to enforce this argument and she gave in, but did not give up her conviction that seniority gave her certain rights over her brother.

This strong-minded woman had left her husband on the grounds that he ran after other women and got drunk more often than she considered acceptable. She remained unattached in spite of offers from eligible men, because she was well aware that her relatively high degree of personal autonomy depended on her single state. All her family (including her brothers, who tended to be more pacific in nature) stood in awe of her anger and had awarded her a biblical nickname that signified a despotic tyrant. This same woman was a passionate reactionary; she espoused entirely orthodox views on the place of women in Fijian social life, and was respected by villagers at large for holding to the forms of what is considered *vakavanua* ('in the manner of the land'). All her arguments appealed to what was *vakavanua*, and she made full use of conflicting formulations of the same construct to rationalize her conduct. Most important, however, is that the arguments put forward by the woman derived from an operational construct of the 'if p, then q' variety that is basic to logic. That she was trying to argue logically from a notion that can only be described as a-logical does not alter the fact that an attempt was made to bring logic to bear on the situation.

Bloch's (1974) observation that once one has entered into ritual it inevitably constrains the potential for argument against it, is relevant here. Thus this woman's behaviour never challenged the ritualized *spatial* constraints of above/below; these were, as Bourdieu would say, inscribed in her day-to-day practice. So at the very time of the argument described above, she was seated *i ra*, below her younger brother, who was seated *i cake*, above at the head of the cloth; she had served his meal and was waiting until he should be nearly finished before she began to eat herself. But she did attempt a logical refutation of her brother's assertion of authority, one derived from a conceptual conflict within the hierarchical construct itself. Her failure to 'win' the argument was compounded not only of the imperviousness of ritual to argument that takes place within ritual constraints, but also of her fear of her brother's greater physical force. The woman's arguments were not a deliberate and conscious challenge to the status quo; they concerned only the specific nature of the interaction between gender and seniority. Nevertheless, it is clear that argument culled from conceptual conflicts *within* a discourse of practice simply *are* a challenge – one that can be 'resolved' only by violence.

Thus, in so far as a scheme such as that for above/below is inscribed in body posture and other behaviour that does *not* enter into discourse, it is defended from change. But to the extent that this same scheme is part of discourse, it can be – and is – challenged by any conceptual conflict inherent in it; such challenges are possible because pure logic may be brought to bear on conflicting formulations.

However, when such conceptual conflicts surface in argument they nevertheless tend to be overcome, not because they are impervious to questioning but because they can be dismissed by violence.

So I would argue that while people may be 'objectively enchanted' or unconsciously coerced by their own cognitive constructs, there are always points at which any inherent conflicts surface under the strain of particular conditions. In the domains of both chiefship and kinship the principle of hierarchy is at odds with that of balanced reciprocity, the latter being exemplified respectively in the relation between landspeople and seapeople and in the equality of cross-cousins. When these conflicts surface in an encounter between a high chief and his people or a man and his wife, they can be settled only by violence. This is still true of marriage in Fiji, but it is no longer true of chiefship.

In the past Fijian chiefship was bolstered by violence – for example cannibalism, the slaying of widows, the killing of commoners on occasions such as the building of the chief's house or the launching of his new war canoe. Moreover, a much-hated chief – one who exploited his people beyond their endurance – would be killed by them, and the known history of accession to important chiefships is often one of murder (for example of an elder by a younger brother, of a man by his brother's son, and so on; see for instance Reid, 1977: 14). I do not suggest that the deposing of a bad chief was a challenge to the system; obviously it was not. Rather, I argue that escalating violence is an inevitable corollary of the conflicts inherent in a practice that imposes hierarchy by dint of 'containing' highly salient notions of equality. It is this violence, as much as the 'enchantment' deriving from the process of cognitive construction of a hierarchy-scheme, that historically made chiefship dominant in Fijian political relations. So it was that the first response to colonization was escalating cannibalism and warfare. In contemporary Fijian marriage it is violence that, in the end, puts paid to any argument derived from the conflict between the equality of cross-cousins and hierarchical relations within marriage.

The notion of above/below as the cognitive product of a process of modulated construction, taken together with the historical and ethnographic data, at once confirm the doxic function of symbolic practice and question its supposed imperviousness. For Bourdieu, continuity is the product of an ideology that is uniform across persons; the corollary of this is that cultural change can arise only out of ideological conflict and the integration of the habitus is such that, within culture, there cannot be more than one ideology. Cultural change requires the heterodoxy entailed by a meeting of two cultures, as in colonization or in the class structure of industrial societies. I have shown above that this formulation of the source of heterodoxy is inadequate. It allows for the complexity of cultural constructs, but it does *not* allow for the way this very complexity gives rise to significant differences between people in respect of their 'meaning'. Differences across sex in the hierarchy-scheme suggest that heterodoxy may be generated *within* culture and so give rise to conflict like that described above. Indeed, cognitive differences across persons may at once provide the foundation for historical change *and* a clue to its nature.

This is not to suggest that the historical process is the *same* as the process of cognitive development. However, given that culture is historically constituted, the nature of cognitive differences across persons has implications for the nature of the historical process. As we shall see below, differences across sex in the construction of above/below throw new light both on gender constructs and on their historical transformation since colonization.

Gender and the historical transformation of above/below

That girls held to a notion of a conceptually separate female hierarchy when they were close to a mature notion of women's status *vis-à-vis* others in the context of *yaqona*-drinking came as a surprise to me. Certainly there are occasions when women engage in activities that are largely organized by and for women, but any moderately important occasion, including intervillage meetings of the Women's Association, always takes place under the auspices of men (for example the women's seminar described in Chapter 5). So as an observer I would not have supposed that girls might conceive of relations among women as if men had no significance for women's status amongst themselves. Men take part in exclusively male activities, but boys do not conceive of male statuses as independent of 'people' statuses. Given the similarity of the criteria used by boys and girls to constitute adult statuses, I have now to explain how the two sets of criteria become differentiated so that girls develop a notion of a distinct female hierarchy.

I have argued elsewhere (Toren, 1988) that the lower status of women (considered as an inclusive category) is historically derived from their exclusion from key ritual contexts – the consumption of human sacrifices and *yaqona*-drinking – where ancestral *mana* was made manifest in tribute to chiefs and dispensed to adult men via redistribution of the chiefly food and drink. Here I briefly summarize this argument.

Traditionally a man's status as an 'owner' of land and his transformation of that land to produce acceptable offerings were the basis of his right to have access to the power of his ancestors. A woman given as 'object' in marriage was separated from her own ancestors' land; after marriage she ate the food provided by her husband's ancestors, since it was they who made the land fertile. Today it is still true that a married woman eats on sufferance, as it were. Even the fish she catches are hers from her husband's ancestors; this is implicit in the notion that if a woman is pregnant *and does not yet know it*, she ruins the fishing for all the women present. The term *bukete* – pregnant – derives from *bukebuke*, a mound of earth where yams are planted or, perhaps, from *bu*, green coconut and *kete*, belly or basket – both yams and coconuts being male products. It seems that if a woman has not yet acknowledged that she will bear a child by virtue of her husband's fertility, his ancestors withhold from her the fish that complement 'true food', itself an analogue of male fertility. Marilyn Strathern (1984) has shown how the 'objectification' of women in marriage rituals in gift economies cannot be equated with the subject-object relation between people and things in commodity economies. Thus because objects in Fijian exchange always have 'people' qualities – are gifts, not commodities – a woman retains her subjectivity in marriage. So she can never be quite alienated from her natal lineage, and retains as it were residual rights that make her children *vasu* – able 'to take without asking' from men of their mother's lineage. But in marrying 'out', in being made the object of a gift exchange rather than a party to it, a woman is separated from her land *and* her ancestors and made beholden to her husband's ancestors.

Ancestral *mana* was dispensed 'downwards' via the high chief of a country and was appropriate only for adult 'owners' by virtue of their rights in the land whose ultimate owners were their founding patrilineal ancestors. Here I remind the reader that in old Fiji young men as well as women were forbidden to drink *yaqona*; young men were included in *yaqona* ritual only as attendants. *Yaqona* was the prerogative of adult men, as was the flesh of human sacrifices to the gods. Men as well as women were then, as now, adults by virtue of marriage and parenthood. But lineage exogamy and virilocal residence meant, and still mean, that women become adult in a context where they are *not* 'owners' – that is, holders and users of patrilineally inherited land rights. Thus, even as adults, women could be excluded from *yaqona*-drinking and the consumption of sacrifices on the grounds that they had no natal right to *mana* from ancestors whom they had 'denied' by marriage, nor to that from their husband's ancestors, who were not their own. Their place in their husbands' homes could only be below, for they had only an indirect access to *mana*: through men.

This reading of the everyday ritual inferiority of wives is paradoxically confirmed by the ritual superiority in myth of the 'unique' in-marrying husband. He is that 'chief from over the sea' who marries the land chief's daughter and becomes the *vu* (root) of the chiefly clan and high chief of the *vanua*. In Chapter 4 I argued against Sahlins (1976) notion that wife-takers are superior to wife-givers in Fiji; in a later analysis of the myth of the stranger chief and the installation of chiefs (1981, 1985: 73–103) Sahlins argues further that the exchange in myth and practice 'of raw [virgin] women against cooked men is paradigmatic of the entire chiefdom economy' (ibid.: 101); that is, that the economy is based on tribute and redistribution. He notes, as I have done, that 'Fijians equate sexual possession with consumption of the woman' (ibid.: 89) and makes the giving of the woman in marriage a tributary act that anticipates the stranger's chiefly offering of 'cooked men'. I agree with Sahlins that the gift of a virgin in marriage is in some sense a 'sacrifice' (Quain, 1948: 340) and may be equated to the cannibal sacrifice of men. However, for reasons I give below, I view these exchanges as denoting not tribute and redistributuion, but rather the balanced reciprocity between land and sea.

In the Sawaieke myth, the land chief Narai challenges the stranger chief, who responds with the gift/sacrifice of dead men; Narai then takes the stranger to live with him and work for him and later acknowledges his personal *mana* with the gift/sacrifice of his daughter. However, the stranger is *not yet* paramount; as I noted in Chapter 4, the in-marrying chief is, by definition, cross-cousin both to the woman he marries and to her brothers; with the latter his relations of equality continue *after* marriage. He also owes 'respect and obedience' to his father-in-law, to whom he is *gone* (child). This relation is balanced by the fact that the child of his marriage will be *vasu* to his wife's brothers and will take what he wants from them 'without asking'. Thus in the general history [*i tukutuku raraba*] of Sawaieke country, the first person to be titled Takalaigau is said to be the son of the foreigner chief to whom Narai gives his daughter and, later, the chiefship with his 'high chief's comb'. It is this set of relationships that makes the chiefship an ambiguous source for the generation of other hierarchical relations. So how does the 'stranger chief' become paramount? The answer lies in the ritual of the installation *yaqona*, for it is here that the *mana* of the stranger is made superior and all-encompassing.

The foreigner chief is *mana* by virtue of descent from his foreigner ancestors, as is the land chief by virtue of his indigenous descent; in the installation, the land chief confers upon the stranger chief the additional advantage of a privileged access to the gods of the land. The marriage of the stranger chief to a daughter of the land makes way for his later installation as paramount, but the logic of Fijian marriage exchanges constitutes the subordination of the wife – not that of either her father or her brothers. In the Sawaieke myth of the advent of the stranger chief, he offers the bodies of *uncooked* men as tribute to the land chief, an act that is balanced by the subsequent gift of the land chief's virgin daughter. However, she not only continues to live but herself gives birth to others; she is the analogue of the 'land food' her own people cannot eat when they are in the company of seapeople just as the stranger, as a warrior, is a fisher of men who cannot eat of his catch in the company of landspeople. In this exchange the *mana* of the two chiefs is equal – a balanced 'effectiveness'.

However, this exchange of effectiveness is also a competitive and thus an escalating one. Its resolution is achieved in the supreme act of *mana* that is possible for the land chief – that of 'creating a chief'. The land chief's *mana* is both realized and compromised in this act, for in conferring on the other a privileged access to the indigenous gods, the land chief creates his own ritual subordination to the foreigner. The land chief creates a paramount chief by 'making him drink' the installation *yaqona* – an act that is at once foreshadowed and reiterated on a daily basis in *yaqona*-drinking. Here, as I showed in Chapter 5, the form of the ritual makes tribute *appear* to outweigh the competitive and ultimately balanced exchanges between kin over time. Thus the political is not just 'an aspect of the cosmological' (Sahlins, 1985: 81), but an ideological transformation of material relations. Today, in Sawaieke, the paramount authority of a Takalaigau and the potency of his *mana* are still at once created and accepted at the point where he is served *yaqona* under the aegis of Narai, the leader of the land chiefs, who in so doing creates his own ritual inferiority. So Narai accords to himself the status of a young man in relation to a chief or, more radically, of a woman in relation to her husband. However, precisely because he is *not* a young man, nor wife to the man whose executive he has become, he retains his own status as chief.

This evidence from history and myth helps to explain how, while chiefly birth is *said* to be the most important factor for differential status, women in general can still be taken to be lower in status than men. Where adult women are salient to men as in-marrying wives rather than as sisters, they may come to be seen as outsiders; moreover, where marriage converts into hierarchy a relationship that was previously one between equals, women in general may come to be seen as subject to the authority of men.

But these data do not, on their own, provide sufficient evidence that girls would have conceived of female statuses as constituted independently of 'people' statuses. Indeed, one might think that this was a recent phenomenon linked to the Women's Associations. These were instituted in 1924 and are mentioned so often in girls' essays that they appear to be *the* salient factor for the notion of a separate female hierarchy. We have therefore to look at the historical and ethnographic evidence more closely in tandem with the modulated construction of above/below.

If I am correct in supposing that adult women were the more easily excluded from key ritual contexts because it was not appropriate for them to approach ancestors whom they had either abjured or who were not their own, women's current inclusion in *yaqona*-drinking would seem to be connected with their inclusion in Christian rituals on the same general basis as men. Since the Christian God has displaced the ancestors as the ultimate source of transcendent power and women have direct access to that power in prayer and observance of Christian beliefs, they can no longer be properly excluded from rituals that ultimately connect with lesser powers. The same reasoning takes in too the inclusion of young, unmarried men and women. However, in Christian ideology a child's duty is to its parents and a woman's to her husband – precepts that are constantly reiterated in sermons and informal religious talks. So, given that it is women as wives who are most salient to adult men, it is hardly surprising that when women entered into *yaqona*-drinking they took up the place that was *i ra*, below (or along with) the young men who in former times would have only prepared but not drunk the *yaqona*, but whose position below the *tanoa* marked their junior status.

With respect to children's notions of gender and their under-standing of the hierarchy manifest in space, the girls'perceptions of adult female status as relevant only with respect to other women becomes explicable, as does the fact that it is women or women and young men who define the pole below in *yaqona*-drinking, while it is 'Mother' who defines this pole within the household. All these women are some man's wife and in this respect they are all 'outsiders', if only with reference to their husband's household. Even when married within the village a woman is, in her husband's household, unambiguously below.

In his installation a chief becomes 'father of his people' and the hierarchy of the household is made to characterize the community at large – because the land chief renders himself ritually inferior to the chief he installs, whose bidding he will now do, as a young man does his father's or a wife her husband's. That the power of a man over his wife is axiomatic is implicit in the extract from a sermon quoted by Peck (1982: 348), where the preacher represented both God and Satan as wanting to 'marry' the congregation; God is represented as having both *loloma* ('caring love', 'pity') and *dodomo* ('sexual love', 'desire') for His people, as wanting 'to put a wedding ring on your finger...'. The imagery is such that the people would then be 'wives' to God, in a position where they owed unquestioning obedience to Him. In so far as the imagery of *yaqona*-drinking is that of 'the household writ large', a high chief's wife has to take up the same position in the *yaqona* context that she occupies in her husband's home. However *vis-à-vis* other women she occupies a pre-eminent position, so they have to be seated below her. In effect therefore, in spatial terms, it *appears* that all women are below men, even if the formal description of rank/seniority statuses would show some women as having higher statuses than the majority of men.

So it is that girls between the ages of ten years eight months and thirteen years two months who wrote essays about their prospective future and used largely the *same* criteria as did boys to denote adult status could refer only to women and children and not to 'people' when writing about their imagined future high status. For if once they include men in the reckoning, their status as women who lead, order, teach, advise, etc., is no longer tenable. Their awareness of their own mothers' positions at home and of senior and highly salient women in contexts like *yaqona*-drinking has to be accommodated to their concurrent awareness of these same women's effectiveness, competence, and real (but perhaps covert) influence with their menfolk. This experience means that any just appreciation of women as adults requires that men be largely left out of consideration – and this is what girls do.

Conclusion

The doxic function of symbolic practice can never produce complete closure; thus it does not preclude the existence of heterodoxy even within the relatively autonomous culture of pre-colonial Fiji. Here heterodoxy was a function of gender constructs and relations between adult men and women. This heterodoxy provided the basis for a historical transformation of the status of women – a transformation that is still in process. The fact that a woman's status varies as a function of her relation to a man raises the question of which relationship, that of wife or that of sister, is most salient for Fijian hierarchy.

This question cannot be resolved, because while it is clear that hierarchy at the village level makes women as wives the crux of status relations amongst men, the dual nature of the female gender construct makes it possible for women as sisters to be more salient at the level of those chiefly families who have national significance. Rank distinctions operate more exclusively at the 'topmost' level of Fijian society than at the level of the village, and there is a high rate of endogamy among the chiefly families of Bau, Rewa, Cakaudrove, and Lau – these being the largest and most significant of the old kingdoms, and very important for the current politico-economy of the state. Here the notion of significant rank differences between 'major chiefs' and 'minor chiefs' demands that women as sisters be of high salience for men who occupy the highest-status positions in the contemporary Fijian state.

I have argued elsewhere (Toren, 1987) that these data throw into question Ortner's notion that: 'It is inherent in the nature of hierarchies that certain non-gender-based principles of social organization take precedence over gender itself as a principle of social organization' (1981: 196). She described hierarchy in Polynesia as based primarily on relative rank, with age and gender being regarded as 'only secondarily' important. Data on the process by which Fijian children construct over time a hierarchy-scheme reveal the relative salience of its different components and show that rank, seniority and gender *cannot* be axiomatically isolated from one another. For the children who produced the data, rank and age were equated at the outset so that 'high chief' and 'father/senior male' were most salient above, while 'mother'/'women'/'women and young men' were most salient below. These data alone make it clear that notions of rank, seniority and gender (and the nature of the interaction between them) are being constructed concurrently in the minds of Fijian persons, and thus that no one of them can be accorded theoretical priority over any other.

By dint of combining the methods of anthropology with those of cognitive psychology and a certain amount of historical data I have, I would argue, effectively done as Bourdieu recommends when he says that we must 'inquire into the mode of production and functioning of the pratical mastery which makes possible both an objectively intelligible practice and also an objectively enchanted experience of that practice' (1977: 4). Moreover, by actually examining the course of children's cognitive construction of a complex principle of hierarchy by reference to the above/below axis I have shown how differences in that process across persons have important implications. Thus, the fact that the differential response of boys and girls centred on gender showed the process of 'learning hierarchy' to be bound up with the process of becoming a gendered person.

Here I have to reiterate a point made earlier on: analysis of the children's data demonstrates that *all* the factors that are significant for the cognitive construction of a hierarchy-scheme have to be articulated to the primary salience of the above/below axis. The hierarchy-scheme of a fourteen-year-old will be enriched and extended by further knowledge of notions of transcendent power, the significance of *yaqona*-drinking and of mythical relations between ancestors or between foreigner chiefs and native wives, and so on. In the adult hierarchy-scheme this further information builds on a foundation laid down in the child's early experience of ritual; the continuing high salience of the rituals that take place within the space described by the above/below axis in the house, village hall, and church lie in the material stability of their components. For my own data, then, I would suggest that it is the valuation of space that underlies both the continued importance of hierarchy in Fiji and its simultaneous transformation over time, both in the minds of Fijian persons and in the historical record.

These kinds of observations argue for the necessity of a radical rethinking, in social and cultural anthropology, of our as yet largely untheorized conception of learning and of the nature of mind. This rethinking entails that we pay as much attention to *how* cultural knowledge is acquired as we do to *what* this knowledge is. Here the challenge is to formulate a model of cognition that gives due weight to differences across persons, to constructs predicated on invariant properties of the physical environment, and to anger, fear and other emotions – especially with respect to the extent to which people may be said to be 'objectively enchanted' by their own cognitive constructs.

I have noted elsewhere that the apprehension of meaning is, cognitively speaking, in itself a rational process – whatever its products look like (Toren, 1984). Here I suggest further that all cognitions inevitably have a symbolic dimension – if only because, when brought into being by particular persons, any given concept is made to reference both predictable and unpredictable aspects of experience by virtue of the continuing constitution of meaning over time – aspects of experience that may or may not be made explicit.

Further, where any new elaboration of meaning *is* made explicit and enters into others' understanding, we find the process by which meaning may be understood as the product of a specific cultural history. Thus any 'concept' – a term I have largely avoided throughout because of its connotations of boundedness, of being finished – has to be descibed in terms of a *continuum* of meaning whose dimensions may be made to manifest as either 'sign' or 'symbol' but which, from an analytical point of view, can be understood only as always both.

Meaning can be constrained, but it cannot be fixed; thus Vološinov argued as long ago as 1929 that understanding language 'amounts to understanding its novelty and not to recognizing its identity' (1929,1986: 68). This observation holds true, I suggest, for understanding ritual. As the product of human cognitive processes 'meaning' cannot be located anywhere outside the minds of human subjects – for it is only momentarily instantiated in the product of their interactions. This is *not* to imply – absurdly – that meaning is so labile as to preclude communication and the continuity of communication, but rather that it is always in the process of 'becoming'. This 'becoming' is possible by virtue of the way we make meaning out of our experience and in so doing have (at least in part) to submit to the meanings others have made, even while our own meanings are becoming the stuff of someone else's experience. That this is indeed so is, I suggest, borne out by my Fijian data, which show how a diversity of subjective notions of the meaning of ritual may yet allow for unanimity in ritual practice and so work to fix as 'unchanging' a historically specific kind of social relations that is nevertheless changing in practice.

APPENDICES

Appendix 1 Children's drawings of a gathering

GIRL 7/0   DRAWING TYPE 4 : 🔺 i cake 🔺◯◯⊙ i ra

GIRL 8/3.   DRAWING TYPE 4: 🔺 i cake 🔺◯◯⊙ i ra

GIRL 7/6   DRAWING TYPE 5 : △ i cake ○⊙ i ra

i cake

i ra

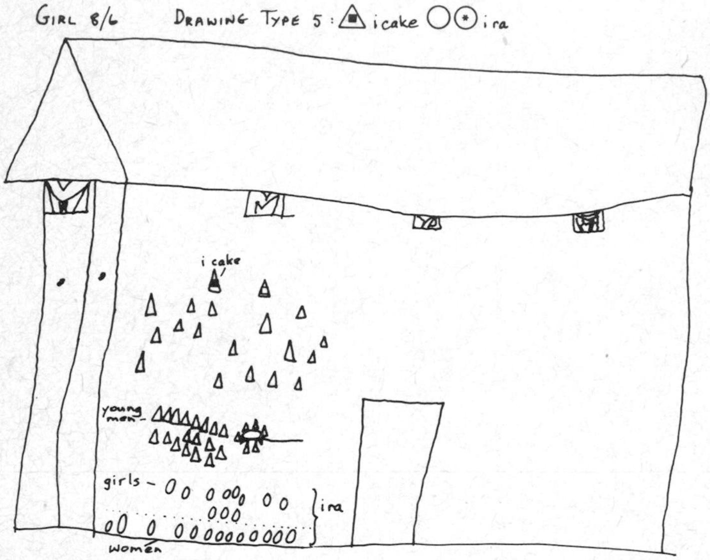

GIRL 8/6   DRAWING TYPE 5 : △ i cake ○○⊙ i ra

i cake

young
men

girls

i ra

women

Boy 7/3 Drawing Type 5: ▲ i cake ◯ i ra

Boy 4/2 Drawing Type 5 ▲ i cake ◯⊛ i ra

GIRL 5/6   DRAWING TYPE 6 : △ △ △ i cake △ ⊛ i ra

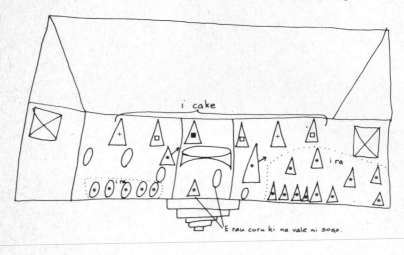

i cake

i ra

E rau curu ki na vale ni soqo.

GIRL 11/0   DRAWING TYPE 6 : △ i cake △ ⊙ i ra

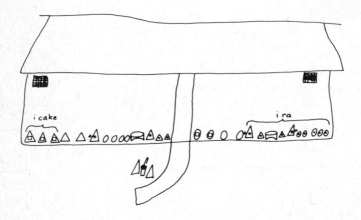

i cake

i ra

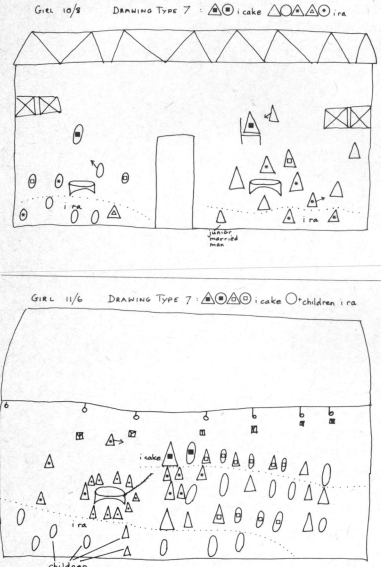

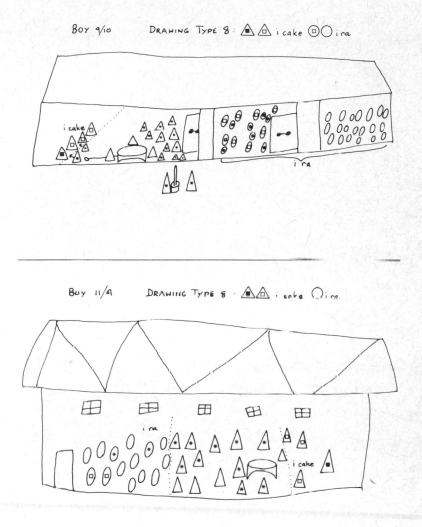

Boy 12/10   DRAWING TYPE 9 : ▲△ i cake △⊙⊙ i ra

Boy 13/8   DRAWING TYPE 9 : ▲△ i cake △⊛ i ra

Vakacava na marama?   Sa bera mai.
Ni ra lako mai na marama e ra na dabe evei?
E ra na dabe sara i ra.

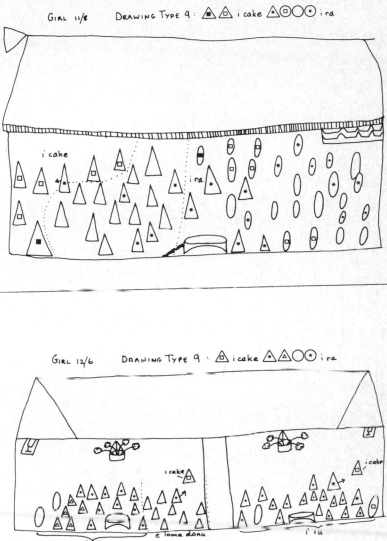

GIRL 13/0   DRAWING TYPE 10 : ▲△ i cake △○⊙ i ra

BOY 14/2   DRAWING TYPE 10 : ▲△ i cake △*△○ i ra

Appendix 2   Response to prepared drawings

The results below are derived from children's responses to prepared drawings depicting people drinking *yaqona*, at meals, and at meetings. These drawings and an English translation of the accompanying instructions are included below. Note that the drawings were presented to children in two sets. The first set of drawings were those numbered 1, 3, 5 and 9; the second set were those numbered 2, 4, 6, 7, 8 and 10. The children were divided into groups of three or four. For each group the drawings in a set were randomized to minimize order effects across children. Children in Classes 1 and 2 were seen individually so that I could write answers for them. Note that this task was designed as an investigatory exercise rather than as a definitive experiment. Nevertheless, it proved possible to use the data to test the hypothesis that children would respond differentially to the situations depicted.

The prediction being tested here was that for drawings depicting meals and *yaqona*-drinking, the children would be more likely to make consistent use of the plane of the page to distinguish status categories on the *cake/ra* axis than they would for the drawings depicting situations described as 'meetings'. The drawings of *yaqona*-drinking and meetings were rated by independent judges (as well as by myself) using a measure that gave a score of 1 to a response judged to be 'not using *cake/ra*', a score of 2 to a response judged to be 'inconsistent' and a score of 3 to one judged to be 'consistent'. The tables below allow a comparison between the assessment of independent judges and my own.

(i) *Summary table of means*

Name of judge	BOYS						GIRLS					
	Meetings		Yaqona		Meals		Meetings		Yaqona		Meals	
Toren	2.48	<	2.81	>	2.76		2.29	<	2.79	=	2.79	
A	2.4	<	2.82				2.3	<	2.74			
B	2.44	<	2.82				2.37	<	2.81			
C	2.48	<	2.78				2.36	<	2.85			
D	2.45	<	2.8				2.3	<	2.8			
x=	2.45	<	2.81	>	2.76		2.32	<	2.8	>	2.79	

(ii) *Summary table of significance levels*

Name of judge	Toren	A	B	C	D
re. BOYS					
H0: *Yaqona*=Meetings	18>	18>	18>	17>	17>
H1: *Yaqona*>Meetings	3<	3<	3<	7<	3<
	5=	5=	5=	2=	6=
Significant at: (one tail)	0.001	0.001	0.001	0.032	0.001
re. GIRLS					
H0: *Yaqona*=Meetings	17>	16>	17>	17>	18>
H1: *Yaqona*>Meetings	2<	5<	1<	2<	1<
	2=		3=	2=	2=
Significant at: (one tail)	0.001	0.013	0.001	0.001	0.001

Appendix 3   Prepared drawings and instructions

Drawing 1: Look at this picture. Some men and some young men are sitting outside. They are sitting outside on a mat. They are having a meeting. When the meeting is over they will drink *yaqona*. When the *tanoa* is brought, who will look after the *yaqona*? Choose the ones who will look after the *yaqona* and then colour them in. Who are the men and who are the young men? What about the high chief, is he present? If the high chief is present then write his name underneath that figure. Please write where each of the young men is seated [literally 'their organization of sitting the men and the young men one by one'].

Drawing 2: Please look at this drawing. Some men and some young men are ready to drink *yaqona*. They are sitting outside. But look, the mat has not yet been drawn in. Please draw in the mat yourselves. Takalaigau [the high chief] and Tui Navure [a *yavusa* chief] should be here too, but they are not yet drawn in this picture. Please draw the two of them yourselves. Where are they seated? Draw the two of them and write their names underneath the men you have drawn. What about the other males – who are men and who are young men? Where are the men sitting? Where are the young men sitting? Please write down where they are each seated.

Drawing 3: Please have a good look at this picture. The men and the young men are sitting in the village hall in Sawaieke. They are ready for a village meeting. Have a good look at the village hall – the big doors 'below' have not yet been drawn in. Please draw in the big doors. Takalaigau and his herald Tunimata are also present. Choose them and then write their names underneath those men. Where is Takalaigau sitting? Where is Tunimata sitting? Who are the other men? Who are the young men? Choose them and then write their names so that it is clear who that male is.

Drawing 4: Please look at this drawing. The men and the women are drinking *yaqona* in the Sawaieke village hall. Who are the women? Who are the men? What about their seating arrangement? Where are the men sitting? Where are the women sitting? Perhaps the high chief is present – if he is present then write his name underneath the man you have chosen to be him. Please also draw in the big doors 'below' in the village hall – the big doors have not yet been drawn in in this drawing. Just draw them in yourselves.

Drawing 5: Please look at this drawing. The man and the young men are having a meeting in the village hall. Who is sitting in the chair? Please write his name beside his chair. Who are the other men? There are some young men present too – who are they? Choose some of the figures as men and some as young men. Is the one who is seated in the chair sitting *i cake* or *i ra*? If he is sitting *i cake* then write the word *i cake* beside his chair, but if you think he is sitting *i ra*, then write the word *i ra* beside his chair.

Drawing 6: Please look at this picture. It is another day. The men and the young men are discussing something important about development. Who is seated *i cake* and who is seated *i ra*? Who is sitting in the chair? Who is sitting on the mat beside the one in the chair? Who are the men? Who are the young men? Write down the words 'man' or 'young man' so that it is clear who are men and who are young men.

Drawing 7: Please look at this picture. Some women, some young men and some men are drawn there. They are ready to drink *yaqona*. Have a good look at the way they are seated. What about the door that is shown here – is it the door at the side of the house or is it the kitchen door? Please write 'kitchen door' or 'side door' on top of the door. Who are the men? Write the word 'man' under those figures [literally 'persons'] you have chosen as men. Who are the women? Write the word 'women' underneath those persons. What about the high chief? Is he present in the picture or not? If he is present then please write his name under the one you have chosen as high chief. If he is not present, then write on the side of the drawing: 'the high chief is not present here'. Who is the male who is entering – a man or a young man? Where will he sit? Please draw an X in the place where he will sit. What about the way people are seated? Please write down where each of the people are seated.

Drawing 8: Have a good look at this drawing. The women and girls are drinking *yaqona*. Have a good look at their organization. Who are the women? Who are the girls? Write the correct word beside the person you have chosen as girl or woman. Who are sitting above? Who are sitting below? Please write where each of the women and girls are sitting. Perhaps a chiefly lady is present in this picture. If she is present then write her name underneath the woman you have chosen as chiefly lady. If no chiefly lady is present, then please write beside the drawing: 'there is no chiefly lady here'.

Drawing 9: Please look carefully at this drawing. Sunday lunch is prepared in your house. But look, everything that should be in this picture has not yet been drawn. The first thing is the kitchen door. Please draw in the kitchen door yourself. The second thing is the pots; please draw in the pots beside your mother. What about your father? Please choose one [figure] for your father and write the word *tamaqu* ['my father'] beside him. A guest has been invited – who is that guest? Please write his or her name beside the person you have chosen to be guest. Who are the other people? Please write their names – your younger brother [or sister] or your older brother [or sister] or whoever.

Drawing 10: It is another Sunday [continues as above].

1.

2.

3.

4.

5.

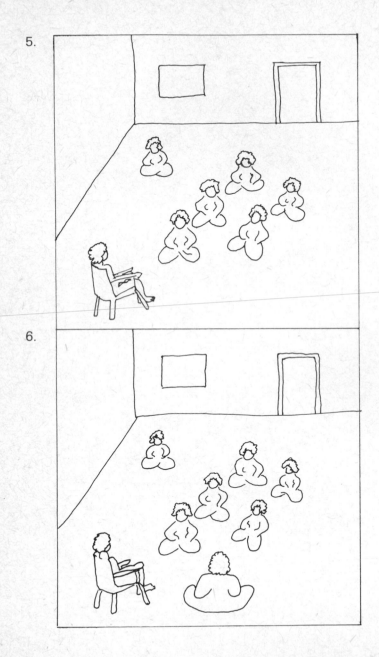

6.

7.

8.

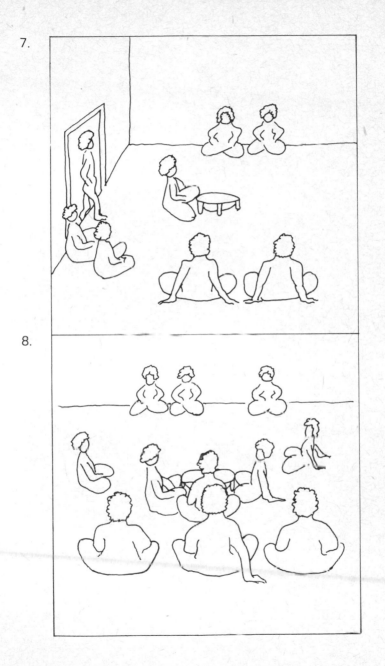

9.

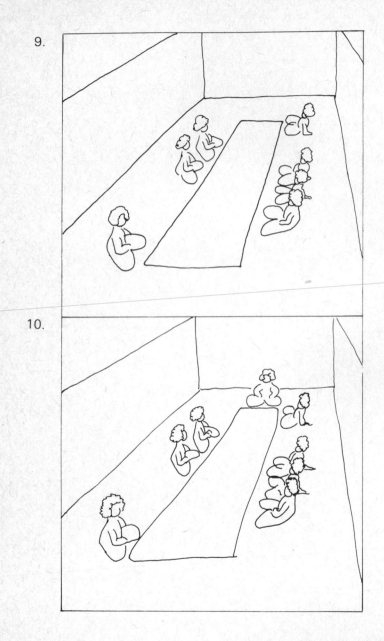

10.

Bibliography

AMRATLAL, J. *et al.* (1975) 'Women's role in Fiji', Suva: South Pacific Social Sciences Association, in association with the Pacific Women's Conference.

ARNO, A. R. (1976a) 'Ritual of reconciliation and village conflict management in Fiji', *Oceania*, 47(1): 49–65.

—— (1976b) 'Joking, avoidance and authority: verbal performance as an object of exchange', *Journal of the Polynesian Society*, 85(1): 71–86.

BELSHAW, C. S. (1964) *Under the Ivi Tree: Society and Economic Growth in Rural Fiji*, London: Routledge & Kegan Paul.

BLOCH, M. (1974) 'Symbols, song and dance and features of articulation', *European Journal of Sociology*, XV: 55–81.

—— (1985) 'Cognition and ideology', in R. Fardon (ed.) *Power and Knowledge: Anthropological and Sociological Approaches*, Edinburgh: Scottish Academic Press.

—— (1986) *From Blessing to Violence*, Cambridge University Press.

BOTT, E. (1972) 'Psychoanalysis and ceremony', in J. S. La Fontaine (ed.) *The Interpretation of Ritual*, London: Tavistock.

—— (1981) 'Power and rank in the kingdom of Tonga', *Journal of the Polynesian Society*, 90. 7–82.

—— (1982) *Tongan society at the time of Captain Cook's visits: Discussions with Her Majesty Queen Salote Tupou*, Wellington: The Polynesian Society Inc.

BOURDIEU, P. (1971) 'La maison Kabyle ou le monde renversé', in P. Maranda and J. Pouillon (eds) *Echanges et communications: Mélanges offerts à Lévi-Strauss*, The Hague & Paris: Mouton.

—— (1972, 1977) *Outline of a Theory of Practice*, London, New York etc.: Cambridge University Press.

BOWERMAN, M. (1977) 'The acquisition of word meaning: an investigation of some current concepts', in P. N. Johnson-Laird and P. C. Wason (eds) *Thinking: Readings in Cognitive Science*, Cambridge University Press.

—— (1980) 'The structure and origin of semantic categories in the language-learning child', in LeCron, Foster and Brandes (eds) *Symbol as Sense*, London & New York: Academic Press.

BREWSTER, A. R. (1922) *The Hill Tribes of Fiji*, London: Seeley, Service & Co. Ltd.

BRUNER, J. S. (1980) *Beyond the Information Given*, London: George Allen & Unwin.

—— (1987) 'The transactional self', in J. S. Bruner and H. Haste (eds) *Making Sense*, London & New York: Academic Press.

BUCKLEY, J. P., FURGIULE, A. R. and O'HARA, M. J. (1967) 'The pharmacology of kava', (Shorter Communications) *Journal of the Polynesian Society*, 76: 101–102.

BURTON, J. W. (1910) *The Fiji of Today*, London: Charles Kelly.

CALVERT, J. (1858, 1982) *Fiji and the Fijians*, vol. II, *Mission History*, Suva: Fiji Museum.
CAPELL, A. (1938) 'The word *mana*: a linguistic study', *Oceania*, IX: 89–96.
—— (1941, 1973) *A New Fijian Dictionary*, Suva: Government Printer.
CAPELL, A. and LESTER, R. H. (1941) 'Local divisions and movements in Fiji', *Oceania*, XI, 4: 315–341, XII, 1: 21–48.
—— (1945) 'Kinship in Fiji', *Oceania*, 16 (2, 3, 4): 109–43, 234–53, 297–318.
CARGILL, D. (1977) *The Diaries and Correspondence of David Cargill 1832–1843*, ed. with introduction by A. J. Schutz, Canberra: Australian University Press.
CHAPELLE, T. (1978) 'Customary land tenure in Fiji: old truths and middle-aged myths', *Journal of the Polynesian Society* 87: 71–88.
CLAMMER, J. R. (1973) 'Colonialism and the perception of tradition in Fiji', in Talal Asad (ed.) *Anthropology and the Colonial Encounter*, London: Ithaca Press.
—— (1976) *Literacy and Social Change*, Leiden: E. J. Brill.
CLUNIE, F. (1977) *Fijian Weapons and Warfare*, Suva: Fiji Museum.
COHEN, L. B. and STRAUSS, M. (1979) 'Concept acquisition in the human infant', *Child Development*, 50: 419–24.
COLLOCOTT, E. E. V. (1927) 'Kava ceremonial in Tonga', *Journal of the Polynesian Society*, 36(141): 21–47.
COOK, B. E. (1975) *Na Kai Kadavu: a study of bilingualism, acculturation and kinship in the Fiji Islands*, unpublished PhD thesis, Stanford, California.
DEANE, W. (1921) *Fijian Society, or the Sociology and Psychology of the Fijians*, London: Macmillan.
DERRICK, R. A. (1946) *A History of Fiji*, Suva: Government Press.
—— (1951) *The Fiji Islands, A Geographical Handbook*, Suva: Government Printing Department.
DIAPEA, W. (1928) *Cannibal Jack*, London: Faber & Gwyer.
ERSKINE, J. E. (1853, 1967) *Journal of a Cruise among the Islands of the Western Pacific*, London: Dawsons.
FIRTH, R. (1929) *Primitive Economics of the New Zealand Maori*, London: Routledge.
—— (1936, 1957) *We, the Tikopia*, London: George Allen & Unwin.
—— (1967) 'The analysis of *mana*: an empirical approach', pp. 174–94 in *Tikopia Ritual and Belief*, London: George Allen & Unwin.
—— (1970a) 'A basic religious rite – the kava', in *Rank and Religion in Tikopia*, London: George Allen & Unwin.
—— (1970b) 'Postures and gestures of respect', in J. Pouillon and P. Maranda (eds) *Echanges et Communications: Mélanges offerts à Claude Lévi-Strauss*, The Hague: Mouton.
—— (1970c) 'Sibling terms in Polynesia', *Journal of the Polynesian Society*, 79, 3: 272–87.
—— (1970d) 'The triumph of complete conversion', in *Rank and Religion in Tikopia*.
FISON, L. (1880) 'Land Tenure in Fiji', *The Anthropological Journal* (Royal Anthropological Institute), X.
—— (1904) *Tales from Old Fiji*, London: Alexander Moring Ltd, the De La More Press.

FLAVELL, J. H. (1963) *The Developmental Psychology of Jean Piaget*, New York, etc.: Van Nostrand Reinhold.
—— (1977) *Cognitive Development*, Englewood Cliffs, NJ: Prentice-Hall.
FORMAN, C. W. (1982) *The Island Churches of the South Pacific: Emergence in the Twentieth Century*, Maryknoll, New York: Orbis Books.
FRANCE, P. (1969) *The Charter of the Land*, Melbourne: Oxford University Press.
FURTH, H. G. (1969) *Piaget and Knowledge*, Englewood Cliffs, NJ.: Prentice-Hall.
GEDDES, W. R. (1945) *Deuba, A Study of a Fijian Village*, Wellington, NZ: Memoirs of the Polynesian Society 22.
—— (1948) *An Analysis of Cultural Change in Fiji*, unpublished PhD thesis, London School of Economics and Political Science.
GELL, A. (1985) 'How to read a map: remarks on the practical logic of navigation', *Man* (N.S.), 20: 271–86.
—— forthcoming, *Character Armour: A comparative analysis of tattooing in the South Pacific.*
GERAGHTY, P. A. (1983) *The History of the Fijian Languages*, Honolulu: University of Hawaii Press.
GIFFORD, E. W. (1929) *Tongan Society*, Honolulu: Bernice P. Bishop Museum Bulletin 61.
GOLDMAN, I. (1955) *Ancient Polynesian Society*, Chicago: University of Chicago Press.
GORDON-CUMMING, C. F. (1882) *At Home in Fiji*, Edinburgh: William Blackwood & Son.
GROVES, M. (1963) 'The nature of Fijian society', *Journal of the Polynesian Society*, 72: 272–91.
HANDY, E. S. C. (1927) *Polynesian Religion*, Honolulu: Bernice P. Bishop Museum Bulletin 9.
HARRIS, P. and HEELAS, P. (1979) 'Cognitive processes and collective represent-ations', *Archives of European Sociology* XX: 211–41.
HASHIMOTO, K. (1984) 'Fijian Vcinggaravi – semantic analysis of feasting', *Journal of the Japanese Association of Ethnology*, 49: 27–8.
HENDERSON, C. G. (1931) *Fiji and the Fijians (1935–56)*, Sydney: Angus & Robertson.
HERR, B. (1981) 'The expressive character of Fijian dream and nightmare experiences', *Ethos*, 9(4): 331–52.
HOCART, A. M. (1912) 'On the meaning of *Kalou*', *Journal of the Royal Anthropological Society*, XLII: 437–49.
—— (1913a) 'The Fijian custom of *tauvu*', *Journal of the Royal Anthropological Institute*, XLIII: 101–8.
—— (1913b) 'Fijian heralds and envoys', *Journal of the Royal Anthropological Institute*, XLIII: 109–18.
—— (1913c) 'On the meaning of the Fijian word *turanga*', *Man* 13: 140–43.
—— (1914) 'Mana', *Man* 14(46): 97–101.
—— (1915a) 'The dual organization in Fiji', *Man* 15–16: 5–9. (Note: SOAS volume incorrectly bound; this paper is to be found in vol. 16, rather than vol. 15 where it should be.)
—— (1915b) 'Chieftainship and the sister's son in the Pacific', *American Anthropologist*, 17: 631–46.

—— (1929) *Lau Islands, Fiji*, Honolulu: Bernice P. Bishop Museum Bulletin 62.

—— (1936, 1970) *Kings and Councillors*, Chicago & London: University of Chicago Press.

—— (1952) *The Northern States of Fiji*, Occasional Publication No. 11, London: Royal Anthropological Institute.

HOGBIN, H. I. (1936) 'Mana', *Oceania*, VI, 3: 241–74.

HOLMES, L. D. (1958) *Ta'u. Stability and Change in a Samoan Village*, Wellington, NZ: The Polynesian Society Inc.

HOOPER, S. PHELPS (1982) *A Study of Valuables in the Chiefdom of Lau, Fiji*, unpublished PhD thesis, University of Cambridge.

HULL, C. L. (1920) 'Quantitative aspects of the evolution of concepts', *Psychological Monographs* 28, no. 123.

JOHNSTON, T. R. ST. (1918) *The Lau Islands (Fiji) and their Fairy Tales and Folk Lore*, London: The Times Book Co.

KAEPPLER, A. L. (1985) 'Structured movement systems in Tonga', in Paul Spencer (ed.) *Society and the Dance*, London & New York: Cambridge University Press.

—— (1971b) 'Rank in Tonga', *Ethnology*, 10(2): 174–93.

KAPLAN, M. (1988) 'The coups in Fiji: colonial contradictions and post-colonial crisis', *Critique of Anthropology*, 3: 93–116.

KEESING, R. (1970) 'Shrines, ancestors and cognatic descent: the Kwaio and the Tallensi', *American Anthropologist* 72: 755–75.

KNAPMAN, B. and WALTER, M. (1979–80) 'The way of the land and the path of money: generation of economic inequality in Eastern Fiji', *Journal of Developing Areas*, 14: 201–22.

LEACH, E. (1972). 'The structure of symbolism', in J. S. La Fontaine (ed.) *The Interpretation of Ritual*, London: Tavistock.

LECRON, FOSTER and BRANDES (eds) (1980) *Symbol as Sense*, London & New York: Academic Press.

LEGGE, J. D. (1958) *Britain in Fiji 1858–1880*, London: Macmillan, in association with University of Western Australia.

LESSIN, A. (1971) *Governmental Change in Sawana, a Tongan Village in Fiji*, unpublished PhD thesis, University of California (Los Angeles).

LESTER, R. H. (1938) 'Notes from Fiji', *Oceania* IX, 2: 156–69.

—— (1940) 'Betrothal and marriage customs of Mbau, Fiji', *Oceania* X: 273–85.

—— (1941, 1942) 'Kava drinking in Viti Levu, Fiji', *Oceania* XII, 2: 97–121; XII, 3: 226–54.

LEVY, R. I. (1973) *Tahitians: Mind and Experience in the Society Islands*, Chicago: University of Chicago Press.

LEWIS, G. (1980) *Day of Shining Red*, Cambridge University Press.

LOMALOMA, S. (1985) *Education Accessibility in Fiji*, unpublished MA thesis, London School of Economics.

LUONG, HY VAN (1986) 'Language, cognition and ontogenetic development', *Ethos* 14(1): 7–46.

MCNAUGHT, T. J. (1974) 'Chiefly civil servants? Ambiguity in district administration & preservation of a Fijian way of life 1896–1940', *Journal of Pacific History*, 9: 3–20.

—— (1977–79) 'We seem no longer to be Fijians: some perceptions of social change in Fijian history', *Pacific Studies*, 1–2: 15–24.

—— (1982) *The Fijian Colonial Experience: a study of the neotraditional order under British colonial rule prior to W.W.II*, Canberra: Australian National University.

MAMAK, A. (1978) *Colour, Culture and Conflict: A study of Pluralism in Fiji*, New York & Rushcutter Bay, Australia: Pergamon Press Ltd.

MAMAK, A. and ALI, A. (1979) *Race, Class and Rebellion in the South Pacific*, Winchester, MA: Allen & Unwin.

MARINER, W. (1827) *An Account of the Natives of the Tonga Islands*, 2 vols, compiled by John Martin, Edinburgh: Constable. Republished New York: AMS Press (1979).

MEAD, G. H. (1934) *Mind, Self and Society*, Chicago, University of Chicago Press.

MEAD, M. (1930) *Social Organization of Manua*, Honolulu: Bernice P. Bishop Museum Bulletin 76.

MERVIS, C. and ROSCH, E. (1981) 'Categorization of natural objects', *Annual Review of Psychology* 32: 89–115.

MILNER, G. B. (1948) 'The language of house-building', *Transactions and Proceedings of the Fiji Society*, 4: 9–14.

—— (1952) '*Ko Viti: A Kena i Tovo Vakavanua* ('Fiji and its social custom, etc.), typescript. For commentary see 'A study of two Fijian texts', *Bulletin of the School of Oriental and African Studies*, XIV: 346–77.

—— (1968) 'Problems of the structure of concepts in Samoa: an investigation of vernacular statement and meaning', PhD thesis, University of London.

—— (1969) 'Siamese twins, birds and the double helix', *Man*, 4: 5–23.

—— (1972) *Fijian Grammar*, Suva: Government Press.

MIMICA, J. (1988) *Intimations of Infinity. The Mythopoeia of Iqwaye Counting System and Number*, Oxford etc.: Berg.

NATION, J. (1978) *Customs of Respect: the traditional basis of Fijian communal politics*, Canberra: Australian National University, ANU Development Studies Centre Monograph No. 14.

NAYACAKALOU, R. R. (1955) 'The Fijian system of kinship and marriage', *Journal of the Polynesian Society*, 64: 44–56.

—— (1975) *Leadership in Fiji*, Melbourne: Oxford University Press.

—— (1978) *Tradition and Change in the Fijian Village*, South Pacific Social Sciences Association, with The Institute of Pacific Studies, University of the South Pacific.

NEISSER, U. (1967) *Cognitive Psychology*, New York: Appleton.

—— (1976) *Cognition and Reality*, San Francisco: Freeman.

NORTON, R. (1977) *Race and Politics in Fiji*, New York: St Martin's Press.

ORTNER, S. B. (1981) 'Gender and sexuality in hierarchical societies: the case of Polynesia and some comparative implications', in S. B. Ortner and H. Whitehead (eds) *Sexual Meanings*, Cambridge & New York: Cambridge University Press.

PECK, P. J. (1982) *Missionary Analogues. The Descriptive Analysis of a Development Aid Program in Fiji*, PhD thesis, University of British Colombia.

PIAGET, J. (1954) *The Child's Construction of Reality*, New York: Basic Books.

—— (1968, 1971) *Structuralism*, London: Routledge & Kegan Paul.

—— (1972) 'Intellectual evolution from adolescence to adulthood', *Human Development* 15.

PIAGET, J. and INHELDER, B. (1969) *The Psychology of the Child*, London: Routledge & Kegan Paul.

QUAIN, B. (1948) *Fijian Village*, Chicago: University of Chicago Press.

RAVUVU, A. (1971) 'Dependency as a determinant of kinship terminology', *Journal of the Polynesian Society*, 80: 480–84.

REED, A. W. and HAMES, I. (1967) *Myths and Legends of Fiji and Rotuma*, Wellington, Auckland, Sydney: A. H. & A. W. Reed.

REEVES, E. (1898) *Brown Men and Women: the South Sea Islands in 1895 and 1896*, London: Swan Sonnenschein & Co.

REID, A. C. (1977) 'The fruit of Rewa: oral traditions and the growth of the pre-Christian Lakeba state', *Journal of Pacific History*, 12: 2–24.

RICHARDS, A. (1939) *Land, Labour and Diet in Northern Rhodesia*, London: Oxford University Press.

RICOEUR, P. (1978) 'The metaphorical process as cognition, imagination and feeling', *Critical Inquiry*, 5: 143–59.

ROGERS, G. (1976–80) 'The father's sister is black: a consideration of female rank and power in Tonga', *Journal of the Polynesian Society* 86: 157–82.

ROKOTUIVIWA, P. (1975) *The Congregation of the Poor*, Suva: South Pacific Social Science Association with Unesco Curriculum Development Project.

ROTH, G. K. (1936) (ed.) *Fiji: Handbook of the Colony*, 4th edn, Suva: Government Printer.

—— (1953) *Fijian Way of Life*, Oxford University Press.

SAHLINS, M. (1958) *Social Stratification in Polynesia*, Seattle: University of Washington Press.

—— (1962) *Moala: Culture and Nature on a Fijian Island*, Ann Arbor: University of Michigan Press.

—— (1976) *Culture and Practical Reason*, Chicago & London: University of Chicago Press.

—— (1981) *Historical Metaphors and Mythical Realities* (Structure in the early history of the Sandwich Islands kingdom), Ann Arbor: University of Michigan Press.

—— (1983) 'Raw women, cooked men and other "great things" of the Fiji Islands', in P. Brown and D. Tuzin (eds) *The Ethnography of Cannibalism* Special publication, Society for Psychological Anthropology.

—— (1985) *Islands of History*, Chicago & London: University of Chicago Press.

SANTS, J. (ed.) (1980) *Developmental Psychology and Society*, London & New York: Macmillan.

SAYES, S. (1984) 'Changing paths of the land', *Journal of Pacific History*, XIX (1).

SCARR, D. (1970) 'A Roko Tui for Lomaiviti: the question of legitimacy in the Fijian administration 1874–1900', *Journal of Pacific History*, 5: 3–31.

SCHEFFLER, H. (1971) 'Dravidian-Iroquois, the Melanesian evidence', in L. R. Hiatt, C. Jayawardena and I. Hogbin (eds) *Anthropology in Oceania*, Sydney: Angus & Robertson.

SCHUTZ, A. J. (1978) (ed.) *Fijian Language Studies: Borrowing and Pidginization*, Bulletin of the Fiji Museum 4.

SCHUTZ, A. J. and KOMAITAI, R. T. (1971) *Spoken Fijian*, Honolulu: The University Press of Hawaii.

SCRIBNER, S. (1985) 'Vygotsky's use of history', in James V. Wertsch (ed.) *Culture, Communication and Cognition*, Cambridge University Press.

SEEMAN, B. (1862, 1973) *Viti: an Account of a Government Mission to the Vitian or Fijian Islands 1860–61*, London: Dawsons of Pall Mall.

SHORE, B. (1976) 'Incest prohibitions and the logic of power in Samoa', *Journal of the Polynesian Society*, 85: 275–90.

—— (1982) *Sala'ilua – A Samoan Mystery*, New York: Columbia Press.

SHWEDER, R. A. (1984) 'Anthropology's romantic rebellion', in Shweder, R. A. and LeVine, R. A. (eds) *Culture Theory, Essays on Mind, Self and Emotion*, Cambridge University Press.

SMITH, L. B., SERA, M. and GATTUSO, B. (1988) 'The development of thinking', in R. J. Sternberg and E. E. Smith (eds) *The Psychology of Human Thought*, Cambridge University Press.

SPATE, O. H. K. (1959) *The Fijian People: Economic Problems and Prospects*, Council Paper No. 13, Legislative Council of Fiji, Government Press, Suva.

SPENCER, D. M. (1941) *Disease, Religion and Society in the Fiji Islands*, Philadelphia: American Ethnological Monograph 3.

SPERBER, D. (1974) *Rethinking Symbolism*, New York & London: Cambridge University Press.

—— (1979, 1980) 'Is symbolic thought pre-rational', in LeCron, Foster and Brandes (eds) *Symbol as Sense*, London & New York: Academic Press.

STEWART, R. A. C. (1980) *From the South Pacific: Profiles in Human Experience*, Suva: University of the South Pacific, Extension Services.

STRATHERN, M. (1984) 'Subject or object? Women and the circulation of valuables in Highlands New Guinea', in R. Hirschon (ed.) *Women and Property, Women as Property*, London: Croom Helm.

STRAUSS, M. S. (1979) 'Abstraction of prototypical information by adults and 10-month-old infants', *Journal of Experimental Psychology: Human Learning and Memory* 5: 618–32.

THOMPSON, L. M. (1940) *Southern Lau, Fiji: An Ethnography*, Honolulu: Bernice P. Bishop Museum Bulletin 162.

THOMSON, B. (1908, 1968) *The Fijians, A study of the decay of custom*, London: Dawsons of Pall Mall.

TIPPETT, A. R. (1968) *Fijian Material Culture*, Honolulu: Bernice P. Bishop Museum Bulletin 232.

—— (1980) *Oral Tradition and Ethnohistory: the transmission of information and social values in early Christian Fiji 1835–1905*, Canberra: St Mark's Library.

TOREN, C. (1980) 'A critique of two theories of cognition: Hallpike (1979) and Sperber (1979)', presented to the Seminar in Anthropological Theory, London School of Economics in November 1980.

—— (1984) 'Thinking symbols: a critique of Sperber (1979)', *Man* (N.S.) 18: 260–68.

—— (1987) 'Children's perceptions of gender and hierarchy in Fiji', in G. Jahoda and I. M. Lewis (eds) *Acquiring Culture: Cross-cultural studies in child development*, London: Croom Helm.

—— (1988) 'Making the present, revealing the past: the mutability and continuity of tradition as process', *Man* (N.S.) 23: 696–717.

—— (1989) 'Drinking cash: the purification of money in ceremonial

exchange in Fiji', in M. Bloch and J. Parry (eds) *The Morality of Money*, Cambridge University Press.
TREVARTHEN, C. (1988) 'Universal cooperative motives: how infants begin to know the language and culture of their parents', in G. Jahoda and I. M. Lewis (eds) *Acquiring Culture: Cross-cultural studies in child development*, London: Croom Helm.
TURNER, J. W. (1984) 'True food and first fruits – rituals of increase in Fiji', *Ethnology* 23(2): 133–42.
—— (1986) 'The water of life: kava ritual and the logic of sacrifice', *Ethnology*, 25: 203–14.
TURNER, T. (1973) 'Piaget's structuralism', *American Anthropologist*, 75, 2: 351–73.
URBANOWICZ, C. F. (1975) 'Change in rank and status in the Polynesian kingdom of Tonga', in T. R. Williams (ed.) *Psychological Anthropology*, The Hague & Paris: Mouton.
VAN BAAL, J. (1966) *Dema: description and analysis of Marind-Anim culture (South New Guinea)*, The Hague: Martinus Nijhoff.
VOLOŠINOV, V. N. (1929, 1986) *Marxism and the Philosophy of Language*, Cambridge, MA & London: Harvard University Press.
VYGOTSKY, L. S. (1934, 1986) *Thought and Language*, New York: The MIT Press.
—— (1978) *Mind in Society*, Cambridge, MA & London: Harvard University Press.
WAGNER, R. (1986) *Symbols That Stand For Themselves*, Chicago & London: University of Chicago Press.
WALTER, M. A. H. B. (1974) 'Succession in East Fiji: institutional disjunction as a source of political dynamism in an ascription oriented society', *Oceania*, 44(4): 301–22.
—— (1975) 'Kinship and marriage in Mualevu: a Dravidian variant in Fiji?', *Ethnology* 14: 181–95.
—— (1978) 'Analysis of Fijian traditional social organization – confusion of local and descent grouping', *Ethnology*, 17(3): 351–66.
—— (1978–9) 'An examination of hierarchical notions in Fijian society: a test case for the applicability of the term "chief"', *Oceania* 49: 1–19.
—— (1979) 'Mother's brother and the sister's son in east Fiji – descent perspective', *Ethnology*, 18(4): 365–78.
WATERHOUSE, J. (1866, 1978) *The King of the People of Fiji*, New York: AMS. Reprint of the 1866 edn published by Wesleyan Conference Office.
WATTERS, R. F. (1969) *Koro: Economic Development and Social Change in Fiji*, Oxford: Clarendon Press.
WERTSCH, J. V. (ed.) *Culture, Communication and Cognition*, London & New York: Cambridge University Press.
WILLIAMS, T. (1858, 1982) *Fiji and the Fijians*, Suva: Fiji Museum, ed. G. S. Rowe. A reprint of the 1858 London edn.
WINCH, P. (1958, 1970) 'The idea of a social science', in B. R. Wilson (ed.) *Rationality*, Oxford: Basil Blackwell.

Index of Names

Ali, A., 21, 271
Amratlal, J., 291, 271
Arno, A. R., 44–6, 271

Belshaw, C. S., 29, 42, 53, 141, 271
Bligh, Captain, 19
Bloch, M., 229, 232, 236, 271
Bott, E., 45, 100, 271
Bourdieu, P., 6–8, 13, 15, 225, 230, 233, 236, 245, 271
Bowerman, M., 14, 16, 271
Brewster, A. R., 52, 54, 57–8, 101, 170, 271
Bruner, J. S., 6, 271
Buckley, J. P., 95, 271
Burton, J. W., 20, 271

Cakobau, 20, 22, 103
Calvert, J., 19, 20, 46, 272
Capell, A., 27, 31, 43, 47, 66, 79, 104, 272
Cargill, D., 272
Chapelle, T. 47, 272
Clammer, J. R., 19, 20, 66, 272
Clunie, F., 19, 272
Cohen, L. B., 14, 16, 272
Collocott, E. E. V., 100, 272
Cook, B. E., 22, 272

Deane, W., 96, 272
Derrick, R. A., 20, 22, 272
Diapea, W., 19, 272

Erskine, J. E., 20, 165, 188, 272

Firth, R., 31, 45, 100, 104–5, 272

Fison, L., 66, 100, 272
Flavell, J. H., 10, 218, 220, 273
Forman, C. W., 129, 273
France, P. 20, 47, 65–6, 273
Furgiule, A. R., 95, 271
Furth, H. G., 8, 273

Gattuso, B., 14, 277
Geddes, W. R., 21, 41, 46, 48, 69, 90, 134, 137, 188, 273
Gell, A., 15, 188, 273
Geraghty, P. A., 22, 273
Gifford, E. W., 100, 273
Goldman, I., 1, 273
Gordon-Cumming, C. F., 273
Groves, M., 43, 50, 85, 273

Handy, E. S. C., 104, 273
Harris, P., 10, 273
Hashimoto, K., 76, 273
Heelas, P., 10, 273
Henderson, C. G., 19, 125, 273
Herr, R, 64, 126, 273
Hocart, A. M., 29, 31–3, 43, 50, 57, 59, 61, 66–7, 74, 75, 80–1, 85, 101, 105, 137, 188, 273
Hogbin, H. I., 104, 274
Holmes, L. D., 100, 274
Hooper, S. Phelps, 29, 42–3, 52, 56, 63, 73–4, 67, 87, 98, 100, 101, 103, 105, 163, 274
Hull, C. L., 15, 274

Inhelder, B., 8, 218, 276

Johnston, T. R. St., 81, 274

Kaeppler, A. L., 100, 274
Kaplan, M., 21, 274
Keesing, R., 43, 274
King George of Tonga, 20
Knapman, B., 25, 274
Komaitai, R. T., 74, 276

Leach, E., 100, 274
Legge, J. D., 103, 274
Lessin, A., 20, 274
Lester, R. H., 22, 29, 33, 43, 52, 55, 66, 78, 100, 272, 274
Lévi-Strauss, C., 12
Levy, R., 171, 174, 183–4, 274
Lewis, G., 231, 274
Lomaloma, S., 179, 274
Luong, Hy Van, 14, 16, 274

McNaught, T. J., 98, 141, 274
Ma'afu, 20
Mamak, A., 21, 275
Mariner, W., 100, 275
Maru, Ratu Sir K., 22
Marx, K., 15
Mead, G. H., 15, 275
Mead, M., 45, 100, 275
Mervis, C., 16, 275
Milner, G. B., 30, 75, 188, 275
Mimica, J., 6, 275

Nation, J., 67, 87, 131, 138, 142–3, 158, 275
Nayacakalou,R. R., 1, 21, 41–3, 46, 51, 55, 69, 80, 129, 143–5, 166, 275
Neisser, U., 11, 275
Norton, R., 21, 275

O'Hara, M. J., 95, 271
Ortner, S. B., 1, 245, 275

Peck, P. J., 31, 105, 142, 275
Piaget, J., 6–8, 10, 12, 14–6, 218, 220, 275–6

Quain, B., 25, 29, 43, 51–2, 54, 64, 66, 68, 85, 171–2, 183–4, 188–9, 240, 276

Ravuvu, A., 44, 276
Reid, A. C., 237, 276
Richards, A., 14, 276
Ricoeur, P., 233, 276
Rogers, G., 45, 276
Rokotuiviwa, P., 134, 276
Rosch, E., 16, 275
Roth, G. K., 22, 47, 67–8, 141, 276

Sahlins, M., 1, 29, 30, 33, 42–3, 51–4, 63, 85, 87, 101–2, 141, 188, 233, 240, 242, 276
Saussure, F. de, 8
Sayes, S., 20, 276
Scarr, D., 145, 276
Scheffler, H., 43, 276
Schutz, A. J., 74, 173
Scribner, S., 233, 277
Seeman, B., 19, 277
Sera, M., 14, 277
Shore, B., 45, 100, 277
Shweder, R. A., 5, 277
Smith, L. B., 14, 277
Spate, O. H. K., 139, 166, 277
Sperber, D., 232, 277
Stewart, R. A., 187–8, 190, 277
Strathern, M., 239, 277
Strauss, M. S., 14, 16, 272

Thompson, L. M., 29, 31, 33, 43, 48, 53, 81, 188, 277
Thomson, B., 52, 74, 188, 277
Tippett, A. R., 134, 144, 277
Toren, C., 15, 29, 137, 239, 245–6, 277
Trevarthen, C., 9, 278
Turner, J. W., 80, 100, 104, 278
Turner, T., 278

Urbanowicz, C. F., 87, 278
Vološinov, V. N., 7, 8, 247, 278
Vygotsky, L. S., 6, 8, 231, 233, 278

Wagner, R., 231, 278

Walter, M. A. H. B., 43, 102, 142, 274, 278
Waterhouse, J., 19, 31, 55, 278
Watters, R. F., 139, 278
Williams, T., 19, 31, 100, 188, 278
Winch, P., 3, 278

Index of Subjects

Accommodation, 10–12, 217, 219, 220, 226
Administrative officials, 144
Adultery, 49
Affines, 65, 167
Age, 10, 18, 19, 37, 199, 201, 206–8
Allegiance, 139, 155, 160
Alliance party, 21, 139, 158
Ancestor gods, 102, 106, 125–6, 137, 163
Ancestors, 30–1, 45, 50, 66, 105, 123–4, 227, 239, 240
Ancestral *mana*, 100, 167
Ancestral wrath, 31
Argument, 150–3, 158, 236
Arrogance, 131, 159, 174, 195, 218
Assimilation, 10–12, 217–9
Avoidance, 43–4, 54–5, 57, 96, 190, 203, 218, 224

Babies, 171, 175
Balanced exchange, 54, 242
Balanced reciprocity, 1, 19, 63–5, 73, 80, 86, 88, 107–9, 117, 237, 240–1
Barkcloth, 79, 80
Bau, 22, 46, 66, 245
Beatings, 53, 183
Behavioural constraints, 25
Bemba, 14
Betrothal 54, 78
Bilateral kinship, 42
Birth, 169
Body posture, 2, 34–5, 181, 218, 236

Bride service, 78
Burial, 31

Cannibalism, 19, 237
Cardinal points, 74–5
Cash crops, 22
Catholics, 119, 130
Central government, 3, 21, 23, 138, 146
Ceremonial confinement, 188
Ceremonial exchange, 111, 114, 193
Cession, 20, 103
Chairs, 34, 133, 135–6, 162–3, 209
Chiefdom, 22, 240
Chiefly descent, 73
Chiefs, 73, 131, 133, 159, 162, 165, 245; and people, 64, 79, 80, 82–3, 88–9, 108–9, 117, 133, 150, 155, 165–6
Chiefship, 88, 102, 237, 241
Chief's grave, 31
Childhood stages, 169
Childishness, 171–2, 174, 218
Children's drawings, 197–210, 228, 251–60
Children's essays, 190–4, 210–11
Children's labour, 178–9
Christ, 123
Christian ideology, 243
Christianity, 20, 142
Christians, 102, 119
Church, 3, 17, 24, 119–37, 230; and tradition, 142–4; and women, 134, 243; and *yaqona*, 129, 131; calendar, 121;

competitions, 122; funds, 73, 121; leaders, 147; hierarchy, 119–20, 128–30; seating, 131–7, 196, 222; services, 122
Circumcision, 187
Clan, 17, 30, 66, 82; chiefs, 67, 69, 79, 128; composition, 70–3; ranking, 72–83, 141, 128
Clap, 35, 99
Cloth, 56–9, 61–2, 227, 236
'Cloth' (*see malo*)
Coercive power, 166
Cognitive construction (*see also* modulated construction) 17, 18, 219, 216–28, 230, 245
Cognitive development, 4, 5, 9
Cognitive differences, 222, 238, 245
Cognitive domains, 3, 10, 14
Cognitive equilibrium, 10
Cognitive processes, 2, 217, 228
Cognitive schemes, 12, 220, 230, 234
Cognitive system, 16
Cognitive theory, 18
Collective representation, 7, 8
Colonial administration, 21
Colonisation, 20, 102
Committees, 144
Common entrance, 31, 35, 37, 75
Commoners, 42, 73, 118
Communal meal, 72
Conceptual continuum, 3, 247; conflict, 226, 234, 237
Concrete operations, 7, 9, 14; referents, 217, 219, 225, 227
Confederations, 20
Conflict, 235, 238
Consciousness, 12–13, 15, 220
Consensus, 5
Conservation, 9
Constructive processes, 5
Constructivism, 7, 10
Conversion, 20

Cooking, 62–3
Copra, 22
Corporate groups, 65
Council of Chiefs, 21, 25, 138, 145, 160
Country Council, 138, 144, 157–62
Cross-cousins, 42–3, 50–6, 64–5, 84, 94, 96–8, 109, 235, 241; and marriage, 85–6
Cultural relativism, 5
Culture, 4–5, 7, 13
Curing, 104

Dancing, 53–4, 90, 98–9
Democracy, 21, 145–6, 166
Democratic processes, 163, 166
Descent, 66
Desire, 50, 64, 125
Development, 110, 138–9, 142
Devils, 123, 125–6, 176
Diplomacy, 20
Discipline, 168, 182–7
Discourse, 13, 15, 16, 233–5
Divine order, 150; power, 167
Division of labour, 39–41, 62–3, 129, 189, 219
Domain specificity, 10, 14
'Door of the cooking irons', 31, 62
Doors, 84, 134–5
Doorways, 33, 35
Doting, 172–3
Doxa, 15, 16, 234
Dravidian terminology, 85
Dualism, 85
Dual organization, 85

Eating together, 57
Egalitarianism, 19, 233
Elder sister, 41, 61, 68, 72, 170, 190, 224, 235
Eldest child, 45, 170
Elected representatives, 139, 146, 163, 165

Embodiment, 7
Endogamy, 42
Environment, 8, 9, 12–14, 229, 246
Environmental influence, 11
Equality, 17, 29, 55, 64–5, 73, 83–4, 88–9, 98, 109, 136, 202, 204, 215, 235, 237
Equals, 167
Equilibration, 11, 12, 217, 219–21
Etiquette, 90
Exchange of drink, 90; of foods, 63–4, 168
Exchange relations, 29, 51, 65, 73, 79, 80, 85, 89, 231
Exogamy, 66, 239, 240

Facing chiefs, 107–10, 136, 165
Facing each other (*see also* *veiqaravi*) 107, 109, 117
Facing God, 135–6
Family history, 33
Fear, 149, 159, 180, 182–7, 246
Feasts, 62, 67
Fishing style, 62
Fiji-Indians, 21–2
Flirtation, 95, 203
Food presentation, 78; provision, 37, 56; taboos, 58, 78–9, 81–2
Fund-raising, 81
Friendship, 50

Games, 178
Gathering, 90–9
Gender, xii, 18, 37, 39, 41–9, 118, 133, 167, 187–94, 202–5, 208, 214, 218, 221, 222–5, 228, 243, 245; and seniority, 45–8, 59, 62, 68, 168, 205–8, 219, 221, 223, 233
Genetic epistemology, 8
God, 1, 45, 105–6, 122–3, 126–7, 137, 143, 163, 176, 243

Gods 241
God's blessing, 131
Graves, 31

Habitus, 15, 16, 238
Heads of government, 145
Heralds, 104, 112, 144
Heredity, 168
Heterodoxy, 238, 244
Hierarchical scheme, 18, 235, 245
High chief, 87, 101, 145, 147, 157, 200, 202, 216
History, 4, 7, 10, 13, 15, 233
Historical transformation, 17, 234, 238–44
Honorific titles, 30, 128, 160
Honoured door, 33, 35, 84
House, 3, 17, 230
House-building, 33
House-design, 29–34, 86
House foundation (*see also yavu*) 29, 31, 78, 140
Household, 17, 58; and community, 18, 87, 129, 243–44; head, 48, 59, 123, 171, 235; membership, 39; ranking, 67
House site, 30
Humility, 36, 157

Ideological order, 196
Ideology, 7, 237–8
Incest taboo, 43–4, 94, 97
Indians, 21
Indirect rule, 20
Individual, 13
Inquisitiveness, 172, 176–7
Installation of chief, 58, 80, 102, 143, 240, 242–3
Installation *yaqona*, 100, 101, 242
Insults, 188, 189

Jealousy, 54

Joking, 50–1, 56, 88, 94–8, 114, 203

Kabyle, 13
Kinship, 29, 41–9, 58, 65, 231, 237
Kinship terminology, 43
Kin terms, 180–2
Kisses, 172

Land, 239–40; and sea, 63, 81–2, 84–5, 88, 108, 109; chief, 84, 240–1, 243; rights, 47; tenure, 66
Lands Commissions, 21, 47, 65, 67, 72, 141
Landspeople, 72, 79, 81, 86, 241
Language, 7, 22, 25, 247
Lau, 22, 245
Leaders, 59, 68, 134, 147, 170
Leadership, 221
Lineage, 57, 66; gardens, 30; head, 68; ranking, 69–72;
Literacy, 20
London Missionary Society, 19
Love, 55, 168, 184–5, 243

Madua (*see also* shame) 18, 47, 149
Magic, 105–6, 123
Malo (*see also* clan chiefs) 79, 80, 157, 159
Mana, 102, 104–6, 167–8, 226–7, 239–42
Marriage, 44, 47–8, 52–64, 169, 231, 241, 242
Matrilateral links, 42
Meals, 18, 31, 38–9, 56–64, 90, 213, 217, 222, 227, 230
Meaning, 4–5, 8, 230, 234, 246–7
Mediating process, 8
Mediation, 13
Meetings, 18, 213, 226, 227
Menstruation, 188

Metaphor, 232–3
Methodist instruction, 173, 180
Methodist minister, 119–20, 129–30, 136, 149
Methodist preacher, 48, 133, 153
Military coup, 21
Mind, 5, 13, 246–7
Misfortune, 45
Missionary, 20
Modulated construction, 10, 12, 13, 15, 17, 222, 234
Myth, 76, 78, 82–3, 85, 140, 240–1

Namesakes, 170
Naming of child, 170
National Federation Party, 21
Neolocality, 39, 40

Obedience, 174, 187, 218, 241
Oceania, 30
Ordered speech, 155
Orders, 168
Orientation of houses, 1, 75–89, 117
Orthodoxy, 16

Paramount chief (*see also* high chief) 30, 72, 78, 80, 83–4, 88, 135–7, 241
Path of kinship, 42
Patrilineal descent, 42
Peeping, 91–2, 197, 230
Peer group, 169
Peers, 175–6, 179–80, 183, 195, 223
Political offices, 3
Politeness, 24, 25, 35–6, 57, 92, 99, 111, 130, 149, 173–4, 181–2
Polynesia, 245
Population, 21, 23
Power, 194, 222
Practice, 231, 234–5, 245

Prayer, 57, 121–2, 127, 129, 143, 160, 163, 227
Pregnancy, 239
Pre-speech abilities, 14
Presumption, 195
Priest, 144
Prime Minister, 145
Pronunciation, xii
Property relations, 88
Provincial Council, 138, 162–6
Psychology, 5

Rank, 18, 37, 41–2, 62, 137, 167–8, 190, 194, 200, 245; and seniority, 37, 205–10, 214–15
Redistribution, 1, 80, 239, 240
Reflective abstraction, 11, 220
religious office, 3; texts, 22
Residence, 51, 240
Respect, 41, 43–4, 48, 142, 147, 173, 174, 218, 231, 234, 241
Ritual obligations, 24, 69, 76, 80
Ritual presentation of food, 37
Rules, 227, 230–1

Sacrifice, 239–41
Samoa, 45
Sawaieke country, 23, 24, 43, 72, 80–1, 96, 139
Scheme, 9–11, 13, 236
School, 24, 81, 169, 179
Schooling, 24
Seapeople, 72, 79, 81, 86, 241
Selfishness, 57
Seniority, 41–9, 61, 167, 182–7, 222–3, 245
Seniority and gender (*see* gender and seniority)
Serving, 92, 93
Sevusevu, 91, 92, 102–3, 108, 111, 117, 122, 128, 131, 143, 160, 162, 226, 227
Sex, xii, 10, 18–9, 50, 55, 169

Sexuality, 52, 188
Sexual liaisons, 54, 55
Shame, 18, 46–7, 149, 159, 181, 182–7, 218, 234
Sharing food, 39
Siblings, 41, 43–7, 59, 68
Sign, 229
Sisters, 224–5
Sister's curse, 45
Social divisions, 65, 66–7
Sociality, 4, 5
Solevu, 114
Speech, 13
Stage theory, 6, 9, 10, 13
Story telling, 176–7
Stranger chief, 78, 240–1
Strangulation of wives, 19
Structure, 7, 12
Subordination, 241
Subservience, 55
Subsistence economy, 19, 22
Sunday school, 122, 127
Symbol, 228–9, 231–3

Taboos, 33
Tanoa, 109–11, 113–14, 116, 117, 135, 212, 217, 221, 223, 226–8, 230
Tattooing, 188
Tanvu, 96
Teaching methods, 179–80
Teasing, 94–6
Thanking, 95, 96, 114, 193
Theory of Practice, 7
Tonga, 20, 45–6, 88
Tradition, 29
Transformation, 12, 13, 16
Tributary relations, 18–19
Tribute, 1, 64, 81, 88, 103, 162, 240–1

Urban context, 25
Urban dwellers, 22
Uniqueness, 16, 240

Vanua, 23–4, 42, 56, 81
Vasu, 55, 85–6
Veiqaravi, 1, 3, 64, 74, 76, 89, 107, 109, 117
Veitabani, 96, 114
Veitabu (*see also* incest taboos) 94–5, 97
Village: council, 138, 146–57; green, 24; hall, 3, 17, 24; layout, 74–89
Virginity, 52, 54, 240
Visions, 126
Voting power, 163

Warfare, 20, 237
Weapons, 20
Welcoming ceremonies, 157, 162, 165
Wesleyanism, 98, 105, 119
Wesleyans, 19
Worship, 1
Whale's teeth, 80, 98, 157, 169–70
Widows, 47, 68, 237
Winds, 74

Witchcraft, 76, 104, 106, 125–6, 163
Wives, 64, 69, 134, 224–5, 240, 243–4; and sisters, 224–5, 242, 244
Women's Associations, 110–12, 114, 160, 221, 242
Women's labour, 37, 40, 56

Yaqona, 1, 24, 35, 227; ceremonies, 100–7
Yaqona-drinking, 18, 36, 89, 90–118, 102, 129, 213, 222, 227, 230, 232, 243; and birth, 169; and chiefs, 116, 141, 243; and church, 122, 129, 144; and curing, 104, 126; and politeness, 106–7; and exclusion of women, 102, 239
Yavu (*see also* house foundation) 29, 30, 140
Yavusa (*see also* clan) 30, 66
Yavu tabu, 30–1, 143
Young men, 53, 156, 202, 240